The Films of Barbra Streisand

The Films of
Barbra Streisand

Christopher Nickens and Karen Swenson

Citadel Press
Kensington Publishing Corp.
www.kensingtonbooks.com

CITADEL PRESS BOOKS are published by

Kensington Publishing Corp.
850 Third Avenue
New York, NY 10022

All Kensington titles, imprints, and distributed lines are available at special quantity discounts for bulk purchases for sales promotions, premiums, fund raising, educational, or institutional use. Special book excerpts or customized printings can also be created to fit specific needs. For details, write or phone the office of the Kensington special sales manager: Kensington Publishing Corp., 850 Third Avenue, New York, NY 10022, attn: Special Sales Department, phone 1-800-221-2647.

Kensington and the K logo Reg. U.S. Patent and Trademark Office
Citadel Press is a trademark of Kensington Publishing Corp.

Designed by Andrew B. Gardner

First printing

10 9 8 7 6 5 4 3 2 1

Printed in the United States of America

Library of Congress Cataloging-in-Publication Data

Nickens, Christopher.
    The films of Barbra Streisand / Christopher Nickens and Karen Swenson.
        p.   cm.
    "A Citadel Press book."
    ISBN 0-8065-1954-1 (pbk.)
    1. Streisand, Barbra.   2. Motion picture actors and actresses—United States—Biography.   3. Singers—United States—Biography.
I. Swenson, Karen.   II. Title.
PN2287.S783N53   1998
791.43'028'092—dc21
    [B]   98–34651
                                                                         CIP

For Brad Aul, Nicholas Gunn, and Randy Lunsford—
dear friends whose encouragement, loyalty,
and humor are not just appreciated but essential.
And for Michel Parenteau—
whose generous spirit touched us all.

Contents

Acknowledgments ix
Introduction xi
A Biographical Profile 2

The Films: 43
Funny Girl 44
Hello, Dolly! 54
On a Clear Day You Can See Forever 65
The Owl and the Pussycat 76
What's Up, Doc? 85
Up the Sandbox 94
The Way We Were 103
For Pete's Sake 113
Funny Lady 122
A Star Is Born 132
The Main Event 144
All Night Long 152
Yentl 161
Nuts 174
The Prince of Tides 185
The Mirror Has Two Faces 198
Epilogue 208

Acknowledgments

For their support, assistance, and encouragement, the authors wish to thank James Galeano, James Spada, Guy Vespoint, Allison J. Waldman, Gregory Rice, Vernon Patterson, Robert Scott, Lynne Pounder, Tom Galyean, Mike Hawks, Richard Giammanco, Tim Newth, and an assortment of Swensons, Nelsons, and Girdners, big and small.

For contributions originally made for the publication of *Barbra: The Second Decade*, we are deeply grateful to Lee Solters, Peter Afterman, Jay Presson Allen, John Arrias, Kenny Ascher, Gary Bell, Kevin Burns, Artie Butler, Mike Campbell, Harry Caplan, Nick DeCaro, Joe DiAmbrosio, Marty Erlichman, Bob Esty, Stu Fleming, Milos Forman, Ian Freebairn-Smith, Marilyn Fried, John Graham, Paul Grein, Don Hahn, Stephen Holden, Patrick Kehoe, Sally Kirkland, Rusty Lemorande, Peter Matz, Paula Moccia, Barbara Oishi, Marty Paich, Nehemiah Persoff, Jon Peters, Sid Ramin, Phil Ramone, Peter Reilly, Bruce Roberts, Jack Roe, Armin Steiner, Larry Storch, Lee Sweetland, and Columbia Records, all of whom graciously gave of their time in order to share background materials and/or reminiscences.

Enormous thanks also to our editors, Allan J. Wilson and Francine Hornberger, for their encouragement, and above all, patience.

Introduction

Barbra Streisand got her first fleeting glimpse of Hollywood in April 1962 when she taped a guest appearance on a Dinah Shore television special at NBC's Burbank studio. Eighteen months later, the town got its first good look at Streisand when she returned for a two-week engagement at the renowned Coconut Grove nightclub in the Ambassador Hotel. America's most talked-about young singer entranced the Grove audiences and landed guest shots on the television shows of Judy Garland and Bob Hope.

She also received her first film offer. Director Sam Goldwyn Jr., son of the legendary independent producer, wanted her to star opposite Peter Fonda in his upcoming drama, *The Young Lovers*. Although she had yearned for movie stardom since childhood, Barbra was unable to even consider Goldwyn's offer as she was committed to other projects, not the least of which was *Funny Girl*, the musical comedy based on the life of Fanny Brice and due to open on Broadway the following spring.

Barbra Streisand didn't return to Hollywood until May 1967, by which time she was the most sought-after entertainer in the world, about to burst into movie stardom. In the decades since, the superstar and the motion picture industry have shared a relationship that, though mutually beneficial, has never been completely free of contention. For many years the only actress whose participation in a film could guarantee its financing, Streisand was acclaimed as a star whose larger-than-life charisma and public appeal seemed a throwback to Hollywood's golden age. Studio executives admired her brilliance and ability to fill theater seats, but they were frequently less than enthusiastic when she aspired to move behind the camera and oversee every detail of her films. Moreover, although she is the winner of all major show business awards, some of her best movie work has been ignored by voters of the Academy of Motion Picture Arts and Sciences. In spite of these snubs, her history with the Oscar—as a two-time winner and multiple nominee—is one that any filmmaker would be proud of. And she has received countless other honors and trophies for her film career, including ten Golden Globes, a record number, won in five separate categories.

Prestigious awards and impressive box-office receipts aside, Streisand's greatest Hollywood legacy may ultimately prove to be the contribution she has made as a role model for talented women who have followed in her footsteps. "Long before Madonna," wrote Jon Pareles in the *New York Times* in 1994, "Ms. Streisand was her own mogul and packager, a feminist with dignity. And long before the latest surge of identity politics and ethnic pride, she refused assimilation by nose job and went on to emphasize her Jewishness in projects like *Funny Girl* and *Yentl*."

Simply by realizing her own ambitions, Streisand helped nurture an environment of opportunity that was practically nonexistent for women before her arrival in films. Now extending her production interests to include television, she remains high on the short list of Hollywood's most powerful women. Though she is proud of the (often grudging) recognition she receives for her pioneering efforts, she admits she never set out to promote any kind of feminist agenda on the sound stages or in the recording studio. "I didn't know the rules," she said recently. "Therefore I didn't know I was breaking any."

From the moment she began her first singing engagement as an inexperienced teenager in a subterranean Greenwich Village nightclub, Barbra's career has been one of trails blazed, molds broken, standards raised, records shattered, precedents set, and, yes, feathers ruffled.

Though she has avoided a string of failed marriages, sex scandals, battles with drugs and alcohol, crushing career setbacks, and other pitfalls that have exacted a toll from so many of her contemporaries, Streisand's public life has been plagued by an eternal controversy. From day one, audiences have been polarized by her looks, her voice, her honesty, her ethnicity, her choice of material, her political beliefs, her wealth, her wardrobe. Often the mere mention of her name can spark impassioned debate. "I happen to despise Barbra Streisand as a performer," said the director Robert Altman, while the author Pat Conroy, whose novel *The Prince of Tides* Streisand turned into a hit film, has called her "a goddess who walks upon the earth."

The barbs directed at her by much of the media frequently take on a more personal, vicious tone than they do in response to the efforts of other accomplished celebrities. The attacks turned especially virulent as she began taking control of her movie projects, as her self-produced and self-directed films took on autobiographical overtones, and as she began asserting herself as an outspoken advocate of Democratic politics, antinuclear policies, gay rights, and other social issues. "I'm a feminist, Jewish, opinionated, liberal woman," she said in 1996. "I push a lot of buttons."

But the criticisms of her as a cranky, controlling prima donna only serve to rouse her broad fan base to new heights of loyalty and devotion. And even her harshest critics have to admit that her show business odyssey has been nothing less than historic. Her multiple talents have made her the most successful and distinguished female superstar of her generation, a legend in her own lifetime who is both mocked as an overachiever and praised as a Renaissance woman. "They're either at your throat or they're at your feet," Stanley Kubrick was fond of saying.

Though the press has always attempted to characterize reaction to Barbra Streisand in black-and-white terms (either you love her or you hate her), the reality is often more complex. Even her admirers can find her "relentless pursuit of excellence" a trial. Karl Malden, her costar in *Nuts*, observed, "She wanted the film, like everything else she does, to be perfect. I respected that . . . enormously; however, she wanted that so desperately that it was sometimes destructive for the morale of the company, and I think, even for herself."

Streisand's enviable position in Hollywood has been attained with a surprisingly skimpy filmography. Though the lengthy respites between movies has contributed to the Streisand mystique,

such a schedule automatically imposes the mantle of "event" on each release—a burden some of the star's lesser efforts can't live up to.

In terms of critical approbation, her movie performances have run the gamut. In the tradition of the most popular stars from Hollywood's past, she is both blessed and burdened with an indelible, dynamic screen presence—a trait that can sometimes work against her sincere efforts to create characterizations that are significantly unlike herself.

In spite of this, Streisand has managed a more varied range of performances than many critics give her credit for,. skillfully portraying such women as Fanny Brice, Yentl, Claudia Draper of *Nuts*, and Katie Morosky of *The Way We Were*—compelling, multilayered characters who share an unshakable sense of purpose but little else. And who could be less alike than Margaret Reynolds, the confused fantasy-prone housewife of *Up the Sandbox*, and Doris Wilgus, the vulgar-yet-vulnerable hooker of *The Owl and the Pussycat*?

Of course, Streisand's stardom is not dependent entirely on her career as an actor and director. In 1999, the respondents of a Reuters/Zogby news service poll named her and Frank Sinatra the Best Singers of the Century. Such titles may be arguable. However, in terms of record sales, with forty-three gold, twenty-seven platinum, and thirteen multiplatinum albums to her credit, she remains the bestselling female recording artist. The recipient of ten Grammy awards—two for career achievement—Barbra's singing projects overlap her acting and directing assignments.

During lulls between films, the singer the *New York Times* has called "a pop answer to Maria Callas" stays firmly in the public consciousness with the release of chart-topping albums. And at an age when most pop artists are years past their ability to sell out stadiums, she remains the world's highest paid concert attraction. If Streisand will forever be thought of first and foremost as a singer, it is fortunate that many of her most stirring vocal performances can be found in her movies.

Though she has appeared in markedly fewer films than many screen giants, Barbra Streisand's movie career has been one of the most celebrated of its time, the stuff of childhood fantasy. Dazzling stardom is, in fact, exactly what she dreamed of as a skinny kid who felt unlovely, "unlistened to, and unseen," in the blue-collar neighborhood and cabbage-scented hallways of her native Brooklyn—about as far from Hollywood in countless ways, if not in actual distance, as any place can be.

The Films of
Barbra Streisand

A Biographical Overview

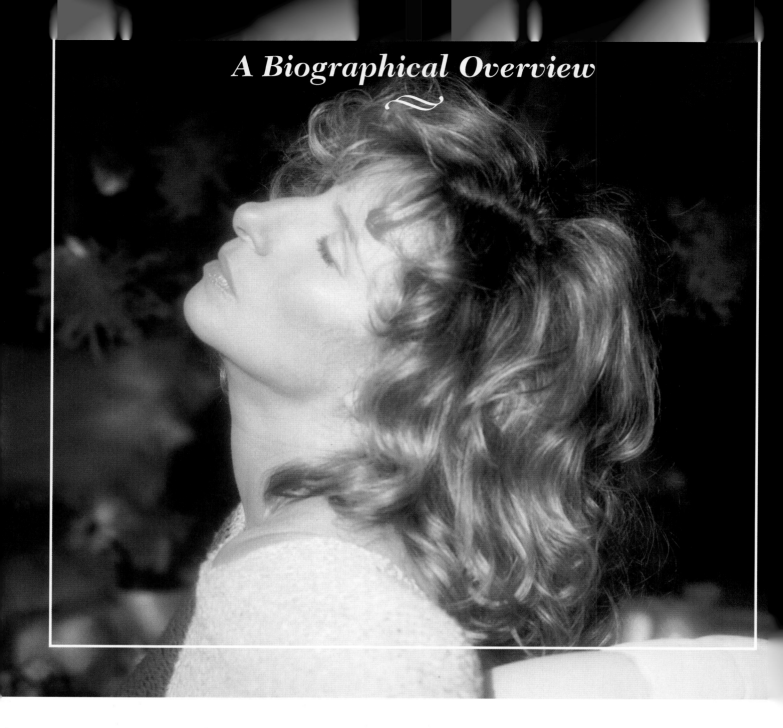

I n so many classic ways, Barbra Streisand embodies the American Dream. Possessed of an iron will, rare talent, and blazing determination, she rose from a childhood in which she cuddled a hot water bottle (in lieu of the doll her mother couldn't afford), to world-class superstardom where she enjoys influential relationships with presidents, princes, and prime ministers. The ugly duckling granddaughter of impoverished immigrants, she soared swanlike from dreary obscurity in Flatbush to heights of fame, acclaim,

and fortune no one would have dared predict. No one, apparently, except Barbra. From about the age of seven she felt instinctively that she was destined to become a great star. She wasn't sure at the time how it would happen, she was simply convinced that it would. Few around her saw any reason to share that conviction.

At seven and a half pounds, Barbara Joan was born to Diana and Emanuel Streisand in the early morning hours of April 24, 1942, at the Jewish Hospital of Brooklyn. Her arrival completed a family that included a son, Sheldon, born in 1935, and further guaranteed that her thirty-four-year-old father wouldn't be drafted into the global conflict the United States had been thrown into just four months earlier with the bombing of Pearl Harbor.

The son of hardworking immigrants from Galicia (a pocket of eastern Europe under Austrian-Hungarian rule bordered by Poland and Russia), Emanuel obtained a master's degree from City College of New York in 1928. He subsequently became a highly respected educator who took a special interest in underprivileged and delinquent youth. Tall, handsome, athletic, and keenly intelligent, Streisand spent one youthful summer as a lifeguard and another hitchhiking through the Canadian wilds. "He'd try anything," his sister Molly said. "He wasn't afraid of anything." In 1930, Emanuel married Ida (subsequently changed to Dinah and finally Diana) Rosen, a plump, pretty nineteen-year-old, whose parents had migrated from Russia.The daughter of a cantor, Diana was blessed with cornflower-blue eyes and a creamy complexion. She also possessed a sweet soprano that was true enough for her to have briefly considered a career in music. After marrying, however, as with most women of her generation and tradition, she aspired only to a life of domesticity in loving support of her husband's promising academic career.

Just three months after Barbara's first birthday, the Streisand family was shattered when Emanuel died. He suffered a seizure, possibly epileptic in nature, that was most likely the result of a head injury he sustained several years before. Emanuel's unexpected death plunged his widow into an inconsolable state of grief exacerbated by financial panic. For the next few years, while Diana took low-paying bookkeeping jobs, her children faced a life in the Williamsburg section of Brooklyn that was devoid of the comforts other kids took for granted.

At the time, Barbara was simply too young to grasp the gravity of what losing her father really meant. Soon, however, its effect on her was profound. "I always felt like an outcast. . . . Everybody else's father came home from work at the end of the day. Mine didn't." Barbara's sense of alienation was heightened by her complicated relationship with her mother. Diana was uncomfortable uttering words of loving encouragement to a child

starved for attention. "When I wanted love from my mother," Streisand recalls, "she gave me food."

Barbara began her education at the Yeshiva of Brooklyn when she was five. Like her father, she proved to be a bright, insatiably curious student, though she lacked discipline—especially when it came to shouting answers to the teachers' questions out of turn. By the time she entered Public School 89, she had become entranced by the glamorous images she saw at the movies and on her neighbor's television sets. She soon developed a potent fantasy life in which she dreamed of the day when she could escape the brick tenements of her neighborhood; when people would not only notice but admire her; when her schoolmates would rue the day they had poked fun at her skinny frame, close-set eyes, and prominent nose—features she had inherited from Emanuel. "I always wanted to be somebody, to be famous . . . you know, get out of Brooklyn . . ."

In 1949, her young life became even more depressing when her mother married Louis Kind, a businessman sixteen years Diana's senior. Barbara immediately distrusted Kind, even after he moved his new family to a better apartment in the Flatbush district. Things did not improve when Diana gave birth to a daughter, Rosalyn (later changed to Roslyn), in January 1951. While Kind would lavish attention on "Rozzie," he went out of his way to ignore Barbara. "He was so loving, kind, and sweet to everyone else," a neighbor recalled, "but he was verbally abusive to Barbara. He would yell at her and say mean things to her and criticize her clothes in front of her friends." In response to Kind's abuse—and her mother's reluctance to put a stop to it—Barbara retreated even further into a private "alternate reality" in which she imagined herself becoming a great star. Her dislike of Kind, however, never extended to his daughter; she adored playing with and caring for her bubbly half sister.

As she approached puberty, Barbara began to be recognized for the talent that would eventually turn her dreams into reality. She would later recall she and the other neighborhood kids "would sit on the stoop and sing together . . . we would harmonize. And I was considered the girl on the block with the good voice." In 1983 she said, "Growing up I used to wonder—what did I have to do to get attention? When I started to sing, I got attention." In spite of a bad cold, she made her

recorded a four-song demo, two selections apiece. Barbara sang "Zing! Went the Strings of My Heart," and "You'll Never Know."

Though she liked the way people responded to her singing, Barbara was inspired to pursue a serious acting career after seeing her first Broadway play, *The Diary of Anne Frank*, when she was fourteen. "Gee, I could play that part [of a teenaged Jewish girl doomed by the Nazi invasion of Amsterdam], I know what it feels like," she thought to herself as she watched Susan Strasberg bring the audience to tears. Soon, Barbara was spending all of her spare time at the library, devouring the biographies of legendary stage actresses Eleanora Duse and Sarah Bernhardt, and immersed in the plays of Shakespeare and Ibsen, novels by Tolstoy and Turgenev, and the acting theories of Stanislavski and Chekhov.

Entering Erasmus Hall High School in 1955, Barbara's intelligence placed her in honors classes for modern history, English, and Spanish. She also joined the freshman chorus. But she continued to feel distanced from her classmates. "I wouldn't know who to talk to," she has said. "I was smart, but the smart kids wearing oxfords and glasses wouldn't look at me, and the dumb kids I wouldn't want to associate with. So I was a real outsider."

During the summer of 1957, when she was fifteen, she wheedled three hundred dollars from her mother, lied about her age, and joined a group of other young apprentices at the Playhouse in Malden Bridge, New York. Her first stage experience had her scrubbing floors and painting

public singing debut at a PTA assembly. She was a hit with everyone except her mother, whose only comment about the performance concerned Barbara being too thin. Thus was established a pattern in which Diana found it preferable to criticize rather than praise her daughter's work. Barbara continued to sing at the occasional wedding or at summer camp—she even auditioned, unsuccessfully, for MGM Records at age nine. In a rare mother-and-daughter endeavor, when she was thirteen she accompanied Diana to the Nota Recording Studios where, for a fee, they scenery in exchange for a walk-on (pulling a goat) in a production of *The Teahouse of the August Moon*. She also earned a chance to play the tomboyish kid sister in *Picnic*. Later in the season, she got her first-ever review for *Desk Set*. "Barbara Streisand," wrote a local critic, "turns in a fine performance as the office vamp. Down boys!"

Returning to Brooklyn, she was more determined than ever to act upon her theatrical aspirations. She never joined dramatics at school, nor did she stand out in the chorus, as she was only interested in pursuing the real thing. During her sophomore year at Erasmus Hall, Barbara worked behind the scenes at night at the Cherry Lane Theater in Greenwich Village, and while a senior, she studied for finals between rehearsals of *Driftwood*, a short-lived play staged in an attic space in midtown Manhattan. She played a female gangster (!) known as The Chief in the scarcely seen production. Graduated from Erasmus Hall in January 1959 when she was sixteen, Barbara ignored her mother's pleas that she go into a less risky field, and she immediately set out to conquer the New York stage.

Barbara was forced to send this less-than-ideal photograph to casting agents when she was eighteen: "I didn't have any money for pictures—[this was] all I had."

With a friend, she was able to rent a small flat for a while in the heart of the theater district on 48th Street. Barbara took any odd job she could find—some courtesy of her brother Sheldon, now an upwardly mobile businessman—and encountered nothing but rejection when she "made the rounds" of the casting offices.

She had youthful ambition in her favor, but her unconventional looks, a figure that had yet to blossom into marketable curves, and her lack of experience worked against her. Indeed, no one knew quite what to make of Barbara at this time. She seemed destined for comic character roles, yet

there was a unique attractiveness about her (which she strove to enhance with exotic makeup, long tapering fingernails, and vintage clothing) that impressed almost everyone. Yet this budding magnetism failed to land her any acting roles.

Constantly losing menial jobs—switchboard operator, clerk at a printing shop—and often without a permanent address, Barbara would sleep in friend's offices, or if need be on an army cot she lugged around the city rather than waste money on rent or food that she could put toward the acting lessons she took from a variety of coaches. Swallowing her pride, she would occasionally

The cast of the nonsensically titled Another Evening With Harry Stoones (left to right): *Sheila Copelan, Virgil Curry, Susan Belink, Diana Sands, Barbra, Ben Keller, Kenny Adams, and Dom De Luise. The Off-Broadway show closed after one performance*

return to Brooklyn for a much needed home-cooked meal. Diana, of course, was horrified by her daughter's gypsylike lifestyle, and she begged her to give up her dreams of a show business career and settle into something sensible such as a job in the school system—where she herself now worked. Barbara would devour the food but ignore the advice. Years later she admitted that Diana's discouragement actually served her well: "I'm thankful to my mother," she said. "My desires were strengthened by wanting to prove to my mother that I *could* be a star."

Early in 1960, Barbara took a job at the Lunt-Fontanne Theater as an usher for *The Sound of Music*, Mary Martin's last great success on Broadway. When she learned that replacements were being sought for the show, she auditioned for casting director Eddie Blum. It would mark the first time she sang in pursuit of a job, and though Blum recognized that she was all wrong for the show, he went out of his way to encour-

age her to add singing to her résumé. "Finally," Barbara recalled, "I *had* to sing. I went on unemployment insurance and got caught in a lie. I was supposed to be looking for work as a switchboard operator, but instead I went looking for work as an actress."

She hooked up with a guitarist who agreed to accompany her, and she talked her boyfriend Barry Dennen into letting her use his sophisticated taping equipment to record her voice. Dennen, with whom Barbara had worked in an ill-fated off-Broadway experiment titled *The Insect Comedy*, agreed to record her—though he had no reason to suspect she had any singing talent. "We spent the afternoon taping," he recalled, "and the moment I heard the first playback [of "Day by Day"] I went insane. . . . This nutty little kook had one of the most breathtaking voices I'd ever heard . . . when she was finished and I turned off the machine, I needed a long moment before I dared look up at her."

On Mike Wallace's P.M. East *talk show, Burt Lancaster responds to Barbra as she reads the lyrics to "Nobody Makes a Pass at Me," a song she recorded for the* Pins and Needles *album.*

Dennen's enthusiastic response convinced Barbara to enter a talent contest at the Lion, a gay bar and restaurant across the street from his Greenwich Village apartment. With her performances of "A Sleepin' Bee" and "When Sunny Gets Blue," Barbara elicited stunned silence followed by thunderous applause from the jaded crowd at the Lion. (One could point to the performance of these two songs as the pivotal moment in Barbra Streisand's career.)

She won the contest, was asked back to sing the following week, and signed her first autograph—most likely the only one she ever signed with her given first name. Shortly thereafter, she dropped the middle "a" from Barbara, establishing herself as an exotic original, while at the same time notifying her former neighbors in Brooklyn and callous producers and casting directors that Barbra—formerly Barbara—Streisand had arrived.

Another bonus from winning the contest at the Lion was a chance to audition at the Bon Soir,

a nearby club located below street level with a larger, more diverse clientele. Signed for $125 a week, Barbra began her first professional engagement, in September 1960, as the opening act for Phyllis Diller. "I'd never been in a nightclub until I sang in one," she said later. "It felt funny to me, like a cliché, something silly." But as Barry Dennen exposed her to his vast record collection of such great, idiosyncratic singers as Billie Holiday, Mabel Mercer, Ethel Waters, and Edith Piaf, Barbra gained new respect for the art of popular singing. She realized that she could still be an actress, but through song.

As a result, she approached each number as if it were a mini-play, creating a different character for each. Her voice, which could slide effortlessly from a silky whisper to a dramatic belt, aided her in this endeavor, allowing her to purr, croon, or even shriek, whatever she felt the song called for. Her eclectic choice of material caused comment, ranging as it did from the dramatic, "I Had Myself a True Love," to the playful, "Keepin' Out of Mischief Now," to the absurd, "Who's Afraid of the Big Bad Wolf."

Learning on the job as she built her act, Barbra realized that her frank, Brooklyn-bred sense of humor was an

asset. Soon, she became almost as well known for her "kooky" between-song patter as for her singing. Night after night, her voice became stronger, her quips funnier, her handling of an audience more graceful. After singing professionally for just six months, this teenager who couldn't read music (but who was obviously blessed with a natural musicianship) was being compared to Judy Garland, Lena Horne, and Fanny Brice. No one had ever seen anything like it in the colorful history of New York's cabaret scene.

It was during her second Bon Soir engagement that Barbra met Martin Erlichman, who became her enthusiastic personal manager. To her great relief, Marty agreed that if Streisand was to reach top stardom—which he firmly believed she would—it would be *because* of her differences, not in spite of them. He discouraged any notions she might have had about changing her songs, her wardrobe, her makeup, her nose. On just a handshake, Marty and Barbra formed a management partnership that would last for decades.

For all of the excitement bubbling around her singing career, what Barbra still really wanted was to act on the New York stage. She got her first opportunity in *Another Evening With Harry Stoones*, an off-Broadway satirical revue in which she sang two solos and shared the rest of the singing and clowning chores with a cast of eight hopeful talents, including Dom De Luise. The show opened on October 21, 1961, at the Gramercy Arts Theater and closed the same evening.

Fortunately for Barbra, Marty immediately booked her at the Blue Angel, a swank nightclub in midtown Manhattan, where she was an even bigger hit than she was in Greenwich Village. Earlier in the year she had also per-

On the brink of fame in 1962.

formed successful club dates in Detroit and St. Louis, but she hadn't gone over in Winnipeg, Ontario, where she was fired for the first and only time in her career. She also returned to the Bon Soir for sell-out bookings in 1961 and '62. Columnist Leonard Harris wrote prophetically of her final performance at the club: "She's twenty; by the time she's thirty she will have rewritten the record books."

Arthur Laurents, author of the smash musical *Gypsy*, saw Streisand at the Blue Angel and arranged for her to audition for *I Can Get It for You Wholesale,* a new musical that Laurents was set to direct for producer David Merrick (with songs by Harold Rome), about the cut-throat garment industry of 1937 Manhattan. Initially considered for an ingenue role, Barbra was instead cast as Yetta Tessye Marmelstein, a lovelorn secretary who was originally conceived as a middle-aged spinster.

Her romance with Barry Dennen now over, Barbra soon found herself falling in love with the show's leading man during rehearsals—and she was touched to discover the feeling was mutual. Tall and dark with a teddy-bearish appeal, Elliott Gould (née Goldstein), was getting his big break in *Wholesale* after toiling as a chorus boy in *Say, Darling* and *Irma La Douce.* A fellow Brooklynite, twenty-three-year-old Elliott was pushed into show business by his star-struck mother—a fact that fascinated Barbra as it was the exact opposite of her experience with Diana.

By the time *Wholesale* returned to New York after out-of-town tryouts, Elliott and Barbra were living together in a cramped apartment on Third Avenue above a seafood restaurant. The young couple loved talking over their mutual dreams of success during excursions in Central Park or strolling hand in hand down Forty-second Street after catching a late-night horror movie.

Barbra's chronic tardiness nearly got her fired from *I Can Get It for You Wholesale,* but when the show opened on March 22, 1962, at the Shubert Theater, her climb toward stardom took a giant leap. Her bombastic performance of "Miss Marmelstein," the comic lament Harold

"Oh why is it always Miss Marmelstein?" Barbra belts out the musical question that will result in a Tony nomination for her show-stopping Broadway debut in I Can Get It for You Wholesale.

Rome had written specifically for her, stopped the show cold. *Wholesale* (and Elliott Gould's performance) received mixed reviews, but Barbra was pronounced a standout, and she became the youngest, newest darling of the Great White Way. Eager not to be typecast as an ethnic comedienne, she continued with a new gig at the Blue Angel, slipping into her ever-more sophisticated *chanteuse* persona for midnight shows following her *Wholesale* performances.

In addition to Elliott Gould, *I Can Get It for You Wholesale* gained Barbra a Tony nomination and a New York Drama Critic's prize for Best Supporting Actress in a Musical. It also allowed the public to hear her on record for the first time. The *Wholesale* original cast album was released just prior to Streisand's twentieth birthday, in April 1962. Not surprisingly, "Miss Marmelstein" was the album's hilarious highlight. A month later, she could be heard on the twenty-fifth anniversary recording of *Pins and Needles,* another Harold Rome show about unions and the clothing business of the thirties.

Both albums were released by Columbia Records, with whom Streisand signed an exclusive recording contract on October 1, 1962, after months of indecision and haggling. Marty Erlichman had received lucrative offers from Atlantic and Capitol, but he was adamant about holding out for Columbia—the Cadillac of the industry. In an extremely rare concession for the time, particularly for a novice, Columbia agreed to allow Barbra *complete* artistic control over her recordings: It was a record-and-release contract which allowed her to sing what she wanted, not what the company dictated.

Erlichman later admitted that he agreed to much less remuneration for Streisand's services in exchange for such control. "It was a difficult thing to do," he said, "because neither of us had any money."

Television offered the rising star important exposure during this period. In April 1961, she made her home-screen debut on *The Jack Paar Show,* and for a year starting in June, she appeared thirteen times on *P.M. East,* a late-night talk and variety show hosted by Mike Wallace on which she kibitzed with Woody Allen, harmonized with Mickey Rooney, and generally served as the show's resident kook/songbird. In May 1962, she was a guest on *The Garry Moore Show,* where she sang "Happy Days Are Here Again" for the first time. Her slow-paced, ironic interpretation brought new heft to the rallying cry of the Democratic party, and it became her first signature song. In August, she joked with guest-host Groucho Marx on *Tonight,* and within the course of the next six months, she was asked back half a dozen times, having become a favorite of Johnny Carson.

In December she made the first of several appearances on *The Ed Sullivan Show,* and two months later she spent a week as Mike Douglas's cohost on his afternoon program aired from Cleveland. During the rest of 1963, she made an impact on the shows of Bob Hope and, most

memorably, Judy Garland. Her electrifying duet with Garland, which cleverly combined "Happy Days Are Here Again" with one of Garland's hits, "Get Happy," made for a classic TV moment, and it earned Streisand her first Emmy nomination.

The Barbra Streisand Album, brilliantly arranged by Peter Matz, and containing songs she had refined in her nightclub act, was released to strong reaction in February 1963. "Miss Streisand is a compelling artist," wrote *Hi Fi/Stereo Review*, "with a full, rich vocal quality that may give you goose bumps when you hear her more dramatic arias." In support of her first album, Barbra embarked on an exhausting club tour that included stops in New York, Chicago, San Francisco, Lake Tahoe, and Los Angeles. In May, she detoured to Washington, D.C., where she sang for President John F. Kennedy, at his

request, at the annual Press Correspondents' Dinner at the Hilton Hotel.

During her booking at Harrah's Hotel in Lake Tahoe, she took a day off to marry Elliott in nearby Carson City on Friday, September 13. As her career momentum intensified, Barbra surely saw marriage to Gould as a stabilizing influence in her life. Unfortunately, *his* career was languishing, and he found himself spending an inordinate amount of time attending to his wife's professional needs.

The nightclub tour was a huge success and bolstered interest in Streisand's recordings. *The Barbra Streisand Album* rose into the top ten on the *Billboard* album chart, making her the best-selling female vocalist in the country. It went on to win three Grammy Awards, including Album of the Year and Best Female Vocal Performance. The release in August 1963 of *The Second Barbra Streisand Album* further cemented Streisand's status as the most exciting new personality since Elvis Presley to hit American show business.

For the remainder of the decade, even in the face of the British invasion and as rock established dominance over the record industry, Streisand remained the top-selling female album artist with releases such as *People, My Name Is Barbra, Je M'Apelle Barbra, Simply Streisand,* and *A Christmas Album.* During one week in October 1965, she had five albums on the Top 100 LPs list.

For Barbra, the year 1963 had been a breakthrough year, and she ended it with a series of one-night concerts in Indianapolis, San Jose, Chicago, Sacramento, and Los Angeles. With money now pouring in, the Goulds were able to move from their small, fishy-smelling apartment to a penthouse duplex once owned by lyricist Lorenz Hart on Central Park West. With a sweeping view of the park, the roomy apartment was just the kind of glamorous domicile Barbra had admired in the movies as a kid. She took great pleasure in decorating her new home, and her choice of red patent leather for her kitchen walls made news.

For years, agent-turned-producer Ray Stark had hoped to film a musical biography of his famous mother-in-law, Fanny Brice, a treasured headliner in the Ziegfeld Follies from 1910 to 1923. Brice's broad comic style, honed in the Yiddish theater, and signature songs "Second Hand Rose," "I'm an Indian," and "My Man" won her legions of admirers. Hilariously gawky and

Barbra and Judy Garland perform an exciting duet on Judy's CBS television show in October 1963. "I admired her tremen-dously," Barbra recalled. "She was brilliant and kind, you know? She was grabbing on to my hand with cold, cold hands because she was so frightened."

clumsy in performance, Brice was—offstage, an elegant clotheshorse and art collector whose refined tastes were well publicized. Brice died in 1951. By the early sixties, she was best remembered as Baby Snooks, a precocious child she

played to comic perfection on the radio of the thirties and forties.

Brice's turbulent marriage to promoter and gambler Nick Arnstein was the stuff of Broadway legend. It was this relationship—which produced daughter Frances, Stark's wife—and Brice's early climb to stardom, that the producer wished to dramatize. At his behest, Isobel Lennart, an Oscar nominee for *Love Me or Leave Me,* delivered a strong screenplay. But even with Stark's impressive industry connections and the success of his first production, *The World of Suzie Wong,* he couldn't drum up interest at the studios. Rejected by Hollywood, he decided to take the project to Broadway, where it finally coalesced in 1962, when Mary Martin expressed interest.

Jule Styne, composer of such standards as "Time After Time" and "I'll Walk Alone" and the scores for *Gentlemen Prefer Blondes, Bells are Ringing,* and *Gypsy,* joined lyricist Bob Merrill (after Stephen Sondheim turned the project down) to create the score for the show, ultimately titled *Funny Girl.* Merrill's most famous songs were "How Much Is That Doggie in the Window," and "If I Knew You Were Comin', I'd've Baked a Cake." His knack for such novelties augured well for the comic songs Fanny would sing in the Follies. Isobel Lennart

Newlyweds Eliott Gould and Barbra Streisand at the Cocoanut Grove night-club in Los Angeles. Two months earlier, Barbra had played the Grove to an enthusiastic auidience sprinkled with movie stars.

adapted the play's script from her screenplay and theater veteran Garson Kanin was signed to direct. Irene Sharaff, fresh from *Cleopatra*—for which she would win an Oscar—agreed to design the costumes, and notorious Broadway mainstay David Merrick joined Ray Stark as the show's coproducer.

When fifty-year-old Mary Martin was deemed too mature—Fanny is a teenager for much of the first act—Carol Burnett, Edye Gorme, and Kaye Ballard were among those considered for the lead. Anne Bancroft, a recent Academy Award winner for *The Miracle Worker,* was close to signing a contract until she realized the song score ranged way beyond her modest vocal abilities.

As if choreographed by the show business gods, Barbra Streisand's ascent in nightclubs, records, and on television coincided with the cast-

ing search for *Funny Girl.* Jule Styne, after having seen her in *I Can Get It for You Wholesale* and in one of her nightclub engagements, became Streisand's ardent champion. (He composed most of the *Funny Girl* score with her voice in mind.) Eventually, he helped convince Stark and Merrill that Barbra, though only twenty, had the talent and steely determination required to star in what was shaping up as a hugely expensive production. Although the decision would not be announced for months, Streisand was signed to play Fanny Brice in October 1962.

Sydney Chaplin, the handsome baritone star of *Bells Are Ringing,* son of movie icon Charles Chaplin, and a notorious womanizer, was hired to play Nick Arnstein. Carol Haney joined the production as choreographer. Lainie Kazan came

All obstacles were over-come, however, when *Funny Girl* opened on March 26, 1964, at the Winter Garden Theater. Barbra delivered a dynamic performance that con-veyed Fanny's youthful dreams of success ("I'm the Greatest Star"), her yearning for love ("People"), and her personal philosophy ("Don't Rain on My Parade"). She riveted the celebrity-jammed audience and earned rapturous reviews.

"*Funny Girl* is just this side of paradise," raved the *World-Telegram and Sun*. "A large and lively evening of entertainment. Barbra Streisand is a joy. She sets an entire audi-ence tingling time and time again." Broadway observers couldn't help but notice that Streisand's own Cinderella story became instantly and forever intertwined with that of Fanny Brice. In an overnight alchemy, star and show blended into one entity, which is why *Funny Girl*

aboard as a Ziegfeld Girl and Barbra's understudy. By the time the show went into rehearsals early in 1964, advance ticket sales were tremendous, thanks in large part to Streisand's ever-growing popularity as a recording artist.

In addition to the usual out-of-town predic-tions of failure and other assorted headaches that plague every musical prior to opening, *Funny Girl* survived a unique set of afflictions that included Merrick backing out, Jerome Robbins replacing Garson Kanin, an alleged romance between Chaplin and Streisand deteriorating into a back-stage feud, and the death of Carol Haney.

is seldom revived successfully. "I knew that I would do [Fanny] justice by being true to myself," Streisand told the press. "*Funny Girl* is about me. It just happened to Fanny Brice earlier."

As a result of the success of the show, Barbra's rags-to-riches saga was detailed in cover stories in *Time* and *Life*, and she was featured in striking fashion layouts in *Vogue* and *Harper's Bazaar*. Her looks, so often ridiculed in the past, became cause for celebration, her hairstyles and make-up emulated. She was called "the girl who catches the light" with "the best legs since Dietrich." Thrift-shop fashions gave way to designs by Pucci and Gernreich; the press dubbed her "La Streisand."

Everything she touched turned to gold. The *Funny Girl* original cast album, released on Capitol, hit number two on the charts, and a version of the show's finest ballad, "People," issued on Columbia, became her first hit single. She would lose the Tony Award to Carol Channing for her performance in *Hello, Dolly!*, but in all other respects, the 1964–65 Broadway season belonged to Barbra Streisand. She would admit years later, however, that the overwhelming attention she received from fans and the media, coupled with a fear that she couldn't possibly live up to audience expectations, drove her into analysis.

Just when it seemed the Streisand career couldn't skyrocket any higher, CBS signed her to a $5 million contract to star in ten hour-long television specials (and a possible series in the future) over a ten-year period.

Early in 1965, Streisand taped the first of her shows, *My Name Is Barbra*, for which she appeared solo despite the network's fervent plea that she include guest stars. (As with her recordings, she had insisted on complete artistic control over her television programs.) Aired in April, the hour was a glamorous, funny, magnetic showcase that allowed Barbra to romp like a child in an oversized set, frolic in Bergdorf Goodman's luxurious department store while singing songs of poverty, and, finally, belt out a concert segment that included her first public performance of Fanny Brice's trademark ballad "My Man."

The show was startlingly innovative, and it introduced millions of Americans to Barbra's talents for the first time since she had conquered Broadway. "She may well be the most supremely talented and complete popular entertainer this country ever produced," raved United Press International in a typical review. A ratings smash, the special remains one of her career milestones. At Emmy ceremonies the following September, *My Name Is Barbra* won five awards, including one for its star. The show also received a coveted Peabody Award and generated not one but two soundtrack albums.

As Streisand's success escalated, Elliott Gould found himself stalled in her ever-lengthening shadow. In the fall of 1965 he attempted a return to the musical stage in *Drat! the Cat!* One of Gould's songs in the play, "She Touched Me," was

Barbra (as Fanny Brice) and Johnny Desmond (as Nicky Arnstein) share a romantic moment in Streisand's Broadway triumph, Funny Girl. *"I couldn't steal the show from her if I stood on my head and yodeled," Desmond said.*

recorded (with a change of gender) by Barbra in the hope that it would call attention to her husband's show. But it was too late. Ironically, while the song did nothing for Gould's flop musical, "He Touched Me" went on to become one of his wife's defining recorded performances.

Shortly after her Broadway run in *Funny Girl* ended in December 1965, Streisand began production of her second CBS special. *Color Me Barbra* followed the three-act blueprint of its pre-

With the guidance of composer Michel Legrand, Streisand records tracks for Je m'appelle Barbra.

decessor, though this time the extravaganza was shot in flattering color. In the Philadelphia Museum of Art, Streisand portrayed singing versions of heroines of several classic paintings. In a circus setting she clowned with the animals and bounced on a trampoline, and a final concert sequence highlighted her confidence and sensuality. "The show is a one-woman tour de force of song and sex appeal," *Newsweek* declared. *Color Me Barbra* was another ratings triumph and its soundtrack album a bestseller.

By the time her special aired on March 30, 1966, Streisand was rehearsing—with British actor Michael Craig as Nick Arnstein—for the London opening of *Funny Girl* at the Prince of Wales Theater. "I found out I was pregnant opening night," she revealed in 1997. "No one wanted to tell me . . . they didn't know what effect it would

have on me to know I was pregnant before [the performance.] I might have said, 'Forget the show.'" With every performance sold out in advance, the star waited nearly two months to announce her pregnancy, and though she was forced to miss a few performances, she fulfilled her fourteen-week commitment.

The press, to her disgust, had dubbed her upcoming bundle of joy a "million dollar baby," because its arrival would cut short a potentially lucrative national concert tour Streisand was planning upon her return to the United States.

As it was, she was able to appear in six cities to tremendous response prior to returning to Manhattan to await motherhood. "When I was pregnant, at least the last four months," she said later, "I was a woman. No deadlines or curtains to meet. Whenever I thought of what was growing

Barbra poses with the Emmy she received on September 15, 1965, for her first television special, My Name is Barbra. *Two years earlier she had received her first nomination for her guest appearance on* The Judy Garland Show.

inside me . . . it's a miracle, the height of creativity for any woman."

On December 29, after being in labor for more than six hours, Barbra Streisand gave birth to a son, Jason Emanuel. In one of her first interviews as a new mother, Streisand reflected on the challenges of raising a boy: "You realize that they are these little people, and they want to be held, and they cry, and they get hurt, just like women. Unfortunately, society has put these pressures on men to be strong, and it's quite unfair. It's nice to find a man who's as vulnerable as he is strong."

In April 1967 Barbra taped her third television special, and it proved to be the first major miscalculation of her career. Designed to pay tribute to the vaudeville era, *The Belle of 14th Street* broke the one-woman-show format by enlisting guest stars Jason Robards and stage legend John Bubbles. Still recovering from Jason's birth and facing the filming of her first movie in a matter of weeks, Streisand felt she lacked the energy to attempt another solo outing. Unfortunately, the entire production lacked energy. When the special was aired in October, critics and fans alike greeted it with indifference, and a soundtrack album was canceled in reaction to the show's disappointing reception.

In May, Barbra arrived in Hollywood to begin rehearsals of the movie version of *Funny Girl*. Her contract with Ray Stark two years earlier had guaranteed the film—but only after she agreed to perform in the London run of the show. After early discussions with other studios, Stark reached an agreement with Columbia Pictures which guaranteed Streisand the chance to immortalize her performance on film. In addition, she had recently been contracted to make the movie version of *On a Clear Day You Can See Forever* for Paramount, and would soon be announced as the star of *Hello, Dolly!* for Twentieth Century–Fox, to begin production immediately following completion of *Funny Girl*. No neophyte film actress had ever entered the movie business under such remarkable conditions.

Surprisingly, just as *Funny Girl* was beginning production, Streisand returned to Manhattan to perform a free concert in Central Park before a crowd in excess of 135,000 people—one of the largest audiences ever assembled to hear a single performer up to that time. Seen by many as a symbolic farewell from the star to her hometown, the June 17 show became another career landmark, although she admitted later that she suffered extreme stage fright as a result of death threats she received in response to her support of Israel in the just-ended Six Day War. The album version of the concert was released over a year later to coincide

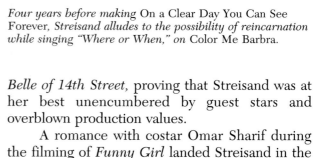

Belle of 14th Street, proving that Streisand was at her best unencumbered by guest stars and overblown production values.

A romance with costar Omar Sharif during the filming of *Funny Girl* landed Streisand in the gossip columns, as did reports that she was bossing her director and cinematographer on the sound-stages. But the terrific success of the film when it opened in September 1968 guaranteed her the movie stardom she seemed destined for. Unfortunately, *this* career milestone coincided with personal heartache. In February 1969 she and Elliott Gould announced their estrangement. Irrespective of the Sharif dalliance, the marriage had been troubled for some time, as Gould found it increasingly difficult to watch the ongoing public glorification of his wife. It seemed no coincidence that upon his separation from Streisand, Gould's career finally ignited.

The announcement later in the month that Barbra had been nominated for an Academy Award as the year's Best Actress surprised no one, although her decision to go with her estranged husband to the ceremonies on April 14, 1969, raised some eyebrows, as did the costume she chose to wear. A shimmering black net pants suit worn over a nude body stocking, the Scassi-designed outfit looked elegantly youthful until it was blasted with intense stage and photographers lights. Under those conditions, it appeared as if Tinseltown's most controversial new star was actually nude beneath the peek-a-boo netting. The audience at the Dorothy Chandler Pavilion was shocked when she walked toward the stage to accept her award, with what looked like her nearly-bare behind on display. They laughed a moment later, however, when she greeted the Oscar with "Hello, gorgeous," her famous opening line in *Funny Girl.*

Considering the mean-spirited press Streisand had endured since coming to Hollywood, and the influence it must have had on Academy voters, it was a small miracle that she won the award—albeit in a tie with Katharine Hepburn for her extraordinary performance in *The Lion in Winter.* In addition to the Academy honor, 1969 brought Streisand other prestigious

with the premiere of *Funny Girl. A Happening in Central Park* contained many of Barbra's hits, comedy bits she hadn't performed since her earliest club dates, and a gorgeously sung "Sleep in Heavenly Peace," a daring selection for a balmy summer evening. The *Central Park* television special erased much of the negative memory of *The*

18

In costume for a vaudeville-era striptease (sung to the strains of "Alice Blue Gown"), Barbra looks to director Joe Layton on the set of The Belle of 14th Street.

awards. She was named "Entertainer of the Year" by both *Cue* magazine and the Friars Club, a venerable all-male theatrical organization, and though she lost the Tony Awards she had competed for in 1962 and 1964, the Antoinette Perry Organization presented her with a special trophy as "Star of the Decade."

In July, Streisand became the first star to play the new International Hotel in Las Vegas with a month-long engagement for which she received close to a million dollars. (She had first appeared in the gambling capital for considerably less money in 1963 as the unconventional opening act for Liberace at the Riviera.) Streisand's highly

A pregnant Barbra makes light of the rain during a stadium concert in Atlanta, one of the stops on her brief 1966 tour.

as smoothly as could be expected, considering the film's massive production challenges. *On a Clear Day You Can See Forever* encountered even less trouble. But after just two years in the movie business, Streisand found it essential to break away from the grandiose musicals that had established her stardom, so as not to be left in the dust with the emergence of the new, harder-edged, reality-based Hollywood. Her unrestrained comic performance as a hooker opposite George Segal in *The Owl and the Pussycat* brought her screen image squarely and hilariously into the seventies.

Streisand began her second decade of superstardom with a relationship that provoked international headlines. For several months she was seen in the company of progressive Canadian prime minister Pierre Elliott Trudeau in Montreal and New York. It was later alleged that Trudeau had proposed marriage, and in her candid 1977 interview with *Playboy*, Streisand revealed, "I thought it would be fantastic. I'd have to learn how to speak French, I would do only movies in Canada. I had it all figured out. I would campaign for him and become totally politically involved in all the causes, abortion and whatever." Although the marital fantasies were apparently fleeting, Streisand and Trudeau formed an enduring friendship.

The contemporizing of Barbra's screen persona corresponded with an updating of her musical image as well. With the exception of the *Funny Girl* score, her last few albums had failed to live up to sales expectations. *What About Today?*, an ill-conceived 1969 stab at "relevant" material by Lennon and McCartney and Paul Simon among others, had only confused record buyers with its Broadway-style arrangements.

Though she resisted at first, Streisand was finally convinced by producer Richard Perry to record a collection of songs by the likes of Carole King, Joni Mitchell, and Randy Newman. The first single, "Stoney End," a rocker penned by Laura Nyro, was released late in 1970, and it climbed the charts as no Streisand single had since "People." The *Stoney End* album debuted in February 1971 and reached the top ten. Some traditionalists were displeased with the "new Barbra," but others, particularly younger listeners, appreciated the risk taken and the mainly positive results. A second pop collection, *Barbra Joan*

touted opening at the International was criticized for its studied elegance and lack of warmth. She took the criticisms to heart and strove to improve the show during the course of the engagement. She returned to the hotel—later renamed the Las Vegas Hilton—for successful stands in 1970–71 and 1971–72. She also returned to the Riviera in 1970 to fulfill an obligation she had put off for six years. This time, sans Liberace, she was a smash.

Aside from a publicized squabble with costar Walter Matthau, production on *Hello, Dolly!* went

The Goulds make an entrance at the New York premiere of Barbra's sensational movie debut, Funny Girl, *in September of 1968. They would announce their separation six months later.*

Streisand, was rushed out six months later, and it, too, became a solid hit.

Following production on *The Owl and the Pussycat,* Barbra took a year off from her movie career. After making back-to-back films since arriving in Hollywood, she needed a respite. "I look forward to working less and simplifying my life," she said, "to fulfilling some of my potential as an individual and as a woman. What I'd like is more time— time not only to read the stacks of political journals that have been piling up, but also time to read *Good Housekeeping* to find out different ways to decorate my son's sandwiches."

In 1972 she returned to the screen in Peter Bogdanovich's screwball comedy, *What's Up, Doc?,* costarring her then-flame, Ryan O'Neal. The huge success of the film put further distance between Barbra and her first screen image as the star of old-fashioned musicals. In April, she reinforced her appeal to her contemporaries when she joined Carole King, James Taylor, and Quincy Jones at the Forum in Los Angeles for a fund-raising concert to benefit the presidential campaign of George McGovern. *Live Concert at the Forum,* released in October, captured Barbra's performance on vinyl.

Her next film, *Up the Sandbox,* met with a mixed reception. Though the overall production was panned, it appeared at a time when the Equal Rights Amendment was being hotly debated, and critics praised Streisand's thoughtful performance and the film's unique examination of the confusion many women were feeling about society's expectations of them. Even so, the ticket-buying public was unimpressed.

Under the banner of her newly formed company, Barwood Films Ltd., *Sandbox* marked Streisand's first foray into motion picture production in association with First Artists, an independent firm she established in 1969 with Paul Newman and Sidney Poitier. The three actors hoped that First Artists would allow them to produce films under their own auspices, so that they would be dependent on the major studios only for

distribution. Streisand, Newman, and Poitier would still honor existing contracts, but they saw First Artists as an opportunity to make less expensive, more personalized projects that the major studios might have passed on. Certainly *Up the Sandbox* fell into that category.

Streisand had much better luck with her next film, released in October 1973. *The Way We Were* united her with Robert Redford in a sweeping love story that brought out the charismatic best in both stars. One of the top-grossing pictures of the year, *The Way We Were* earned Barbra a Best Actress Oscar nomination. In addition, her performance of the title song enhanced the film's soundtrack and hit number one on the singles chart—her first record to do so. The song went on to win the Oscar and the Grammy as Song of the Year.

On November 2, 1973, CBS aired *Barbra Streisand . . . and Other Musical Instruments*, her first television special in five years. Streisand had been seen only rarely on the home screen since becoming a film star, so there was great anticipation surrounding *Musical Instruments*. Though not without highlights ("I Got Rhythm," "I Never Has Seen Snow," and duets with Ray Charles), the show was overproduced, received lukewarm reviews, and would prove to be the final special to air under Streisand's 1965 CBS contract. The soundtrack from the show was not a hit.

To follow the critical and popular success of *The Way We Were*, Streisand chose *For Pete's Sake*, a sitcom-like vehicle that made money but did nothing for her reputation. In one respect, however, the movie proved vitally important to her future both as a woman and as a star. The wig she wore in the picture was designed by Jon Peters, a young, dynamic Beverly Hills-based hairstylist-turned-millionaire. Dark, handsome, and bearded, Peters was reputed to be both "the hairdresser to the stars" and a flamboyant ladies' man. He and Barbra began a turbulent affair that would survive harsh criticism for nearly a decade. To the chagrin of Streisand's famous agent, Sue Mengers, Peters soon became active in Barbra's career; he felt he could help her move her career in a new, funkier direction. "I didn't fall in love with Barbra independent of her star trip," Peters admitted. "I was fascinated by her and, of course, by Hollywood."

"Marty the Martian" was a comic highlight of Barbra's free Central Park concert "happening" held in the summer of 1967 and telecast over a year later.

Streisand models the Arnold Scass-designed evening paja-mas she would later wear to the Academy Awards.

The outfit took on a much different—and controversial—nature when flooded with light from flashbulbs and television cameras.

The first Streisand/Peters collaboration was *ButterFly*, an album of songs by a diverse roster that included Bob Marley, David Bowie, Bill Withers, and Paul Anka. Most critics disliked it when it was released in October 1974, but *ButterFly*'s sales warranted a gold record. Veteran Streisand admirers expressed concern that their favorite star—now seen more often in jeans and T-shirts than haute couture—was tossing aside her usual good taste in favor of Peters's desire to turn her into a rock star. Marty Erlichman, too, didn't agree with Jon's desire to bring the goddess down to earth; by 1977 he ceased to function as Barbra's manager.

In order to extricate herself from the multi-picture contract she had signed with Ray Stark a decade earlier, Streisand agreed to film a sequel to *Funny Girl* that would trace Fanny Brice's life after her divorce from Nick Arnstein and through

In December of 1969, Barbra attended the nightclub debut of her half-sister, Rosyln Kind, at the Plaza Hotel in Manhattan. Rosyln has forged an intermittently successful singing and acting career that has never been unique enough to allow her to fully emerge from Streisand's shadow.

her subsequent marriage to showman Billy Rose. Though *Funny Lady* failed to live up to its predecessor's standards, it drew many rave reviews and proved a major box-office success for Columbia Studios during the 1975 Easter season.

In the wake of the critical drubbing suffered by *ButterFly,* Streisand turned production chores on her new album, *Lazy Afternoon,* over to composer/ arranger—and future Broadway maven—Rupert Holmes. The resulting song collection, which included "Moanin' Low," placed in a big-band setting, and a disco version of "Shake Me, Wake Me," was one of the best of Streisand's career, pleasing both critics and fans when it was released in October 1975. *Classical Barbra* made its appearance four months later. A unique effort in which she delivered elegant, if not dynamic, interpretations of songs and lieder by Debussy, Orff, Handel, and other composers, the album's hypnotic quality earned Streisand a Grammy nomination for Best Classical Vocal Soloist Performance.

"She can't go on playing Ray Stark's mother-in-law forever," said Jon Peters as he and Barbra geared up for her tenth and most controversial film, *A Star Is Born.* Set in the chaotic world of rock music, the filming of this tragic love story attracted vicious criticism from the moment the project was announced. It proved a tremendous hit with the public, however, and became the highest grossing Streisand film to date. *A Star Is Born* redefined her image, brought her a new generation of fans, and thrust her into the pop music main-

stream as never before. "Evergreen," the hit ballad she composed for the film, went on to win the Oscar for Best Original Song and a Grammy for Song of the Year; Streisand's performance was honored with a Grammy for Best Pop Vocal, Female. The tremendous success of the film, and its multi-platinum soundtrack album, established Peters and Streisand as producers to be reckoned with.

In the summer of 1977, Columbia released *Streisand Superman,* a potent pop collection that hit big and reinforced the contemporary persona Streisand had projected in *A Star Is Born.* Though such subsequent albums as *Songbird* and *Wet* were of inconsistent quality, they helped her reach a new peak of public acceptance. Over the next few years, Barbra enjoyed her greatest success as a pop vocalist with radio-friendly hits that included "My Heart Belongs to Me," "Woman in Love," "You Don't Bring Me Flowers" with Neil Diamond, "Enough Is Enough/No More Tears" with Donna Summer, and "Guilty" with Barry Gibb. By 1979, *US* magazine had named Streisand and Summer the top female recording artists of the 1970s.

Back on television in May 1978, Streisand performed four songs with the Los Angeles Philharmonic Orchestra as the finale of an ABC-TV special, *The Stars Salute Israel at 30*. Prior to singing "Hativka," the Israeli national anthem, Streisand chatted with Golda Meir via satellite from Tel Aviv.

Taking longer and longer breaks between her professional obligations, Barbra spent much of her time enjoying the verdant parcel of Malibu land that she and Jon Peters were now calling home. Located in exclusive Ramirez Canyon, the "ranch" as it was misleadingly called, eventually grew to include a tennis court, swimming pool, and no fewer than five houses, including an authentically designed art deco guest cottage that Streisand masterminded.

With Jason now eleven, and Jon Peters's nine-year-old son Christopher (from his marriage to Lesley Ann Warren), rounding out her family, Barbra thrived in the woodsy splendors of her Malibu retreat. "I love it here," the former Brooklynite told the press. "You are very much in touch with the earth, and with the natural things that happen. I never used to walk or ride a bike. I never breathed deeply before. The pressures of the business can destroy you . . . the thing that keeps me sane is living here. It's away from it all." Streisand also maintained a handsome Mediterranean-style home closer to the center of things in Holmby Hills, a few blocks west of the Beverly Hills Hotel.

Returning to the screen after two and a half years, Barbra once again teamed up with Ryan O'Neal, in *The Main Event*, a strident battle-of-the-sexes comedy that possessed none of the breezy charm of *What's Up, Doc?* Although the movie pulled in hefty box-office grosses upon release in the summer of 1979, it drew some scalding criticism for the inconsistency of Streisand's role—and performance—and the screenplay's vulgar humor.

To write and produce her next album, *Guilty*, Barbra called on Barry Gibb of the Bee Gees, then basking in the unbelievable success of the soundtrack for *Saturday Night Fever* and a string of subsequent hits. Thanks to Gibb's melodious compositions, his sure production hand, and Streisand's airborne vocals, *Guilty* emerged in October 1980 as the seamless pop statement that fans had been waiting for since *A Star Is Born*. It proved to be Barbra's most popular album to date, climbing to the top of the charts in close to a dozen countries—even the former U.S.S.R. The album has since been certified platinum many

In January 1970, Clint Eastwood and Barbra posed with Golden Globes they had won from the Hollywood Foreign Press Association as World Film Favorites. Later in the year they would both release musicals from Paramount with disappointing box-office results.

Four-year-old Jason Gould and his mother are ambushed by photographers at a screening of Willie Wonka and the Chocolate Factory.

times over, and though it was nominated for four Grammys—including Album of the Year—only Streisand and Gibb's lilting duet of the title song won an award.

Guilty's popularity carried over into the early spring, but it didn't help sell tickets when Streisand's new comedy with Gene Hackman, *All Night Long,* was released in March 1981. The film, which a minority of critics felt exuded a delicate European charm, failed to entice audiences and became the biggest flop of Barbra's movie career.

In November 1983, after years of frustrating delays, studio turndowns, seemingly insurmountable roadblocks, and twenty-four months of grueling production in England and Czechoslovakia, Streisand's pet film project, her directorial debut, *Yentl,* opened to predominantly good reviews and strong box office. As the first woman to produce, direct, cowrite, and act—and sing—in a major film, Barbra received lavish praise, balanced by predictable cries of megalomania. In January she became the first woman to win a Golden Globe for directing. A lack of major Academy Award nominations for *Yentl,* however, was labeled a scandal and led a boisterous crowd to demonstrate outside the Oscar ceremonies the following spring.

In many ways, the pressure of making *Yentl* took an irreparable toll on Barbra's relationship with Jon Peters, who had vacillated about the movie for years. By the time the film opened, the couple had ended their volatile ten-year romance. Following a brief spell of dating, Streisand began an affair with tall, curly-haired Richard Baskin, a composer and heir to the Baskin and Robbins ice cream empire. Typically, as the relationship deepened, Streisand called on Baskin's musical expertise as she recorded a new album. Looking for a break from the almost symphonic *Yentl* score, the singer decided on a pop effort, one that Columbia hoped would spawn a number of hit singles as *Guilty* had four years earlier.

An uneasy mix of ballads, dance music, and rock, *Emotion,* released in October 1984, was branded a "formularized, predictable pop effort." The album barely crawled into the top twenty—despite two stylish videos Streisand made to promote it. In the three years since the release of *Guilty,* the world of pop music had undergone one of its periodic upheavals. The advent of MTV and the emergence of new stars left little room on the singles charts for even the most revered veterans. Over the next few years, despite continued success with her albums, Streisand would receive less and less airplay on Top 40 radio stations. It was a situation that harked back to the sixties for the singer as did, coincidentally, her next album.

In July 1973, Barbra was at work on the London set of Barbra Streisand...and Other Musical Instruments *with piano prodigy Dominic Savage.*

"Anybody could have done the songs on [*Emotion*] as well or better than I could have done them," Streisand told the *New York Times* a year later. "It was time for me to do something I truly believed in." To the delight of critics and fans, she did precisely that when she released *The Broadway Album* in November 1985. Reuniting with Peter Matz, who had offered brilliant musical support on her first few albums, she delivered masterful renditions of Broadway classics by Gershwin, Sondheim, Bernstein, and Rodgers and Hammerstein. William Friedkin directed her in a handsome video for "Somewhere," and though the song wasn't a top-selling single, it became an instant Streisand classic. *The Broadway Album* brought Barbra Streisand back to her musical-theater roots, and the record-buying public found the results overdue and irresistible. Reaching number one, the release earned her the sixth Album of the Year nomination of her career. In still another move linked to the early days of her career, Barbra reunited with Marty Erlichman, and he continues to function as her manager to this day.

On September 6 of the following year, Streisand staged her first concert in fourteen years in a grassy meadow on her Malibu property. A benefit for the newly formed Hollywood Women's Political Committee, *One Voice* supported five Democratic senatorial candidates who espoused nuclear disarmament and progressive social and environmental causes. Before a star-studded audience that had paid $5,000 per couple to attend, and backed by just a handful of musicians, Streisand performed intimate versions of some of her signature songs and—for the first and only time—"Over the Rainbow." "We must find new ways to communicate with each other," she said between songs, "to understand each other, to be compassionate toward each other. We inhabit this tiny planet together, and if we are to survive, it will be together or not at all."

Though earnestly felt, the entertainer's preachings struck some as condescending, yet no one could deny her power to raise money: The evening grossed $1.5 million, substantially more, the press noted, than had been raised at a nearby Reagan fund-raiser on the same evening. *One Voice* was aired as a television special on HBO at the end of the year, and an album of the event was released the following April. Proceeds from the various *One Voice* incarnations were utilized to establish the Washington, D.C.–based Streisand Foundation, which by 1998, had donated over $20 million to organizations dealing with breast cancer, AIDS, children's concerns, environmental advocacy, and other political and social causes.

As unlike *Yentl* as it could be, Barbra's first film project in four years was a harrowing courtroom drama about a prostitute accused of killing a client. *Nuts* costarred Richard Dreyfuss and allowed Streisand an opportunity to deliver a powerful performance that earned her a Golden Globe nomination. Ultimately, in spite of enthusiastic previews and excellent reviews, the 1987 film

27

strengths, her direct approach to music, acting, people, and yes, making love. To me she is beautiful. I know some people make fun of her nose, but let me tell you, she can smell a phony with it a mile away."

True to form, Barbra brought Johnson into her next project, an album of contemporary songs that would follow a love affair full circle from hopeful beginnings to a bittersweet end. Unfortunately, by the time the couple's duet of "Til I Loved You" hit radio stations, their romance was all but over, a development that sabotaged any success the single might have enjoyed. The follow-up album, of the same name, released in November, proved to be disappointing.

For her second directorial attempt, Streisand chose to film Pat Conroy's best-selling novel, *The Prince of Tides.* The movie, released in 1991, became a showcase for the commanding performance of Nick Nolte as an unhappily married southern football coach who must come to terms with his seriously dysfunctional family. Streisand took a subordinate role as Nolte's controversial love interest, the New York psychiatrist who is treating his sister.

In a move that courted criticism but which proved ideal for the film, Barbra cast twenty-five-year old Jason Gould as her character's troubled teenaged son. Shortly before the release of *The Prince of Tides,* a supermarket tabloid "outed" Jason, claiming that he and a male model had been joined in a "marriage" ceremony that Barbra had refused to attend. Though leaving public discussion of her son's sexual orientation up to him, Streisand retorted, "I don't care if my son marries a chimpanzee; I would be at the wedding." (In 1996, Jason directed and starred in *Inside Out,* a fifteen-minute seriocomic film in which he played the son of a superstar who must come to terms with having his homosexuality made public by the tabloids. Elliott Gould appears in the film as Jason's understanding father. *Inside Out* was well received at the Sundance Film Festival and has been shown at various gay and lesbian festivals around the country.)

failed to perform to box-office expectations, and garnered no Academy Award nominations.

By this time, Barbra's relationship with Richard Baskin had cooled; the couple had settled into a warm, companionable friendship. Shortly after *Nuts* opened, Streisand began a highly publicized new romance that was played out in tabloid headlines. She met Don Johnson, the sexy star of the popular TV show *Miami Vice,* while they were both spending the holidays in Aspen. Soon they were attending boxing matches, basketball games, and high-profile celebrity parties together.

Well-known for his womanizing, Johnson had been married three times—once to the much younger Melanie Griffith—and he seemed an unlikely romantic prospect for Barbra. "I've been with thousands of women," Johnson admitted to a British journalist, "but Streisand is supreme, unequaled in all the ways that count. I love her

Jon, Barbra, and musician Tom Scott go over charts for Streisand's Butterfly *album, released in October 1974. Jon may have loved Barbra, but critics felt differently abou the album he produced for her.*

The Prince of Tides opened nationally on Christmas Day, 1991, to uniformly positive reviews and outstanding business. When award season rolled around several weeks later, Nick Nolte became a Golden Globe recipient for Best Actor, while Streisand was thrilled to receive a nomination from the Directors Guild. *The Prince of Tides* was nominated for six Academy Awards, including one for Best Picture—but not for direction. When the movie failed to win any Oscars, Streisand took solace in the knowledge that the worldwide box-office totals were the best of her career.

Aside from a soundtrack for *The Prince of Tides,* Streisand's main 1991 album release had been in the planning stages for years. *Just for the Record* included sixty-five tracks tracing her singing career from the recording of "You'll Never Know" she made at thirteen to a 1988 version of the song she blended with the original. The four-CD set, which also featured several of her award-acceptance speeches, included duets with Judy Garland and Ray Charles as well as many other songs which had never been available commercially.

On January 19, 1992, Barbra made a brief appearance during a hilarious segment on *Saturday Night Live* that featured Mike Myers in drag as Linda Richman, an obsessed Streisand fan and host of *Coffee Talk*, a tacky cable TV show. The skit showed Linda Richman, chatting with Madonna and Roseanne about *The Prince of Tides*, and declaring Barbra to be so wonderful she's "like butter." Streisand's surprise walk-on shocked and delighted the three stars and the studio audience. A few nights later, during ceremonies at Radio City Music Hall, Stephen Sondheim presented Barbra with a Grammy Legend Award, which she dedicated to her fans.

On November 18, Streisand was presented the Commitment to Life Award from AIDS Project Los Angeles at the organization's annual gala. An all-star lineup that included Elton John, Liza Minnelli, Clint Black, and Wynonna Judd delivered exciting versions of songs from *West Side Story*. Barbra joined Johnny Mathis for a medley of "I Have a Love" and "One Hand, One Heart," and soloed on "Somewhere."

For several years, Streisand was criticized for not taking a more active stand in the fight against AIDS. It was appreciated that she had contributed a great deal of money to the cause, but some activists felt she should have made her support more public, as had stars such as Elizabeth Taylor, Madonna, and Bette Midler. However, much of this criticism was swept aside as a result of this evening, which—largely because of Streisand's participation—raised a record $3.9 million.

In December 1992, fifty-year-old Barbra Streisand signed a new $60 million contract with Sony/Columbia that placed her in a league with Madonna, Prince, and Janet and Michael Jackson—all of whom had recently made similar (some lesser) deals with their record companies. Streisand's agreement encompassed both records and films, and would guarantee the star a $5 million advance against every album and a 42 percent royalty rate that translates to nearly $3 per CD sold. Her film fees would be based on whether she simply acted in a feature or took on directing and producing chores as well.

The first album produced under the new contract, *Back to Broadway,* was released in July 1993. The collection contained two dramatic showstoppers from Andrew Lloyd Webber's new spectacle, *Sunset Boulevard;* and a duet of "The Music of the Night" from *Phantom of the Opera* star (and former *Hello, Dolly!* costar), Michael Crawford. A strong effort that lacked the sparkle of the first Broadway collection (some critics found it overproduced), *Back to Broadway* earned Streisand two Grammy nominations.

Later in the year, she joined a roster of stars for what would become Frank Sinatra's final recording sessions. She crooned "I've Got a Crush on You" with Sinatra for his popular *Duets* album released on Capitol. Years past his vocal prime, Sinatra still managed to bring a poignant magnetism to his collaboration with Streisand, whose sinuous vocals complemented his world weariness. Thanks to state-of-the-art technology, Barbra and Frank were able to record their lyrics separately—Frank even adding a note or two by phone—a technique that somehow doesn't spoil the record's pleasurable sense of intimacy.

Barbra's live performances for Clinton and AIDS Project L.A. led to speculation that she might be considering a long-awaited return to concertizing. Her singing appearances had become so rare since the early seventies that even the performance of a single song—at the Oscar or Grammy ceremonies, for instance—became an event. Aside from the abbreviated schedule of concert dates she undertook during her pregnancy in 1966,

Following the presentation of her award by Warren Beatty, Streisand delivered a powerful speech against apathy and intolerance that drew even greater response from the audience than had her rare singing performance. After railing against right-wing extremists such as Pat Buchanan, she advocated a boycott of Colorado as a winter vacation destination in the face of recently passed antigay legislation by the state. "I am against discrimination of any kind," she later told Barbara Walters emphatically, "and this is an amendment that is discriminatory."

Streisand had been instrumental in rallying Hollywood's most influential Democrats behind Bill Clinton, and she performed at a fund-raiser for his campaign in September, helping to raise over $1.5 million. More politically outspoken than she had ever been, she weathered criticism for her close friendship with the first family. In January, she was the pièce de résistance of Clinton's inaugural celebration: In Landover, Maryland, she closed a concert at the U.S. Air Arena that had featured performances by Michael Jackson and Fleetwood Mac. She sang Clinton's favorite, "Evergreen."

Streisand had never toured. Her most consistent schedule of live performances had occurred during her once-a-year Las Vegas engagements from 1969 through 1971. As the years rolled on, the singer admitted that she suffered increasingly from a paralyzing stage fright heightened by audience expectations; the more legendary she became, the more people wanted to see her sing live, and the more she feared disappointing them.

Thus a great deal of hoopla greeted the announcement in the fall of 1993 that Streisand would open the gargantuan MGM Grand Hotel in Las Vegas for two concerts over the '93–'94 New Year's weekend, for a fee that allegedly amounted to $20 million and a guarantee from the hotel's owner, Kirk Kerkorian, that he would donate $3 million to charities of Streisand's choice. Eager aficionados from all over the world put through over a million telephone calls on the November day the upscale tickets, priced from $100 to $1,000, went on sale. "My fans, the public, they want to see me perform," Streisand told Barbara Walters. "It's almost like something I withhold from them, and in a way maybe I was . . . I was ready to sing, I was ready to face this kind of fear . . . because it's a way of touching people and have them touch me."

Barbra enlisted the aid of longtime friends and collaborators, lyricists Marilyn and Alan Bergman and composer Marvin Hamlisch, to design a multimedia show that would trace in song and patter her youthful inspirations, her years of therapy, her humor, and her social and political beliefs—while allowing for the inclusion of many of her hit songs. The sold-out concerts in Las Vegas were greeted ecstatically by fans and warmly by critics. "Streisand combined in these two hours all that she has learned as an artist," the *Los Angeles Times* reported. "Drawing upon her experience in movies and music, Streisand injected the production with a director's sense of atmosphere and occasion, an actress's feel for character and intimacy, and a singer's vocal beauty and command."

As fans had hoped, once Streisand got her act together, and it had proven such a smash, she took it on the road for a limited tour. She opened in April 1994 in London, where she received a dose of nasty attention from the tabloid press but got to reunite backstage with Prince Charles, whom she had met in Hollywood in 1974. In his

31

Michael Douglas poses with Paul Williams and Barbra as they greet the press after accepting Golden Globe Awards for writing "Evergreen," the love theme from A Star Is Born.

autobiography, published soon after, Charles admitted to a long-standing crush on Barbra, calling her "my only pinup . . . she is devastatingly attractive . . . with a great deal of sex appeal."

From England, Barbra moved on to Washington, D.C., Detroit, Los Angeles (Anaheim), San Jose, New York, and back to Los Angeles to make up for dates she had postponed earlier due to a severe case of laryngitis. At every stop, she was greeted by thunderous ovations, fawning celebrities, and a preponderance of great reviews. She also made charitable appearances, primarily for children's causes, along the way.

With their atmosphere of a homecoming, Streisand's New York dates at Madison Square Garden were particularly electrifying. Her final

song was broadcast live on Times Square's Jumbotron screens. "As Barbra hit the final soul-searching notes of the evening's last song, 'Somewhere,'" wrote columnist Liz Smith, "I thought the top of my head—and the roof of the Garden—would come off! All about her were hysterical, but Barbra was in total, brilliant control—the calm, glittering eye of her own self-created hurricane. What a woman! What a talent! Barbra is a star for the ages."

HBO taped the final show of the tour in July at the Arrowhead Pond in Anaheim, and when *Barbra Streisand: The Concert* aired on August 21, 1994, it registered as the highest-rated entertainment special in the cable channel's history. At the Emmy awards ceremony in September 1995, *The*

Concert earned five trophies, including one for Barbra—her first Emmy in thirty years. *Billboard* later named the commercially released home video of *The Concert* the best-selling music video of '95 and '96.

A two-disk album of the concert recorded during the explosive Madison Square Garden dates was released in September and promptly climbed into the top ten. Certified double platinum, the album earned Streisand two Grammy nominations. At the award ceremonies, however, her only recognition took the form of a Lifetime Achievement honor.

Early 1995 brought her attention for her deeply held, controversial political and social beliefs. On February 3 she delivered an impassioned address entitled "The Artist as Citizen" to an overflow crowd at the John F. Kennedy School of Government at Harvard University. In her talk she defended herself and others in the entertainment industry who speak out politically, and she attacked the notion that arts funding was nonessential when compared to the demands of military budgets. "I'm also very proud to be a liberal," she said. "The liberals were liberating. They fought slavery, fought for women to have the right to vote . . . fought to end segregation, fought to end apartheid. Liberals put an end to child labor."

Three days later, NBC aired *Serving in Silence: The Margarethe Cammermeyer Story,* Streisand's first foray into dramatic television production. Starring Glenn Close in the title role,

Serving in Silence told the story of Colonel Cammermeyer, who was drummed out of her National Guard nursing position—after years of exemplary service—when she admitted that she was a lesbian. Barbra and her Barwood production company partner (and lifelong friend), Cis Corman, had developed the project along with producer Craig Zadan after reading about Cammermeyer's case. "If we can help change some people's opinions," Streisand said in promoting the film, "make them less frightened of something they don't understand; if they can look at this story and feel compassion and perhaps even anger at the military

It's a bird, it's a plane, it's Barbra, posing for photographs to accompany her smash Streisand Superman *album. She wore the same outfit for the cover of* Playboy.

for this injustice, then it will be worthwhile." A ratings winner, *Serving in Silence* won Glenn Close an Emmy for her sensitive portrayal, and the drama went on to win a Peabody award.

Streisand's third directorial effort, *The Mirror Has Two Faces,* received some of the most derogatory reviews she had faced in years when it

opened in November 1996. Labeled a vanity production by many important critics, the movie nonetheless found its boosters who applauded Lauren Bacall's stand-out performance as Barbra's mother.

Streisand had written a "love theme" for the picture which rocker Bryan Adams, and other

(Above) Flanked by her mother, Diana, and her brother, Sheldon, Barbra dedicates the sign that officially renames a Santa Monica school in honor of her father. Barbra's interest in the school, and the subsequent financial endowment, stemmed from studies for her son's Bar Mitzvah.

(Left) Neil Diamond and Barbra are all smiles following their duet of "You Don't Bring Me Flowers," on the Grammy Awards telecast of February 27, 1980. (Photo by Robert Scott)

cowriters, expanded into "I Finally Found Someone," a pop confection recorded as a duet by Adams and Streisand that closed the movie on an ebullient note, and became Streisand's first hit single in fifteen years.

The title of the song, mixed with the sentiment of the movie about a mature couple finding love unexpectedly, mirrored a dramatic development in Barbra Streisand's personal life that began as she was editing the film. In July, at a party thrown by Jon Peter's ex-wife, Christine, Barbra was set up to meet James

Streisand's failure to win any significant Oscar nominations for Yentl *led a group called Principles, Equality and Professionalism in Film to organize a protest outside the Dorothy Chandler Pavilion the night of the Academy Award Ceremonies, 1984 (Photo by Robert Scott)*

Brolin, the tall, handsome fifty-six-year-old actor who is best known as the star of *Marcus Welby, M.D.* and *Hotel*, two long-running television series. It was soon obvious to Peters and her other guests that there was an immediate and intense attraction between Brolin and Streisand.

Shortly after they met, Brolin was called away to the Philippines for a film assignment. During his absence, he and Barbra would spend hours talking on the telephone: she has recalled one evening when she fell asleep on the bathroom floor, the phone cradled in her arm. Later, she accompanied Brolin to Ireland where she would rise at dawn to prepare him breakfast as he faced the challenge of

directing his first feature film. "I think for the first time in my life I'm not afraid to love," Streisand told Barbara Walters. "Jim . . . fills a void that I never thought could be filled. Not having a father it was this kind of deep hole that could never be filled. Not only is he my lover and my friend, my best friend, but he fills the role of my dad at times . . ." "How would I characterize my relationship with Barbra?" Brolin told *McCalls*, "I'm her commanding officer and her slave all in one."

Within months of their first meeting, James joined Barbra in her homey, three-house complex perched atop a Malibu palisade that overlooks the ocean. (In 1993 Streisand turned her former

36

In 1987, Barbra Streisand was given the Grammy Award for Best Female Pop Vocalist for The Broadway Album.

Malibu property over to the Santa Monica Mountains Conservancy, and more recently she sold both her Holmby Hills residence and her penthouse on Central Park West.)

"For a while I didn't think I would [meet anyone]," Barbra told Oprah Winfrey. "I thought, well, God gives people certain gifts, and they say you can't have everything . . ." Brolin adds, "We are always saying, 'How did this happen? How did we get so lucky?' "

Barbra got lucky again when Academy Award nominations were announced in February 1997. Lauren Bacall, who had already won the Golden Globe, had been nominated in the supporting actress category for *Mirror,* and "I Finally Found Someone" had received a nod for Best Song. Natalie Cole was asked to sing the song for the Oscar broadcast after Barbra declined, but when Cole was taken ill, Celine Dion—who was already set to sing on the show—volunteered to sing "I Finally Found Someone."

Later in the year, Barbra and Celine, a devout Streisand fan, collaborated on "Tell Him," a lyrically insipid power ballad that nonetheless supplied a melodic framework within which both singers were allowed to shine. The following January, Barbra learned she would be competing with herself for a Grammy when her duets with Celine and Bryan Adams were both nominated in the same category. Unfortunately, neither song won, and illness forced Barbra to back out of the performance of "Tell Him" she and Celine had planned for the Grammy telecast.

Coinciding with the release of "Tell Him," another television project of Streisand's was aired on Showtime. *Rescuers: Stories of Courage* was a three-installment series of films about non-Jews who went to heroic lengths to rescue Jewish fam-

Barbra in the studio with (left to right) *Alan and Marilyn Bergman and composer Michel Legrand recording the* Yentl *soundtrack.*

ilies from the Holocaust. "This is a series that defines courage," Streisand said, "and how average people . . . given the horrific circumstances of war, often demonstrated the most unbelievable acts of selflessness." Barwood drew a group of actors including Elizabeth Perkins, Linda Hamilton, Dana Delany, and Alfred Molina and directors including Streisand's former colleague Peter Bogdanovich to the project.

In November 1997 Barbra's CD *Higher Ground* debuted at number one on the album chart, making history in the process. With the charting, Streisand became the recording artist with the longest span—thirty-three years—

between first and current number-one albums. "My plan," she wrote in the liner notes, "was to sing a collection of songs that spoke to the hearts of all persons of faith." Her versions of "The Water Is Wide," "Deep River," "On Holy Ground," and the haunting Hebrew prayer, "Avinu Malkeinu," proved to be emotional highlights of the multiplatinum album.

On November 21, Barbra, happy to promote the CD, sat down for an hour-long, entertaining chat with longtime fan Rosie O'Donnell on the latter's popular talk show. The highly rated hour offered a rare glimpse of a relaxed, relatively unguarded Streisand, who was later joined by James Brolin for a kiss and a champagne toast.

Television has played an increasingly pronounced role in Barbra's professional life. Barwood recently signed a multi-million-dollar deal with industry giant King World that will allow Streisand and her associates to develop future long-form TV projects. The second Barwood network television film was broadcast on NBC on May 3, 1998, and it generated unexpected controversy.

The Long Island Incident starred Laurie Metcalf as Congresswoman Carolyn McCarthy, the housewife who ran on a platform that urged the banning of assault weapons following the 1993 murder of her husband—and the maiming of her son—by a crazed gunman on the Long Island Rail Road. The morning after the telecast, Charlton Heston, president-to-be of the National Rifle Association, took out full-page newspaper ads challenging Streisand, as the film's executive producer (and the most famous, exploitable associate on the production), to a public debate about the Second Amendment of the Constitution—which guarantees the right to bear arms. ABC television reportedly offered the two stars a full hour of prime time for the debate, but Barbra declined. Through a statement read by the show's director, Joseph Sargent, she declared that she was not against guns being retained for protection or hunting but that she saw no justification for the legal ownership of assault rifles.

Such contretemps aside, Streisand clearly sees television as a welcoming forum for the kind of issue-related dramas that are increasingly more difficult to get produced as feature films.

After James Brolin announced his engagement to Barbra in May 1997, and she began sporting an elegantly simple solitaire diamond ring, a flurry of erroneous reports had them marrying everywhere from New England to Mexico. Just as speculation about a wedding seemed to have died down, Streisand and Brolin decided rather suddenly to marry on July 1, 1998—the second anniversary of their first meeting.

Amid heavy security (and romantic touches

Barbra happily displays two Golden Globes she won for directing and producing Yentl.

that included white orchids floating in the swimming pool), the ceremony took place in the living room of the main Malibu residence, as the sun was setting, before guests that included family and close friends Marilyn and Alan Bergman, Sydney Pollack, Quincy Jones, John Travolta, and Tom Hanks as well as President Clinton's brother Roger and Barbra's ex beau Richard Baskin. Wearing a Donna Karan-designed gown of off-white topped by a crystal-beaded veil of fifteen feet, Barbra was given away by her son. Brolin's actor-son Josh served as best man, while Barbra's sister Roslyn Kind stood in as matron of honor. Music was supplied by Marvin Hamlisch leading a string-heavy sixteen-piece orchestra.

Following the traditional Jewish ceremony, Barbra sang two new songs to her groom, "Just One Lifetime," and "I've Dreamed of You." The next morning, the Brolins embarked on a honeymoon—not to Barbados, as rumored—but to the nearby Channel Islands, which lie off the coast of Santa Barbara. The couple was allowed only a week-long idyll before Brolin's services were needed for a new season of *Pensacola: Wings of Gold*, his syndicated TV series.

In September 1999, Streisand released *A Love Like Ours*, an album of songs inspired by her happy marriage. Predictably, many critics couldn't resist chiding the accompanying liner notes (overladen with romantic poses of the Brolins), and reviewing the CD with more than a touch of cynicism. Others, however, were moved by Streisand's remarkably youthful vocals of such gems as the bittersweet Gershwin rarity "Isn't It a Pity," the two ballads she sang at her wedding, and a sensual new interpretation of a standout from the stage score of *Funny Girl*, "The Music That Makes Me Dance," a song she hadn't performed since 1966. To promote the album, Barbra spent another hour on the Rosie O'Donnell show, aired on November 16, 1999.

As Streisand's career approaches its forti-

A playful pose that recalls the "kooky" Streisand image of the early 1960s.

eth anniversary, the star has announced no feature-film plans, though she will be active in her role as a producer for television.

In February 1999 it was revealed that Barwood will produce a three-hour remake of Jerry Herman's musical comedy *Mame*, to be broadcast over ABC. Hopes are that Streisand will not only serve as executive producer of the show, but will agree to star in the title role once a suitable script and director are in place. Barwood's television schedule also includes a drama, *Two Hands That Shook the World*, which traces the lives of the slain Israeli prime minister Yitzhak Rabin and Palestinian leader Yassir Arafat, and *Roots and Wings*, about the relationship between a young girl and her grandmother. Streisand's company has also optioned *Romeo and Julie*, a novel by Jeanne Ray that traces the relationship between lovers from rival Italian and Jewish families.

For a reported fee of $13 million, Barbra

returned to the MGM Grand in Las Vegas to perform two Millennium Concerts on New Year's Eve weekend for a top ticket price of $2,500. A more elaborate presentation than the 1994 concert, the *Timeless* show recalled Streisand's early night-club dates, her successes on Broadway, and her movie musi-cals. Included in the program were songs she either hadn't per-formed publicly in decades, ("Miss Marmelstein," "A Sleepin' Bee," "Lover Come Back to Me,") or had sung only in the recording studio ("Alfie," "The Main Event").

Although she contem-plated a worldwide tour follow-ing the Las Vegas dates, Streisand opted instead to per-form four concerts in March in Australia and four shows in the final weeks of September (two each in Los Angeles and New York), which she announced would be the final concerts of her career. Exorbitant ticket prices aside, the finality of these appearances led fans from all over the world to converge on the Staples Center in L.A. and on Madison Square a week later. What they witnessed was a finely tuned, complicated stage presentation headed by a confident, chatty, relaxed Streisand who delivered a vintage program of songs through what one critic alled her "rust-proof pipes."

The New York shows left the crowd—which included Lauren Bacall, Rosie O'Donnell, Drew Barrymore, Tony Bennett, Stephen Sondheim, Alec Baldwin, GleenClose, Secretary of State Madeleine Albright, and Rev. Jesse Jackson—teary-eyed, and Barbra, too, couldn't help shed-ding a few tears onstage as she faced wave after wave of applause from her hometown audience. Fans around the world were able to enjoy the evening's final song, "People," as it was broadcast live over America Online. A day prior to the Los Angeles concerts, Columbia released a double CD, *Timeless: Live in Concert*, recorded during the New Year's Eve Millennium show.

Three weeks after the Las Vegas shows,

Barbra sings an impassioned version of "Papa, Can You Hear Me?" during a performance at Madison Square Garden on the New York leg of her celebrated 1994 concert tour. Streisand's seven Manhattan concerts earned a record $16.6 million. (Photo courtesy of Richard Giammanco)

Barbra Streisand received the Cecil B. DeMille Award from the Hollywood Foreign Press Association for her "outstanding contribution to the entertainment field," at the organization's annual Golden Globe ceremonies and telecast on January 23. In accepting her award from pal Shirley MacLaine, Streisand reflected on her childhood dream of becoming an actor, and she spoke with fondness of William Wyler. Backstage she hinted—as she has several times since her marriage—that she may retire, stating that she wants to "travel and enjoy life" rather than tackle work. "I'd like to direct another movie someday," she told a swarm of reporters, "but I don't have to. Film is a bit like *Alien:* It lives inside of you and then explodes out, leaving you lying on the floor covered in blood, exhausted." In response to another recent query about what her long-term professional goals might be, Streisand said only, "I'm waiting to be inspired."

The Films

Funny Girl
(1968)

❧

A Columbia Pictures Release of a Rastar Productions Picture

CAST

Barbra Streisand (*Fanny Brice*); Omar Sharif (*Nick Arnstein*); Kay Medford (*Rose Brice*); Anne Francis (*Georgia James*); Walter Pidgeon (*Florenz Ziegfeld*); Lee Allen (*Eddie Ryan*); Mae Questel (*Mrs. Strakosh*); Gerald Mohr (*Branca*); Frank Faylen (*Keeney*); Mittie Lawrence (*Emma*); Gertrude Flynn (*Mrs. O'Malley*); Penny Stanton (*Mrs. Meeker*); John Harmon (*Company Manager*); Thordis Brandt, Bettina Brenna, Virginia Ann Ford, Alena Johnston, Karen Lee, Mary Jane Mangler, Inga Neilsen, Sharon Vaughn (*Ziegfeld Girls*).

CREDITS

Producer: Ray Stark; director: William Wyler; assistant directors: Jack Roe, Ray Gosnell; screenplay: Isobel Lennart; book: Isobel Lennart (based on the play); music: Jule Styne; lyrics: Bob Merrill ("My Man" music by Maurice Yvain, English lyrics by Channing Pollack; "Second Hand Rose" by James F. Hanley and Grant Clarke; "I'd Rather Be Blue" by Fred Fisher and Billy Rose); director, musical numbers: Herbert Ross; music supervisor and conductor: Walter Scharf; orchestrations: Jack Hayes, Walter Scharf, Leo Shuken, Herbert Spencer; unit production manager: Paul Helmick; production designer: Gene Callahan; costumes: Irene Sharaff; photography: Harry Stradling; set decorator: William Kiernan; art director: Robert Luthardt; supervising film editor: Robert Swink; makeup supervisor: Ben Lane; makeup artist: Frank McCoy; hairstyles: Vivienne Walker, Virginia Darcy; public relations: Jack Brodsky. Running time: 155 minutes.

For many, *Funny Girl* remains the quintessential Barbra Streisand film in that it allows her talents as singer, comedienne, and dramatic actress to fully flower within a glamorous star-is-born scenario, which in many ways recalls her own breathless climb to the peak of the show-business mountain. A dazzling, demanding showcase, the picture afforded Barbra, a screen newcomer, an almost unheard of opportunity. Yes, she had won accolades and awards for her performance as Fanny Brice in the stage versions, but there was no guarantee that she could parlay those triumphs into the movie stardom she had coveted since childhood. That she succeeded so magnificently is a tribute not only to her abundant gifts but also to the talents of the seasoned filmmakers with whom she collaborated. The stunning success of *Funny Girl* made Barbra Streisand, overnight, the most sought after actress in Hollywood, but the negative tone of the publicity during its production established an exaggerated image of the star as a troublesome, temperamental prima donna, an image that has haunted her career ever since.

Barbra got off on the wrong foot almost immediately upon her arrival in Hollywood in May 1967 when she showed up late at a lavish party thrown in her honor by the film's producer, Ray Stark. Shy and overwhelmed by the likes of Marlon Brando, John Wayne, Rosalind Russell, Cary Grant, Gregory Peck, Robert Mitchum, Steve McQueen, and Natalie Wood, among many others, Barbra appeared aloof and distracted. "I was aware of how most people thought about me," she recalled defensively, "aware of the deep jealousies and resentment . . . I could *feel* my unwelcomeness."

Irrefutably the most exciting personality-phenomenon to hit town since Elvis Presley, Barbra also represented the first major launching of a star from Broadway to Hollywood since Julie Andrews, who, in the three years since her debut in *Mary Poppins*, had become the world's most popular screen actress. Everyone, from studio executives

A determined young Fanny Brice sings "I'm the Greatest Star."

to gossip columnists, was curious about this Brooklyn girl of barely twenty-five who had breezed into the business armed with contracts for above-the-title leads in three multimillion-dollar musicals without even having submitted to a screen test. (That legendary names—William Wyler, Gene Kelly, and Vincente Minnelli—were eagerly lined up to direct those projects inspired something akin to awe.) Would the Andrews-type lightning strike twice, or would the stage- and television-proven Streisand magic fail to ignite on film as it had with the majority of Broadway imports over the years? Such theatrical greats as Carol Channing, Mary Martin, Ethel Merman, Gwen Verdon, and even Fanny Brice had found the silver screen essentially unfriendly to their brassy personas and unconventional looks.

In an industry built on equal amounts of egotism and neurotic insecurity, there were surely those who hoped Barbra would fall flat on her famous nose. Who, they asked, was this young performer—already an international household name—who had seemingly given so little to receive so much? Talent wasn't the question. Paying one's dues was. "It's funny," Marilyn Monroe had mused aloud a decade earlier, "how success makes so many people hate you. I wish it wasn't that way. It would be wonderful to enjoy success without seeing envy in the eyes of those around you."

Of course, not everyone in the business was against Barbra. She could count on the support of several accomplished allies where it mattered most—on the soundstage. William Wyler (replacing an ill-suited Sidney Lumet) had announced that he was tackling the first musical film of his lengthy career solely for the chance to work with Barbra, who, contrary to press reports, was well aware of Wyler's exalted reputation and was thrilled when he agreed to direct her movie debut. "This girl . . . intrigued me," Wyler said. "She had made such a hit in other mediums. Why not pictures?" The director was a master of production complexities and was particularly adept at scaling down broad, theatrical performances for the subtle demands of the camera. His films had been honored with 125 Academy Award nominations and 40 victories. Actresses as diverse as Bette Davis, Audrey Hepburn, Greer Garson, and Olivia de Havilland had won Oscars under his guidance. Cinematographer Harry Stradling, fresh from his

Oscar win for *My Fair Lady*, assured Barbra that he intended to spare no effort in his quest to photograph the exotic Streisand features as flatteringly as possible for *Funny Girl*.

Several faces familiar to Barbra from the New York and London companies of the show

Lennart's scenario focused on Fanny Brice's youthful climb to stardom in the Ziegfeld Follies, juxtaposed against her turbulent marriage to glamorous gambler Nick Arnstein.

The choice of dashing Egyptian actor Omar Sharif to play the unreliable love of Fanny's life

Nick Arnstein meets Fanny for the first time. "Nicky Arnstein, Nicky Arnstein, what a beautiful, beautiful name…"

joined the production as well. Kay Medford would be re-creating the role of Fanny's mother, Rose Brice; Lee Allen had signed to play Eddie Ryan, Fanny's friend and mentor; and costume designer Irene Sharaff would be retooling her stage designs for Streisand to wear on film. In addition, Herbert Ross, who had mounted the musical sequences for Barbra's breakthrough show *I Can Get It for You Wholesale*, would be doing the same for *Funny Girl* as an adjunct to Wyler's overall direction. Isobel Lennart fashioned the screenplay from her book for the play, which had started as a screenplay in the first place. As it had on Broadway,

surprised many. The show's composer, Jule Styne, had hoped to get Frank Sinatra to play Arnstein, but the singer turned the offer down. "It's the girl's picture," he told Styne. Ray Stark was glad when Frank declined. "Sinatra's all wrong," he said. "We need a big, attractive man. Someone with Cary Grant class." Though Rock Hudson, Tony Curtis, Marlon Brando, Gregory Peck, and television actor David Janssen were suggested as possible candidates, Sharif won the role in large part because Stark and William Wyler observed his classy charm and dark good looks on a daily basis on the Columbia lot, where he was shooting *Mackenna's*

Gold. At the peak of his popularity following charismatic performances in *Lawrence of Arabia* and *Doctor Zhivago,* Sharif was a well-known womanizer (with an understanding wife tucked away safely in Cairo) who admitted that he didn't find Barbra attractive at first but that her appeal soon overwhelmed him. "About a week from the moment I met her," he recalled, "I was madly in love with her. I thought she was the most gorgeous girl I'd ever seen in my life . . . I was lusting after her."

The first publicity photos released from *Funny Girl* captured Omar nuzzling the neck of a giggling Barbra during rehearsals for the show's comic seduction number "You Are Woman." The shots were wire-photoed around the world and created a furor when Egypt condemned Sharif for associating with a Jewish woman; this was shortly after the Arab-Israeli Six-Day War. When the war broke out, according to Wyler, nervous Columbia executives came close to firing Sharif until Wyler and Streisand backed him up. *Funny Girl* was immediately banned in the Arab nations for "furthering Zionist objectives." When told of this, Barbra joked, "You think Cairo was upset? You should have seen the letter I got from my Aunt Rose!"

Rehearsals, preproduction, and prerecording for *Funny Girl* took up most of June and July, with principal photography starting just before August —first on location at an old-fashioned train depot in New Jersey, then in the harbor at the foot of Manhattan (primarily to capture the innovative, complicated "Don't Rain on My Parade" number), and later at the Columbia Gower Street lot in Hollywood. Almost immediately, Joyce Haber, a venomous columnist for the *Los Angeles Times,* labeled Streisand "a full-fledged girl monster" who was telling Wyler how to direct and Stradling how to photograph. "She was a bit obstreperous in the beginning," Wyler admitted. "But things were ironed out when she discovered some of us knew what we were doing."

Expecting the collaborative working atmosphere she had enjoyed on her recording and television projects and lacking a knowledge of traditional soundstage etiquette—between takes she would retreat to her dressing room for private moments with her baby son rather than hang out with the crew—Barbra surely overstepped her bounds at times, typically asking a million ques-

tions and bluntly offering strong opinions about every aspect of the production. Wyler finally had to discourage some of her more general input while at the same time welcoming her insights into the character she had played hundreds of times. "I don't know what other actresses do," Barbra remarked in response to the complaints of her so-called meddling. "Do they just sort of stand around . . . like mummies, get dressed, get told what to do, move here, move there? That can be pretty boring."

It became a running gag on the studio lot that Wyler, legendary for demanding countless retakes from his actors—who was known, in fact, as "ninety-take Willie"—was being asked for "just one more" from Barbra. The perfectionist filmmaker had apparently met his match. "I just loved the way she handled Wyler," costar Anne Francis recalled in 1994. "She would get him so confused because she intellectualized incredibly about her character and what she thought she should be doing at this moment and did he feel she should be doing this or what? She would give him so many ideas at one time that he would just roll his eyes and say, 'Go ahead, Barbra, go ahead.' It was wonderful. She knew just how to handle him. . . ."

Years later, both star and director went to great lengths to deny stories of any rifts between them. "I'm terribly fond of her," Wyler said. "She was very professional, very good, a hard worker, too hard at times. She would work day and night if you would let her. She is absolutely tireless." According to Barbra, ". . . Willie and I had a very good creative relationship. . . . He respected me and I respected him . . . and it worked out fine. All those stories were absolutely untrue. . . ." There are those who believe that some of the overripe tales and outright falsehoods about Barbra's behavior were actually generated by Ray Stark, who apparently ascribed to the old adage that there is no such thing as bad publicity.

Harry Stradling soon realized that Barbra's concerns about his cinematography were rooted in her anxieties about how she would appear onscreen. "She has youth," he remarked, "but she's a difficult girl to photograph." Once Barbra saw Stradling's artfully shot costume, makeup, and hairdo tests, she relaxed and placed herself in his capable hands for the remainder of filming without further complaint. Herbert Ross directed the tests, and he recalled watching them with a terrified Barbra. "It was the first time she'd seen her-self on film. Well, on-screen she looked a miracle. How could anyone have known that her skin was going to have that brilliant, reflective surface, that she was going to look radiant—that was just a wonderful plus." Happily, Barbra turned out to be strikingly photogenic, something much more essential for success in the movies than traditional prettiness. The motion-picture camera simply loved her, just as the microphone did.

Barbra's voice gave her some unexpected trouble as she prepared to record the *Funny Girl* soundtrack. The cesarean section she had under-gone just months earlier had taken a slight toll on the muscles she utilized for the dramatic "belting" that had become one of her trademarks. In addi-tion, airborne dust from resin spread on the soundstage floor for "The Roller Skate Rag" (in which Fanny, out of control on skates, hilariously botches up the entire number) had gotten into her lungs and created further vocal limitations. These deficiencies were relatively minor and more noticeable to Barbra than the thousands who attended either her spectacular free concert in Central Park on June 18 or her performance at the Hollywood Bowl three weeks later. Fortunately, after a few concentrated sessions with a vocal coach, the problems were resolved, and the sound-track recording proceeded, with Barbra in superb voice.

The screen version would emerge as even more of a one-woman spectacular than *Funny Girl* was onstage; songs by Nick, Fanny's mother, and Eddie Ryan were excluded entirely from the movie. Numbers retained from the Broadway score included "If a Girl Isn't Pretty," "I'm the Greatest Star," "His Love Makes Me Beautiful," "People," "You Are Woman," "Don't Rain on My Parade," and "Sadie, Sadie." The movie also con-tained new compositions, such as a title ballad, "Roller Skate Rag," and "The Swan" (for a parody of *Swan Lake*) as well as songs closely associated with Fanny Brice: "I'd Rather Be Blue" and "My Man." Another Brice staple, "Second Hand Rose," had been a 1965 hit for Barbra, and it was utilized as Fanny's audition number for Ziegfeld, but it wasn't included on the soundtrack album.

"They warned me she was temperamental and stubborn. She was," musical supervisor Walter Scharf related. "She . . . is also one of the most original artists I have encountered." Having lived with most of the *Funny Girl* songs for over three years, Barbra performed them with even more understanding and dynamism than she had on the stage. "People" was sung with an appealing new intimacy, and "Don't Rain on My Parade" was given a powerful anthemlike interpretation that ends the movie's first act with a spine-tingling wallop. Writer Pete Hamill was present when Barbra filmed "I'd Rather Be Blue." "She was treating it the way a great performer treats a stan-dard," Hamill wrote. "She was looking deeply into it, past the glib surface, and locating the emotion that was there at the start, before repetition and second-rate artists had corrupted it. . . . She did almost a dozen takes of the scene, and each time it came out fresh. The hired audience of extras was dazzled. So was I."

Midway through production, a gleeful press sniffed out provocative new whispers emanating from the *Funny Girl* soundstages; Barbra had apparently fallen in love with her leading man. While Elliott Gould was in New York filming *The Night They Raided Minskys,* Barbra and Omar were seen out on the town and were rumored to be carrying on in Sharif's suite at the Beverly Wilshire Hotel. Years later, in his autobiography, Sharif said of the coupling, "We were not having an affair. . . . It was a romance, really. . . . We led the very simple life of people in love." A bewil-dered Elliott told reporters that Barbra had admit-ted to him that she was "crazy in love with Omar." The Streisand-Sharif liaison was intense and fairly short-lived, but the damage to the Gould marriage was substantial. Barbra and Elliott would separate within eighteen months.

Filming concluded in December 1967, but Barbra shocked everyone when she asked if they could reshoot the film's finale, Fanny's tearful per-formance of her signature torch song "My Man." Barbra had recorded the vocal track months ear-lier, and she felt it lacked the emotional punch the song required. "It was too musical, too commer-cial, too perfect,"she argued. To the surprise of many, Ray Stark agreed and allowed Barbra to refilm (most of the song) live on the soundstage, something that hadn't been done since the earliest days of sound movies. It was a wise decision. The reshot scene, filmed in lustrous close-up against a stark black background, ends the film on an elec-trifying note.

Barbra was relieved at having completed this

most important project of her career to date but was saddened when the hostility of one of her costars surfaced. Soon after the film wrapped production, Anne Francis told a Hollywood newspaper, "Every day Barbra would see the rushes, and the next day my part would be cut. Barbra ran the whole show. . . ." Blond, beautiful, and a well-liked Hollywood veteran, Francis had been cast as Georgia James, an aging, alcoholic Ziegfeld girl whom Fanny befriends. Georgia had always been a sketchy role at best (it had been dropped from the stage version prior to Broadway), and as filming progressed, it became clear that the role was completely superfluous as well. Many years later, Anne Francis admitted that the comments attributed to her in 1968 had actually been made by her well-meaning but misinformed publicist, a personal friend whom Francis felt she could not publicly contradict. "I had no reason to think that Barbra had anything to do with my scenes being cut," she says today. "I think that was entirely Wyler's decision. He didn't like the character I was playing, didn't think she added anything to the picture. There were a lot of scenes cut on the very day I was to shoot them."

That the original complaints attributed to Francis were widely repeated in the press (even by columnists who knew full well that Wyler would never put up with such nonsense from Barbra or any other actor) indicates how fashionable it was at the time to assume the worst of Barbra Streisand and how much power she was erroneously believed to possess.

Fortunately, when *Funny Girl* premiered in September 1968, at the Criterion Theater on Broadway, the brilliance of Barbra's performance and the overall excellence of the picture outshone the bitchy gossip that had plagued the filming. With a self-assured presence that belied her inexperience as a film actress, Barbra brought forth all of the drive, poignancy, romanticism, comic flair, musical expertise, and sheer magnetism that had characterized her stage performances. And for the screen she projected something extra, a robust sexuality that Fanny Brice would surely have found highly flattering. No doubt, Barbra's chemistry with Sharif, fueled by their offscreen fling, gave off genuine heat. "I don't know where Fanny ends and Barbra

At opening night of the Ziegfeld Follies, Fanny stops the show as a pregnant bride in "His Love Makes Me Beautiful."

Barbra cuddles her infant son, Jason, while still in costume for "The Roller Skate Rag."

or from admirers of Fanny Brice, whose unique qualities—in their view—Barbra failed to capture. In most cases, however, she was hailed as a groundbreaking role model for future stars whose allure might fall into the nonconventional category. She also became the first openly Jewish romantic leading lady in motion-picture history. (In the past, such stars as Theda Bara, Sylvia Sidney, and Lauren Bacall had been discouraged from revealing their backgrounds.) Her determination to wear her heritage proudly was cheered as an important breakthrough.

Funny Girl set a record by remaining at the Criterion for over a year, a rare achievement marked by an anniversary "repremiere," which Barbra proudly attended. The picture proved to be a tremendous international box-office hit, first in road-show release—for which audiences purchased reserved-seat tickets in advance—and then for months after in wide circulation. One of Columbia's all-time moneymakers, the film is scheduled for a limited thirtieth-anniversary reissue.

begins," Ray Stark told reporters following the opening.

Reviews for the film were generally excellent, though some critics carped about the old-fashioned style of the picture, the drag of the slowly paced second act (which had afflicted the stage version as well), and the overdone Ziegfeld girls, who looked more like *Playboy* centerfolds circa 1967 than stage beauties of the World War I era. But nearly everyone agreed that Barbra's performance constituted one of the most sensational movie debuts ever. She did, however, receive a few surprisingly harsh criticisms, some laced with thinly disguised anti-Semitism. These came primarily from writers who had believed the Barbra-as-monster press reports

On February 24, 1969, *Funny Girl* received eight Academy Award nominations, including nods for Best Picture, Best Actress, Best Supporting Actress (Kay Medford), and Best Song, for "Funny Girl." At the ceremonies in April, Barbra emerged the film's only victor in her famous tie with Katharine Hepburn. Further heralding her arrival as an authentic new movie star, Barbra also received a Golden Globe Award for her performance, and she tied with Mia Farrow (*Rosemary's Baby*) for the David Di Donatello Award, Italy's version of the Oscar. As a salute to Streisand's newly minted box-office clout and future potential, the National Association of Theater Owners named her Star of the Year.

Barbra calls Fanny's trademark ballad, "My Man," a "classic victim song."

REVIEWS

"A star is not born in Funny Girl, *despite the dutiful outpourings of publicity for Barbra Streisand's film debut. A star comes of age. . . . Miss Streisand has matured into a complete performer and delivered the most accomplished, original, and enjoyable musical comedy performance that has ever been captured on film. She is an actress, now, who uses her versatile singing voice as a poet uses verse, to intensify and heighten experience. . . . She is beautiful when she chooses to be and has the good sense to look awful when a scene requires it. . . . Amid all the overblown sights and sounds of a Broadway musical turned into a big-budget movie, she scales her performance to consistently human proportions."*

NEWSWEEK

"Let me preface my remarks about Funny Girl *with a statement or three about Barbra Streisand. I have followed her meteoric career. . . . being enthralled by her intense singing style on stage, in numerous recordings and a few television spectaculars. Simply, I love Barbra. But I did not like the film* Funny Girl. *I enjoyed the earlier sequences, but as I watched the film go to pieces and crumble around Miss Streisand's shapely legs in the second half, I felt sorry . . . both for Miss Streisand and the audience. We were both being cheated. We are presented with an overblown, irritatingly fake Hollywood production. . . ."*

VILLAGER

"Barbra Streisand arrives on the screen, in Funny Girl, *when the movies are in desperate need of her. The timing is perfect. There's hardly a star in American movies today, and if we've got so used to the absence of stars that we no longer think about* it much, we've also lost one of the great pleasures of movie going: watching incandescent people up there, more intense and dazzling than people we ordinarily encounter in life . . . she skirts pathos because her emotions are so openly expressed. She doesn't touch us for sympathy in the Chaplinesque way by trying to conceal her hurt. She conceals nothing; she's fiercely, almost frighteningly direct. . . . The end of the movie ["My Man"] in a long single take, is a bravura stroke, a gorgeous piece of showing off, that makes one intensely, brilliantly aware of the star as performer and of the star's pride in herself as performer. The pride is justified."*

NEW YORKER

53

Hello, Dolly!

(1969)

A 20th Century-Fox Release of a Chenault Productions, Inc., Picture

CAST

Barbra Streisand (*Dolly Levi*); Walter Matthau (*Horace Vandergelder*); Michael Crawford (*Cornelius Hackl*); Louis Armstrong (*Orchestra Leader*); Marianne McAndrew (*Irene Malloy*); E. J. Peaker (*Minnie Fay*); Danny Lockin (*Barnaby Tucker*); Joyce Ames (*Ermengarde*); Tommy Tune (*Ambrose Kemper*); Judy Knaiz (*Gussie Granger*); David Hurst (*Rudolph Reisenweber*); Fritz Feld (*Fritz*); Richard Collier (*Vandergelder's Barber*); J. Pat O'Malley (*Policeman in Park*).

CREDITS

Producer: Ernest Lehman; associate producer: Roger Edens; director: Gene Kelly; assistant director: Paul Helmick; screenplay: Ernest Lehman (based on the stage play produced by David Merrick; book of the stage play by Michael Stewart; stage play directed and choreographed by Gower Champion); director, dance and musical numbers: Michael Kidd; assistant choreographer: Shelah Hackett; dance arranger: Marvin Laird; music and lyrics: Jerry Herman; music scored and conducted by Lennie Hayton and Lionel Newman; choral arranger: Jack Latimer; music editors: Robert Mayer, Kenneth Wannberg; orchestrations: Phillip Lang, Lennie Hayton, Joseph Lipman, Don Costa, Alexander Courage, Warren Barker, Frank Comstock, Herbert Spencer; unit production manager: Francisco Day; production designer: John De Cuir; costumes: Irene Sharaff; photography: Harry Stradling; set decorators: Walter M. Scott, George Hopkins, Raphael Bretton; art directors: Jack Martin Smith, Herman Blumenthal; editor: William Reynolds; sound supervisor: James Corcoran; makeup supervisor: Dan Striepke; makeup artists: Ed Butterworth, Richard Hamilton; hairstylist: Edith Lindon; public relations: Pat Newcomb.
Running time: 146 minutes.

If it was universally agreed that the casting of Barbra Streisand in *Funny Girl* was so inspired as to suggest divine intervention, just the opposite could be said of the decision to sign her for the title role in *Hello, Dolly!*

Based on Thornton Wilder's 1954 stage farce *The Matchmaker* (which Wilder had fashioned from his own 1938 comedy *The Merchant of Yonkers*), *Hello Dolly!* tells the lighthearted tale of middle-aged, matchmaking widow Dolly Levi and her schemes to bring three sets of young lovers together against all odds while at the same time securing love and security for herself in turn-of-the-century New York. In the colorful title role, Carol Channing delivered a defining, warm, and wacky performance that revived her career, won her a Tony, and made *Hello, Dolly!* the top smash of the 1964 Broadway season. The infectious title song, as recorded in an irresistible Dixieland style by Louis Armstrong, became an enormous hit at a time when the Beatles were dominating the record charts.

When 20th Century–Fox acquired the movie rights to the musical in 1965 for $2.1 million, it was assumed that Channing would be allowed to re-create her career-best performance in the film version. Producer-screenwriter Ernest Lehman, who had previously adapted *The King and I*, *West Side Story*, and *The Sound of Music* for the movies, thought of casting no one *but* Channing until he screened, in advance, her scenes from *Thoroughly Modern Millie*, a Julie Andrews vehicle filming at Universal in which Channing had taken a flashy supporting role as a madcap heiress. It was her first film assignment in a decade, and Channing had reportedly agreed to appear in *Millie* hoping to convince Fox executives to cast her in *Dolly!* Ironically, the performance—later nominated for an Academy Award—had just the opposite effect on Lehman. "I thought she looked

forced to fire Garland from *Valley of the Dolls* shortly after the *Dolly!* casting choices were made.) Other age-appropriate stars, such as Betty Grable and Ginger Rogers, who were successfully playing Dolly Levi to theater audiences in Channing's wake, were years past their ability to draw crowds to movie theaters. Lucille Ball, Debbie Reynolds, and Shirley Jones were all deemed inappropriate. Lehman was at a loss for months until director Mike Nichols casually said to him over dinner one evening, "Why don't you cast Barbra Streisand as Dolly? She'd be great." After thinking it over, Lehman found himself excited by Nichols's suggestion.

The actress in question wasn't so sure. "I wasn't gonna do it," Barbra said. "I tried to convince them that it would be more emotional if it were the story of an older woman whose time is running out and she has to make the most of it." Finally, however, worn down by Lehman's constant pleading and enticed by—as Fox announced—"the largest single film deal in film history with a performer who has never before appeared in a motion picture" (in the spring of 1967, Streisand was signed before *Funny Girl* went into production), she signed to play Dolly Levi.

The announcement of Barbra's casting raised an outcry and prompted the *Washington Post* to call the idea "knuckleheaded." Carol Channing admirers were as outraged as Streisand fans would have been had Shirley MacLaine been cast in *Funny Girl*. There was much talk about Barbra's being chosen only for her box-office potential, though she hadn't so much as set foot on a movie

a little grotesque, cartoonish," he said. "I honestly felt I couldn't take a whole movie in which Carol was in practically every scene. Her personality is just too much for the camera to contain."

With Channing out of the running, other names—based solely on box-office appeal, such as Elizabeth Taylor and Julie Andrews—were suggested but quickly dropped. Perhaps because she was committed to a new television series, Doris Day was apparently never approached, and Judy Garland, who just a year or two earlier might have been ideal, was never considered, mired as she was in the physical and professional downslide that would lead to her death in 1969. (In fact, Fox was

Michael Crawford, Barbra, and Danny Lockin enjoy a laugh during the filming of "Dancing."

soundstage; there was, as yet, no guarantee she would succeed in films. It was also snidely suggested that she took the role as a way of exacting revenge on Channing, who had beaten her out of a Tony Award. Ernest Lehman announced, "Truthfully, I am wary of the whole subject of Carol Channing. I would say I prefer her on the stage to on film. I chose Barbra," he added, "because she's dynamic, she's a marvelous comedienne, and what she will do with the score will astound people."

Typically, the louder the chorus of protests over her casting crew, the more Streisand rose to the occasion. She rationalized her decision to keep

the role by reminding the public that a woman could be widowed at any age; in fact, the currently raging war in Vietnam had tragically produced thousands of young widows. But the core sentiment at the heart of *Hello, Dolly!* was not about Dolly's widowhood specifically; it concerned, as Barbra herself had already pointed out, Dolly's finding happiness as she faced advancing middle age. For all of her bravado, Streisand knew instinctively that she would face this reality on a daily basis as she struggled to define her interpretation of Dolly Levi.

By the time *Funny Girl* was completed, preproduction on *Dolly!* was well under way. Dance great turned director Gene Kelly was chosen to direct. Walter Matthau, a recent Academy Award winner for his supporting role in *The Fortune Cookie,* was signed to play Horace Vandergelder, the irascible Yonkers merchant on whom Dolly sets her marital sights. A cast of mainly unknowns was chosen to round out the supporting roles: British import Michael Crawford and young dancer Danny Lockin were cast as Vandergelder's adventure-seeking young store clerks whose impetuous trip to Manhattan—at Dolly's suggestion—sets the story in motion. When Crawford interviewed with Kelly for the job, the director told him that the part called for "an attractive idiot. My wife thinks you're attractive," Kelly added, "and I think you're an idiot." Marianne

McAndrew (chosen over Ann-Margret, who was deemed too sexy) and E. J. Peaker were signed to play a sensible young milliner and her giddy assistant, the boys' love interests. Tommy Tune was cast as a suitor of Vandergelder's niece.

Gene Kelly would be accompanied by many familiar talents from the fabled M-G-M/Arthur Freed production unit, including associate producer Roger Edens, choreographer Michael Kidd, and orchestrator Lennie Hayton. Encoring their *Funny Girl* duties would be cinematographer Harry Stradling and costumer Irene Sharaff. The *Dolly!* budget ballooned from a 1965 estimate of $10 million to almost $19 million for a proposed eighty-eight-day shoot. The fifteen-acre "New York Street," ingeniously constructed at the entrance to

In street clothes, Walter Matthau and Barbra rehearse the film's most elaborate number, "Before the Parade Passes By." The two actors had clashed during an earlier scene.

Director Gene Kelly and costume designer Irene Sharaff insist on just the right tilt to Barbra's hat brim.

Fox's Century City lot, cost $1,700,000, while the tab on the indoor set for the Harmonia Gardens, in which Dolly belts the show's popular title tune, ran close to $375,000. Sixty-five percent of the film would be shot outdoors. Having apparently learned little from the *Cleopatra* financial debacle of six years before, the more money Fox committed to the production, the better everyone seemed to like it.

Rehearsals on *Dolly!* began in February 1968. "I came into this picture with my dukes up because I'd heard [Barbra] might be uncooperative. But she's the most cooperative actress I've ever worked with," testified Gene Kelly. "She'll try anything to be good. There has never been any friction between us . . . and I predict there never will be." Kelly started shooting on April 15. Initially, the atmosphere on his *Dolly!* set was amiable enough, but that changed when the filmmakers went east to the Hudson Valley town of Garrison, New York, where an 1890s version of Yonkers had been painstakingly re-created.

On location, the usual tension present on movie sets became unusually distorted as both Streisand and Matthau internalized their feelings about not being all they could be in their roles, while Ernest Lehman and Gene Kelly attempted to take this light confection of a musical and turn it into a realistic piece of Americana. In this regard, Kelly was an odd choice for the project. Twenty years earlier at M-G-M he had innovated—along with codirector Stanley Donen—a new, contemporary approach to the musical formula, resulting in such triumphs as *On the Town* and *An American in Paris. Dolly!* was more of a throwback to traditional Metro titles, such as *The Harvey Girls* and *In the Good Old Summertime,* exactly the kind of nostalgic trifles Kelly had once rebelled against. Furthermore, often swamped by the technical demands of the *Dolly!* shoot, Kelly was unable to offer his leading actress the sure-handed guidance she felt her performance desperately needed.

When, in Barbra's opinion, her original concept of a highly elegant Dolly didn't come off in the first day's rushes, she gravitated toward a more outrageous interpretation. "As the picture progressed,"

Gene Kelly, Louis Armstrong, Roger Edens, Barbra, and Ernest Lehman share a light moment during the recording sessions for the Hello, Dolly! *soundtrack.*

Kelly said, "she tried very, very hard to make her characterization work. If only there had been more time, I'd have tried to help her work out a clear-cut characterization. But we had a tight schedule, and I left it up to her. . . . Her accent varied as much as her mannerisms. She kept experimenting with new things out of sheer desperation, none of which really worked to her satisfaction. And she's such a perfectionist, she became [increasingly] neurotic and insecure [about it]."

The problem, of course, wasn't just a lack of time or even directorial guidance—though undoubtedly Barbra could have used more of both—but the realization that she was indeed, for all of her (and Ernest Lehman's) public protestations, seriously miscast as Dolly Levi in this obscenely expensive production, and that the hoped-for success of the film was resting firmly atop her comely shoulders.

The pressure cooker exploded on a miserably muggy June 6, 1968, the day after Robert Kennedy had been fatally wounded in Los Angeles. The large *Dolly!* cast and crew continued on with their trivialities in the senator's home state of New York. "I was in a mean, foul mood," Matthau conveyed to a reporter from *Esquire.* "I took it hard. I wasn't going to vote for Bobby Kennedy. Still, I was knocked out, and Gene was, too. I couldn't work that day, and it was a hundred degrees in Garrison. Giant [lights with enormous wattage] surrounded us in a complicated outdoor scene. . . . My head felt as though it was being smashed. . . . Suddenly, Barbra sneezed, and I took that as a personal insult. I went into a wild, furious, incoherent tirade about her. Kelly put his hand on my arm and tried to pull me away. That's all I remember, except that I had to get my lines out, and I did not use any profane language— amazing how I can remember that. I don't dislike [Barbra]. I have a kind of fondness for her that is very real. She's a very unique actress. She has a great sense of overlap—and underlap. Anyway, I apologized to her for the fight and said it was all my fault." (Another account of the incident had Matthau screaming, "You might be the singer in this picture, but I'm the *actor!* You haven't got the talent of a butterfly's fart!")

Barbra doesn't remember the sneeze or the apology. Speaking with a friend, writer Joseph Morgenstern, she recalled, "One day I had an idea about something I thought would be funny involving the scene in a wagon. I said, 'What do you think of this?' and people started to laugh. But all of a sudden Walter Matthau closed his eyes and started screaming: 'Who does she think she is? I've been in thirty movies, and this is only her second—the first one hasn't even come out yet—and she thinks she's *directing?* Who the hell does she think she is?' I couldn't believe it. I had no defense. I stood there, and I was so humiliated I started to cry, and then I ran away."

Gene Kelly chimed in with another variation on the event. "It was the classic dispute between actors over who stepped on whose lines," he told columnist Earl Wilson. "They got really angry. Walter roared. Barbra cried for a long time. They quarreled in front of everybody. I said, 'Cut the lights,' stopped everything. We went into a little store and straightened it out. Then we did the scene." But the damage was done. Thanks to biased press reports, the image most people remember was bossy Barbra versus poor, frustrated Walter.

The weather was seasonably hot back in Los Angeles that July, but tempers were cooler. Preparing for the logistic complexities of "Before the Parade Passes By," the rousing number that closes the film's first act, Kelly asked Barbra to come in for a Sunday rehearsal. "It's against [Screen Actors Guild] regulations," he admitted. "But she came, bringing her little boy. I brought my little girl. While the kids played, we rehearsed. Here was this so-called temperamental actress doing her work, tending her child, worrying that both hers and mine might fall off a nearby cliff. That's her cooperative side, her motherly, kind side."

The director would have occasion to sympathize with his leading lady's predicament. "You have to remember," Kelly told the press, "[that] this onetime beatnik kid who made fifty cents an hour as a baby-sitter (and that wasn't too long ago) now has an income of more than a million dollars a year. That's quite a change from Flatbush gamine in thrift-shop clothes to the hottest merchandise in show business. It's difficult for everyone, repeat anyone, to handle that kind of meteoric rise to fame."

Columnist Liz Smith was on the Fox lot when "Before the Parade Passes By" was filmed. "Kelly kept zooming in on Barbra as she sang the last note of the song in the middle of the marching crowd." Smith reported. "He wanted to end on a close-up. Barbra insisted that he should zoom out and leave her as a tiny figure being passed by the [thirty-eight hundred extras marching in the] parade. Kelly, exasperated, finally shot just one take Barbra's way. It's the shot you see in the movie. . . ."

According to Streisand biographer James Spada, Kelly had reason to be frustrated with his star; she had gone behind his back and phoned the producer. "Barbra called Lehman that night and told him, 'Ernie, I think you should know that Gene didn't shoot the last part of the parade number the way you wrote it. He shot straight down so all you could see are a few people marching by the camera. It would be much better the way you originally intended it.' Lehman immediately telephoned Kelly. 'He was very angry,' Lehman recalled, 'but I told him that he'd better shoot it the way I wrote it. . . . He gave me all the reasons why he did it his way.' Finally, Kelly challenged Lehman to come to the set the following day, reassemble the extras, and shoot the scene himself. 'I had never directed traffic! But I . . . shlumped into my jacket and walked over and climbed the boom and did the shot. It's the fabulous shot of Barbra holding that last note seemingly forever while the parade marches on. And I did it! The next day Gene and I were watching the dailies. His shot comes on and he didn't say a word. Later he told me, 'Jesus, my shot was awful. I'm glad you redid it.' "

The only other altercation that marred the final weeks of filming took place on the large, multilevel set of the Harmonia Gardens. Choreographer Michael Kidd and designer Irene Sharaff battled loudly over a train on Barbra's heavily beaded gold gown that was impeding her ability to execute the dance steps in the "Hello, Dolly!" number. Streisand stood by silently as filming was halted and ego-driven tempers flared. Kidd insisted the train be eliminated, while Sharaff argued that the choreography should be changed to accommodate the costume. After Ernest Lehman stepped in and ordered the train shortened, filming resumed without further incident.

Hello, Dolly!—with a final price tag rumored to be in the neighborhood of $24 million—was completed in July 1968 and was ready for release four months later, but frustratingly, Fox was unable to announce a firm premiere date. In 1965, Broadway producer David Merrick had agreed to sell the rights to the show upon the condition that the movie not be released until the play had run its course. By late 1968, as the movie version languished on the shelf, *Dolly!* the musical was still playing to sell-out crowds, with no end in sight. Merrick had kept interest in the show at a high level with clever, successive title-role casting that included Phyllis Diller, Ethel Merman (for whom the show was originally written), and Pearl Bailey in an all-black version, which featured Cab Calloway as Horace. In the wake of the success of *Funny Girl* and Barbra's subsequent Oscar victory, Fox was itching to release *Dolly!* and the studio finally had to agree to reimburse Merrick for any dip in the Broadway show's grosses that could be attributed to the release of the film.

Hello, Dolly! opened to great fanfare at the Rivoli Theater on Broadway on December 16, 1969. In New York filming *The Owl and the Pussycat,* Barbra attended the premiere and caused a small riot when mobs of overzealous fans engulfed her limousine, breaking through safety barriers that fronted the theater. A glamorously attired, though thoroughly terrified, Barbra barely made it through the lobby in one piece. Fox executives who witnessed the melee were heartened by what they saw as an enthusiastic welcome for their multimillion-dollar Streisand gamble. But Ernest Lehman had a less optimistic reaction. "At the premiere . . . it was so clear that all those people had come out to see no one but Barbra," he recalled. "And I thought, My God, they're expecting this to be a Barbra Streisand picture. And it really wasn't. There were long stretches when she wasn't on the screen, when all you saw was those idiot clerks and their idiot girls. I firmly believe a lot of people were disappointed that there wasn't more of Barbra, and that hurt the film."

What Lehman would never fully admit was that by casting an actress just seven years out of her teens to play Dolly, he had robbed the story of the poignancy that had touched theater audiences. Despite Barbra's heartfelt delivery of the monologue that precedes "Before the Parade Passes By," it simply lacked the bittersweet quality a middle-aged actress could have brought to it. It might further be argued that once Lehman decided on Streisand for the role, he could have adjusted the supporting cast accordingly; in scenes where Barbra should appear almost motherly opposite Michael Crawford and Marianne McAndrew, it's clear that she is, in fact, their contemporary. And if Horace had been played by a more attractive, youthful actor (such as Jack Lemmon, for example), his appeal to Dolly would have been more understandable, even in the face of his cranky demeanor. Why would a vibrant *young* woman bother chasing a cantankerous, middle-aged character, embodied by basset-faced Walter Matthau, even if he was a "well-known half a millionaire?" Dolly is clearly the most exciting, magnetic woman in the Harmonia Gardens, a radiant belle of the nineties, likely to have been pursued by Vanderbilts, not rebuked by Vandergelder! Matthau and the supporting players might have been effective foils for an actress of Carol Channing's age, but they didn't complement Streisand in the dewy blush of her youth.

Unsure how to best play a role she had little personal connection to, Streisand gave a wildly varying performance that calls to mind everyone from Mae West and Scarlett O'Hara to Lena Horne and Marilyn Monroe, with liberal doses of Barbra as Fanny Brice inevitably stirred in. It is clearly not the best possible Dolly, but taken on its own terms, the interpretation is charming, often hilarious, and wholly entertaining. And though they share no romantic chemistry, the comic exchanges between Streisand and Matthau are masterfully performed. The less said about the performances of the supporting cast, however, the better. Michael Crawford is particularly ungainly as he struggles with an American accent, and his singing gives no hint of the power he would employ many years later in *The Phantom of the Opera.* Louis Armstrong, however, appears to great effect leading the Harmonia Gardens band in the midst of the "Hello, Dolly!" number. In their all-too-brief musical interplay, Satchmo and Barbra ignite the screen, leaving audiences begging for more.

The *Hello, Dolly!* score was essentially

Dolly makes her glittery entrance into the Harmonia Gardens, cuing the start of the show's famous title song.

unchanged from the Broadway version except for two new songs composer-lyricist Jerry Herman wrote for Barbra. "Just Leave Everything to Me" is a fast-paced ditty that serves to introduce the eccentric Dolly character, and "Love Is Only Love" (a reworking of a song Herman had dropped from his score for *Mame*) is a contemplative ballad in which Dolly reminds herself that life with Horace will lack the fireworks of her first marriage. As Ernest Lehman predicted, Streisand's vocals send the *Hello, Dolly!* songs soaring, although Barbra expressed disappointment that other characters sing her two favorite melodies from the show, "Ribbons Down My Back" and "It Only Takes a Moment."

A predominance of rave reviews for *Hello, Dolly!* indicated a hit. In fact, the first weeks of the showcase engagement ran well ahead of *The Sound of Music,* the current box-office champion. As the movie ran throughout 1970, however, it began to lose momentum; it became clear that the Streisand-Matthau vehicle would prove a disappointment. The soundtrack album, released on 20th Century Records, climbed to only number 49 on the *Billboard* chart.

"The road to *The Late Late Show* is paved with good intentions," Ernest Lehman reflected. He came to believe that his faux pas was trying to open up a play that was, above all, a theatrical—almost vaudevillian—experience, best enjoyed live. In hindsight, he also felt that it was impossible to make "a successful movie version of *The Matchmaker*"; a 1955 attempt had failed for Paramount despite a wonderful cast led by Shirley Booth, Anthony Perkins, Shirley MacLaine, and Robert Morse. Over time, worldwide film rentals, estimated at $40–50 million, combined with the sale to television and eventually home video, would push the grosses for *Hello, Dolly!* over its unwieldy break-even mark. Although Barbra would later refer to it as her "big mistake," industry analysts agree that most of the film's box-office performance was due to her drawing power. On *her* resumé, at least, it was a hit. On February 16, 1970, *Hello, Dolly!* received seven Academy Award nominations, including one for Best Picture. At the ceremonies held in April it won awards for Art Direction, Sound, and Best Adapted Musical Score.

REVIEWS

"Barbra Streisand, the umpteenth Dolly, is magnificent as always in a role that apparently brings out the best in those who attempt it. And the best of Barbra Streisand has got to be the best there is. . . . As a legitimate, straight singer, she is without peer, her loud, clear and strikingly identifiable voice is of inestimable benefit to whatever she chooses to sing. But more than that she is a complete performer. Her comedic talents are exceptional, her comprehension of material perfect. When she is on screen, Hello, Dolly! *bubbles over, but all too often, especially during the first half of the film she is missing."*

NEW YORK MORNING TELEGRAPH

"To immortalize the role of Dolly Levi, a damned exasperating woman and matchmaker, on celluloid, Barbra Streisand was chosen. The decision was economically sound, but artistically unwise. Miss Streisand is too real and honest a performer to carry off a cartoon character like Mrs. Levi. The part calls for a touch of madness and Miss Streisand is too sane."

VILLAGER

"There she stands at the head of the great ornate stairway, her glorious merry-widow figure draped in a ton of jeweled gold, a spray of feathers in her belle epoque topknot. She is smiling her sly, secret, Brooklyn-Jewish-girl-who-made-it-big smile. The film is at its climax, she is the champion female movie star of her time and she is poised for the most played, the most familiar, the most parodied song of the decade. We are expectant. Will she bring it off? Will she top all the toppers? Boys, the kid's a winner. The whole thing's a triumph. She was smiling that sly smile because she knew all the time she was going to kill us."

WOMEN'S WEAR DAILY

On a Clear Day You Can See Forever

(1970)

A Paramount Picture

CAST

Barbra Streisand (*Daisy Gamble*); Yves Montand (*Dr. Marc Chabot*); Bob Newhart (*Dr. Mason Hume*); Larry Blyden (*Warren Pratt*); Simon Oakland (*Dr. Conrad Fuller*); Jack Nicholson (*Tad Pringle*); John Richardson (*Robert Tentrees*); Pamela Brown (*Mrs. Fitzherbert*); Irene Handl (*Winnie Wainwhistle*); Roy Kinnear (*Prince Regent*); Mabel Albertson (*Mrs. Hatch*); Laurie Main (*Lord Percy*); Elaine Giftos (*Muriel*); Leon Ames (*Clews*).

CREDITS

Producer: Howard W. Koch; director: Vincente Minnelli; assistant director: William McGarry; screenplay: Alan Jay Lerner (based on the musical play *On a Clear Day You Can See Forever*); choreographer: Howard Jeffrey; vocal-dance arranger: Betty Walberg; music: Barton Lane; music supervisor, arranger, and conductor: Nelson Riddle; lyrics: Alan Jay Lerner; production designer: John De Cuir; contemporary costumes: Arnold Scassi; period costumes: Cecil Beaton; director of photography: Harry Stradling; aerial photography: Tyler Camera Systems; time-lapse photography: John Ott; set decoration: George Hopkins, Ralph Bretton; editor: David Bretherton; dialogue coach Walter Kelley; sound recording: Benjamin Winkler, Elden Ruberg; choral arranger: Joseph J. Lilley; makeup supervisor: Harry Ray; hairstyles: Frederick Glaser; wardrobe: John Anderson, Shirlee Strahm. Running time: 129 minutes.

O f the three musicals that constituted the first phase of Barbra Streisand's movie career, *On a Clear Day You Can See Forever* had been the least successful while on Broadway; it ran for only 280 performances after opening to mixed reviews in October 1965. Alan Jay Lerner, who served as the show's producer, author, and lyricist, had concocted a fanciful story from his interest in extrasensory perception and the renewed public fascination with reincarnation that resulted from the controversial "Bridey Murphy" story of the mid-1950s. (*The Search for Bridey Murphy* was a nonfiction account of a case in which a Colorado housewife supposedly recalled verifiable details of a past life she lived a century earlier in rural Ireland.) In *Clear Day*, an eccentric young clairvoyant, Daisy Gamble, while under hypnosis, reverts to a past incarnation as Melinda, an elegant eighteenth-century courtesan whose fortune-telling talent leads to her ruination. Romantic complications ensue when Daisy falls in love with Dr. Mark Bruckner, the psychiatrist-professor who is guiding her hypnosis, and he in turn develops a crush on her unattainable Melinda persona.

The Broadway version featured a winning performance from its lead, Barbara Harris, a baby-faced actress with an impish quality that was much admired by theater critics. Alan Jay Lerner, writing with Burton Lane, supplied a score that never approached his finest work (with former partner Frederick Loewe) for *Brigadoon*, *My Fair Lady*, *Camelot*, and *Gigi*. Nevertheless, *Clear Day* boasted two numbers—the title song and "What Did I Have That I Don't Have?"—that became popular with such singers as Eydie Gorme and Robert Goulet. Paramount paid $750,000 for the screen rights in April 1966 and turned the project over to production vice president Howard Koch, who would share producing chores with Alan Jay Lerner. After her engaging screen debut in *A Thousand Clowns* just months before starring in *Clear Day*, insiders surmised that Barbara Harris would, naturally, repeat her deft performance as Daisy Gamble on-screen. However, talented though she may have been, Koch couldn't see

building a multimillion-dollar production around an actress who was still an unknown commodity to the vast majority of moviegoers; he had his eye on a more treasured prize.

When Audrey Hepburn turned him down, he got an inspired idea to cast the most important musical star to come along in years. "I'd seen Barbra on Broadway," Koch said, "and thought she was stunning. She'd already been signed for the movie version of *Funny Girl,* so it was pretty clear that she was going to be a success in Hollywood. We figured she'd be great in *Clear Day."* Courted while playing Fanny Brice on the London stage, Barbra had other things on her mind—not the least of which was the anticipated birth of her child—and politely declined the offer. Koch briefly flirted with other casting possibilities, but he couldn't get Streisand out of his mind. Her image defied traditional Hollywood thinking regarding glamour—perfect for the multiple roles this assignment represented. He was determined to make her an offer she couldn't refuse. He had until the end of 1966 before he needed a commitment. Koch's final offer, which included costar and director approval as well as a fee of $350,000—a substantial increase over her *Funny Girl* salary— was relayed to New York, where Barbra was resting during her final months of pregnancy.

By January 1967, Koch had his leading lady, who found she couldn't resist the acting challenge the project presented. "The two parts in *Clear Day* come close to my own schizophrenic personality," Barbra admitted. "The frightened girl as compared to the strong woman in me. Just heaven!" The problem now was that the film could no longer be produced in 1967 or most of 1968, for that matter, due to Streisand's commitments to *Funny Girl* and *Dolly!* So both Lerner and Koch busied themselves with other Paramount projects; Lerner with his *Paint Your Wagon* and Koch with *The Odd Couple.*

During the rest of 1967, Koch also got to work on Barbra's suggestions for the *Clear Day* production team. Regarding a director, both she and Lerner agreed that Vincente Minnelli was the perfect choice. Minnelli was in semiretirement following such disappointments as *Goodbye Charlie* and *The Sandpiper.* He hadn't made a film in five years, and the last musical he directed was *Gigi,* in 1958—a "last hurrah" of sorts for M-G-M. But as a director of musical films, with an incredible eye for detail and period authenticity, he was without peer. Having also directed many of the screen's legendary musical talents (Garland, Chevalier, Kelly, Astaire), Minnelli found it hard to resist the chance to work with Streisand. After just one meeting, Barbra sensed an easy rapport with her new director. "I love Vincente Minnelli already," she enthused. "I either like someone immediately or dislike them immediately. He didn't come in as the old-time director of many hits, and you're just a girl with one [or two] pictures; he's so open and trusts my instincts so. I guess he must have liked my work or something."

Several changes were made to the play, and several more were in store for the musical score as well. Six tunes were retained from the Broadway show, though in most cases their order within the movie—and therefore much of their dramatic context—was to be altered. "On a Clear Day," sung only by Dr. Bruckner in the play, would now be performed by Daisy as well. "She Wasn't You," another stage solo for the doctor, became Melinda's lament, "He Isn't You." Lerner and Lane also supplied new songs for the film: "Love With All the Trimmings," "Go to Sleep," "Who Is There Among Us Who Knows?" and "ESP." Only two made it into the movie.

The logistics and intricacies involved in "opening up" a play, which basically took place in one room (the professor's study), to make a movie that featured several different and colorful locations created the need for a minimum of eight weeks' rehearsal time. Prerecording, recording, and costume tests caused the picture's budget to swell to nearly $10 million. A highly visible part of the film's expense would be the decision to engage two different costume designers: one for Daisy and one for Melinda. Barbra had long admired the contemporary fashions Arnold Scassi created for a number of high-profile clients, such as Natalie Wood and Joan Crawford. When Scassi showed Barbra some new designs for her personal wardrobe, she felt they would be appropriate for the "mod" look she wanted Daisy to have. With Howard Koch's approval, Scassi was given his first film assignment. Well known for his elaborate designs and sophisticated tastes, British designer and photographer Cecil Beaton was hired to create Melinda's wardrobe. A two-time Oscar winner (for *Gigi* and *My Fair Lady*), Beaton had photographed Barbra early in her career. "I think

I was the first to say she looked like Nefertiti when she was singing in nightclubs," he pointed out.

Harry Stradling was pleased to sign on for his third consecutive film as Barbra's cinematographer. "She's one of the greatest talents I've ever worked with," Stradling said. "She knows photographic quality—what's good and what's not good. She knows what height the camera should be and just where it should be placed for her close-ups, and she's learned all this during the short time she has been in pictures. She's just a very wonderful, really brilliant woman."

As preproduction continued, Howard Koch had yet to cast Barbra's costar. Talks with Richard Harris, fresh from his triumph in *Camelot,* lasted for weeks until the actor finally dropped out when he realized that his part was in danger of becoming a supporting role. Determined to create a teaming that would inspire an unusual chemistry, the producers offered the role to Frank Sinatra, Gregory Peck, and *Gigi* star Louis Jourdan, all of whom passed. Jourdan had, in fact, bowed out of the original Broadway cast of *Clear Day* during out-of-town tryouts, but everyone seemed to like the idea of casting a "sexy Frenchman."

In August, Paramount announced that the tall, dark, and *very* French Yves Montand had been contracted for the role, now renamed Dr. Marc Chabot. A dynamic actor in European films, such as *The Wages of Fear* and the then-soon-to-be-released *Z,* Montand had also acquired a following as a suave balladeer. But he had never made a favorable impression on American moviegoers. His embarrassing performance opposite Marilyn Monroe in 1960's dreadful *Let's Make Love* had been followed by only slightly better work in *Goodbye Again* with Ingrid Bergman. However, when Barbra met him at the studio, she found him charming and flattering (he called her "incomparable"), and she agreed with Lerner and Koch that he would bring a unique Continental flavor to the whimsical *Clear Day* mix.

Preproduction moved ahead smoothly. After an intense two years in the movie business, Barbra had become more accustomed to the ways of Hollywood, and vice versa. There were none of the personality conflicts that had plagued her first two features. "I have to compromise," she admitted in the press. "A little. I know that now. I've come to understand that a little bit of compromise is part of the perfection. A little bit of imperfection is part of the perfect, because perfection is lifeless and dull." To the chagrin of industry gossips, she got on exceedingly well with her *Clear Day* collaborators, though her inexhaustible quest for excellence in herself and others was as appar-

a social call. . . . We kept on working until past midnight. We had a job to do, and we did it—no nonsense about it. This is what I admire in Barbra, she is thoroughly professional."

The *Clear Day* cast would ultimately grow to include Larry Blyden as Daisy's stuffy fiancé; Bob Newhart in the role of a hapless university president; and most interestingly, Jack Nicholson playing Daisy's ex-stepbrother, Tad Pringle. Just months away from his triumphant breakthrough in *Easy Rider*, Nicholson was introduced by Howard Koch to Barbra, who immediately approved his casting. Tad was scheduled to sing "Who Is There Among Us Who Knows?" and Nicholson found the task daunting. "They didn't know if I could even carry a tune," he remembered. "I auditioned [with] just me and [Minnelli] in the room. Me singing 'Don't Blame Me' a cappella . . . it blew my mind." Later, in the recording studio, Nicholson was surprised and delighted when Barbra decided to hum along at the end of his song and when she offered further support on the soundstage. "Streisand treated me great, man," Nicholson said. "I don't think she saw *Easy Rider*, either, so it wasn't because of that. [But] she tried to help me in my scenes, you know?" Streisand and company recorded the *Clear Day* soundtrack at the Samuel Goldwyn studios in Hollywood, a few miles west of the Paramount lot, under the musical supervision of veteran arranger and conductor Nelson Riddle.

Singing, of course, was familiar territory for Barbra, but she called on Deborah Kerr to help her learn flawless interpretations of the British accents, both cockney and near royal, that she needed for the various stages of Melinda's incarnation. In a remarkably short time everyone within earshot agreed that Streisand sounded to the manor born. "Wouldn't it be great if the whole Brooklyn thing was a put-on?" she teased.

Three days before principal photography was to begin, in January 1969, Paramount launched the publicity for *Clear Day* in a grand style that recalled the glittering galas of Hollywood's golden age. The invitations to the Reincarnation Ball, staged at the Beverly Hilton Hotel, read: "Come as the person you would like to have been." Hundreds of celebrities did just that. Barbra, in a

ent as ever. "Pleasing her is very difficult," Cecil Beaton confessed. "It's a constant battle between her and her taste—very exhausting." Arnold Scassi agreed. "We spent a whole day going over the styles she would wear as Daisy," he recalled. "By eight o'clock I was ready to quit. I had been invited to dinner at the Minnellis', so I stood up and said, 'Barbra, I must leave, I have a previous engagement.' She lifted her eyes from the sketches and very quietly said, 'Arnold, why did you come to Los Angeles?' She did not have to say another word. I immediately realized what she meant and that she was right. I was there on business, not on full, curly wig and a white lace gown with a stuffed toy poodle tucked under her arm, impersonated Colette, the beloved French writer of *Gigi*. Vincente Minnelli was almost unrecognizable as the artist Garibaldi. Yves Montand came as the French thief Arsene Lupin. Photographers swarmed around Raquel Welch, who made a very convincing Katharine Hepburn. Other guests in attendance: Omar Sharif (in costume for his role in *Che*); producer Robert Evans (Rudolph Valentino); Phyllis Diller (Kim Novak); Groucho Marx as himself; and Edward G. Robinson as the Sea Wolf. Naturally, with such a star-studded cast, the event was widely covered in movie magazines, society columns, and the international press for weeks.

The first *Clear Day* scenes captured on film were the opening and closing numbers, "Hurry! It's Lovely Up Here," which Daisy croons in the college-campus garden on her way to Dr. Chabot's class, and the film's finale, "On a Clear Day You Can See Forever," which she sings as she leaves Chabot's office for the last time. Both songs were shot at the Rose Garden in Exposition Park, across the street from the University of Southern California. Scenes set in Chabot's classroom and office as well as those of Daisy's rooftop apartment in midtown Manhattan were shot on the Paramount soundstages. The production moved on to New York to shoot exteriors for Yves Montand's showcase, "Come Back to Me," in which Chabot sings (out loud and telepathically atop the onetime Pan Am Building) to Daisy as she darts all over Manhattan locations trying to avoid hearing his voice.

For Melinda's "regression" sequences the *Clear Day* ensemble journeyed to Brighton, England, where it became the first motion-picture company allowed to film in the elegant Royal Pavillion at Brighton. Now a national monument visited by thousands of tourists yearly, the architecturally eclectic "beach house" of former royalty would become the visual centerpiece of the film's most fondly remembered scenes. "It's a combination of the grotesque and the beautiful," Barbra said of the structure. "And it's grotesquely beautiful."

Security was tight for filming within the interior for a banquet scene—filled with elaborately costumed extras—that would serve as an opulent backdrop for "Love With All the Trimmings," the seductive ballad Melinda sings to her future husband, the elegantly handsome young rascal Robert Tentrees, played stiffly by John Richardson. The place settings—cut crystal, gold, and silver—were valued at seventy-five thousand dollars each. Food on the lengthy table was estimated to cost an additional thirty-five thousand dollars.

If anything could upstage this extraordinary scene, it was the sight of Barbra, exquisitely clad in a white crepe décolleté gown and wearing a turban studded with beads and diamonds. The overall effect suggested a buxom Arabian princess. Streisand had, Beaton says, collaborated very closely with him on this costume in particular. The experience reinforced his image of her as "a self-willed creation. It's a pity that Barbra doesn't do more period material. Her face is a painting from several historical eras. She is an ideal mannequin and a compelling actress in elegant period costumes." Minnelli was also impressed. "[Stradling] got the beauty of Streisand without tampering with it," he said. "The contours on her face give her a rare beauty," Stradling offered. Paramount quickly issued striking still photos of Barbra's sexy Melinda to international magazines as more advance publicity for the film and further proof—if any was needed—that the Brooklyn-born ugly duckling had indeed transformed into a glamorous Hollywood swan. (While on location in Brighton, Barbra—whose separation from Elliott Gould had been announced months earlier—indulged in a brief romance with George Lazenby, the handsome British actor who played James Bond in *On Her Majesty's Secret Service*.)

Barbra had been promised an early May completion date so that, following a respite, she could go into rehearsal for her hugely ballyhooed singing engagement that would open the International Hotel in Las Vegas in July. But as the filming continued, obstacles started getting in the way that threatened to infringe on Barbra's opening. Still unfinished, production on *Clear Day* was shut down on May 21. Scenes of students demonstrating in protest (arising from Chabot's revelations that through Daisy's regressions he had apparently proved reincarnation) were scheduled to be shot at a New York college, but negotiations with two separate eastern universities (Columbia and Fordham) had stalled due to the threat of *genuine* student demonstrations. During this uneasy stalemate, Barbra's contract expired. Rumors circulated that she had no intention of completing the film and that she was running up extravagant bills for photo retouching. Though Howard Koch vehemently denied that she was causing any problems whatsoever, the fact that this word spread at all was indicative of the industry's increasing paranoia over a star they had helped to create and their fear that they had lost the power to control her.

Barbra, however, was reasonable about her contract. All she asked for were some props from the production, including etched glass doors from one of the regression sets. Koch recalled she also requested "all the wardrobe she wore. . . . It was good for us because those things are expendable, anyway. I went to her house. . . . It was fun to go there and see all the items from [our] sets." "I made some real money on those windows," Barbra would later confess, laughing. "The studio rented them back from me for five hundred dollars to use in *The Great White Hope.*"

As it turned out, principal photography was completed without any further delays in time for Barbra's Vegas engagement. (The student demonstration, which lasted a brief five to ten seconds on-screen, was finally shot back in Los Angeles at the USC campus.)

"When the picture ended," wrote Minnelli in his memoirs, "Barbra, having noticed that I take only cream in my coffee, presented me with an antique silver coffee service, the sugar bowl missing. On the coffeepot was inscribed: 'To Vincente, whom I adore . . . Love, Barbra.' On the creamer: 'You're the cream in my coffee.' It remains one of my greatest treasures." Minnelli gave her a specially framed sketch of Sarah Bernhardt and told her that she'd eventually play the legendary French Jewish actress. "That made her very happy." A year later, a proposed biography of *The Divine Sarah*, under the guidance of Ken Russell, was discussed, but Barbra rejected Russell's apparently outrageous script, and the project fell apart.

By February 1970, it was clear that the era of the colossal superstar musical was

Streisand models one of Arnold Scassi's designs for "boring" college student Daisy Gamble.

Flanked by producer Robert Evans (with cigar) *and studio vice president Bernard Donnenfeld, Barbra joins other stars filming on the Paramount lot.* From left: *Lee Marvin, Rock Hudson, John Wayne, Yves Montand, and Clint Eastwood.*

coming to an end. Paramount had shouldered some heavy financial responsibilities, and they began to panic. Though no one, including Howard Koch or Alan Jay Lerner, would later accept blame, *someone* at Paramount ordered Minnelli's 143-minute final cut of *Clear Day* shortened by almost 20 minutes. Costs were also slashed for a rather unattractive advertising campaign. They then decided to release the picture in the heat of the summer, amid the light comedies and youth-oriented fare. Reasoning that *Clear Day* didn't show the earmarks of a real winner, they hoped to recoup most of their expenses strictly on Barbra Streisand's marquee value, the disappointing *Hello,*

Dolly! grosses notwithstanding.

Once again, this decision meant further repercussions for Barbra, who was accused of tampering with the film to satisfy her own ego. This impression was reinforced when Yves Montand claimed: "It was to have been more of an equitable sharing of the movie. That was what I thought. . . . They gave Streisand everything she wanted and more." Minnelli and Koch, however, countered that every scene Montand shot that didn't involve both stars was used in the picture. Indeed, almost every single moment excised from the film was from one of Barbra's scenes. Nicholson's "Who Is There Among Us Who Knows?" also ended up on

72

the proverbial cutting-room floor.

On a Clear Day You Can See Forever opened in New York on June 17, 1970, to mostly favorable reviews. Contrary to the negative predictions, the film broke existing house records during its first week. It continued to do steady, respectable business throughout the summer, but as it began to play out, it became apparent that it was far from the summer blockbuster the studio desperately needed. In fact, the production didn't break even until after its subsidiary (foreign and television) sales. "It was not my greatest musical success, but neither was it Paramount's greatest musical failure," Minnelli said years later. Alan Jay Lerner agrees. "I feel rather badly about *Clear Day* because I think it had the makings of a marvelous picture. [But] the office where the doctor works should have looked more realistic instead of being so grand and theatrical. And Barbra's clothes should have been simpler. Instead of being a poor student who has this glorious past incarnation, she showed up in different, bizarre costumes for each scene. That's where Vincente's love of beauty occasionally fails him. If the contrast between her present and past lives had been even sharper, I think it would have solved most of what was wrong with the film."

But the film had more serious shortcomings. The flashback story that leads up to Melinda's execution is difficult to follow, and perhaps most damaging, there is no romance in the picture worth rooting for. The look of constant irritation on Dr. Chabot's face and his increasing disdain for Daisy, a character we empathize with no matter how "boring" or "uninteresting" she is supposed to be, only erodes his already tenuous standing with the

Barbra wears one of Cecil Beaton's excessive costumes that never made it into the film.

audience. Chabot is never totally likable. Therefore, most people couldn't have cared less if Barbra/Daisy/Melinda ever got together with him; they'd much rather have seen a teaming with Nicholson. (At least he smiled and told Daisy she was sexy!) Even a final hypnosis session that indicates Chabot and Daisy will be linked romantically in a future incarnation comes a little too late.

Barbra's performance as Daisy is equally frustrating. She is occasionally tender and vulnerable,

Melinda spots her handsome future husband across the room as she accompanies her current spouse, Lord Percy (Laurie Main, left), to an elaborate banquet at the Royal Pavilion at Brighton.

but many of her comedic scenes are too strident and clearly still influenced by her Fanny Brice characterization. In spite of this, she manages to keep Daisy sympathetic. Her Melinda, however, is virtually flawless: sensual, regal, witty, and classically lovely. In certain moments—prior to singing "He Isn't You"—she even brings to mind the actress first considered for the role, Audrey Hepburn. Through his graceful artistic vision, Vincente Minnelli nurtured a gentleness in the Streisand persona not exhibited previously. These too-infrequent regression sequences offered audiences the kind of unapologetic, gorgeously crafted screen glamour that was all but extinct in the pared-down Hollywood of 1970.

In discussing *his* role in the film, Jack Nicholson recalled: "[My] part was added; it wasn't in the original script. They added it—I should have known—to try to get a young audience, etc. It wasn't well understood by the [middle-aged] people who wrote it. I was supposedly playing a rich hippie. They asked me to cut my hair for the

part . . . ways of dressing and stuff like that, they didn't really understand."

The picture also suffers from Montand's uncomfortable performance, delivered with an accent so thick, it's unintentionally comical at times. Minnelli, though, was "totally satisfied" with the picture and Montand's contribution. Koch said, "I love [Yves] as a person—he's a lovely guy—but I think he was wrong in the final [analysis]. The chemistry didn't work; they didn't rub together. I think she and Richard Harris would have rubbed together." Minnelli didn't agree that chemistry was essential: "People said that Gregory Peck or Frank Sinatra would have been better, but I think Montand was better than either of those two." The point Minnelli might have missed is that Barbra didn't have to work for the audience's sympathy and Montand did.

Sinatra might have lacked chemistry with Streisand as well, but at least he would have sung the songs brilliantly, especially under the auspices of Nelson Riddle, who had arranged some of his classic recordings. (One can easily imagine how electric "Come Back to Me" could have been as belted out by Frank standing astride the Pan Am Building!) As she had with her two previous film scores, Barbra delivered glorious vocals for *Clear Day*. In particular, her exultant performance of the title song rescued it from the finger-snapping nightclub cliché it had become and stamped it as one of her signature numbers. (She revived it to great response for her 1994 concert tour.) Upon release in 1970, however, the *Clear Day* soundtrack album proved a sales flop, hitting a lowly 108 on the *Billboard* chart, and unlike *Funny Girl* and *Hello, Dolly!*—both Best Picture nominees—*Clear Day* failed to garner a single Academy Award nomination. In December 1970, Barbra said, *"Clear Day* I liked. I liked the concept but didn't feel it was fulfilled as a movie. But that's beyond my control, and I don't have any control over my movies."

REVIEWS

"Miss Streisand's particular looks, stunningly abetted by Cecil Beaton costumes, allow Minnelli to create what amount to balletic sequences of uncommon splendor. Miss Streisand, for instance, sings one song ["Love With All the Trimmings"] entirely as background to a flirtation scene of high coloration and sexuality. . . . The nature of the play requires her to be a totally different person in these regression scenes, and she is. She is with the technique and conviction beyond many more experienced actresses. If Miss Streisand will just get Funny Girl *out of her system there might be no limits to her growth and diversification."*

HOLLYWOOD REPORTER

"It is that rare meeting in the musical field of a respectable score and an intriguingly original book with a talented cast and a director of great subtlety and style. . . . Minnelli works so well with Stresiand that for the first time in a musical she functions as part of the team. Clown and chanteuse are merged into one and she is not afraid to sacrifice a scene to someone else."

FILMS ILLUSTRATED

Barbra as the elegant Melinda — precisely the kind of glamorous heroine Barbara Joan had dreamed of playing as a youngster in Flatbush.

The Owl and the Pussycat
(1970)

A Columbia Pictures Release of a Rastar Productions Picture

CAST

Barbra Streisand (*Doris*); George Segal (*Felix*); Robert Klein (*Barney*); Allen Garfield (*Dress Shop Proprietor*); Roz Kelly (*Eleanor*); Jacques Sandulescu (*Rapzinsky*); Jack Manning (*Mr. Weyderhaus*); Grace Carney (*Mrs. Weyderhaus*); Barbara Anson (*Miss Weyderhaus*); Kim Chan (*Theater Cashier*); Stan Gottlieb (*Coatcheck Man*); Joe Madden (*Old-Man Neighbor*); Fay Sappington (*Old-Woman Neighbor*); Marilyn Briggs (*Barney's Girl*); Dominic T. Barto (*Man in Bar*); Marshall Ward, Tom Atkins, Stan Bryant (*Gang in Car*).

CREDITS

Producer: Ray Stark; associate producer: George Justin; director: Herbert Ross; assistant director: William C. Gerrity; screenplay: Buck Henry (based on the play *The Owl and the Pussycat* by Bill Manhoff); music composer and arranger: Richard Halligan; music editor: William Saracino; lyrics: Blood, Sweat and Tears; unit production manager: Robert Greenhut; production designer: John Robert Lloyd; production assistant: Leo Garen; costumes: Marian Doughtery; photography: Harry Stradling, Andrew Laszlo; set decorator: Leif Pedersen; art directors: Robert Wightman, Phillip Rosenberg; script supervisor: Marguerite James; design supervisor: Ken Adam; title design: Wayne Fitzgerald; supervising film editor: Margaret Booth; editor: John F. Burnett; sound: Arthur Piantadosi, Dennis Maitland; makeup: Lee Harmon, Joe Cranzano; hairstylist: Robert Grimaldi; wardrobe: Shirlee Strahm, George Newman. Running time: 95 minutes.

In light of the disappointing box-office returns for *Hello, Dolly!* and *On a Clear Day You Can See Forever*, it became obvious that even Barbra Streisand, Hollywood's most in-demand new star, couldn't resuscitate the old-fashioned, extravagant musical film—an entertainment that was becoming less and less appealing to youth-dominated movie audiences seeking relevance and realism. Such acclaimed films as *Medium Cool, Easy Rider, Bob & Carol & Ted & Alice*, and *The Graduate* were now reflecting the tastes of a generation torn and challenged by civil unrest, the sexual revolution, political assassinations, the drug-soaked counterculture, and the Vietnam War.

At twenty-seven, Barbra was the youngest, though hardly the only, victim of this change in movie-going tastes, Fred Astaire and Petula Clark had failed to generate much audience interest in *Finian's Rainbow*. *Sweet Charity* flopped for Shirley MacLaine and director Bob Fosse. The novelty of a singing Clint Eastwood hadn't made a hit of *Paint Your Wagon*, and just four years after the global popularity of *The Sound of Music*, Julie Andrews's film career was about to nosedive with the failure of *Star* and *Darling Lily*, two hugely expensive musicals.

Some in Hollywood wondered if Streisand would survive the apparent demise of the tradition-bound film genre that had catapulted her to screen stardom. Fortunately, *The Owl and the Pussycat* came along at precisely the moment when she needed it most.

Barbra had first seen Bill Manhoff's battle-of-the-sexes comedy in London in 1966, where it was playing following a successful Broadway run that had starred Alan Alda as aspiring writer Felix Sherman and Diana Sands (the gifted black actress who had worked with Barbra in the ill-fated *Another Evening With Harry Stoones* in 1961) as Doris, a "hopeless, hapless hustler." Ray Stark purchased the *Pussycat* screen rights in 1966 for a reasonable $100,000, intending to cast Elizabeth

Felix and Doris confront each other at the start of their wild night together.

Taylor and Richard Burton. When that deal fell through, Stark shelved the property until two years later, when he presented it to Streisand, who was under contract to him. Although she once called *Pussycat* "an obligation to fulfill," it was clear that Barbra was delighted with the prospect of portraying a down-to-earth, contemporary young character in a ribald comedy—her first nonmusical role since her days as a teenager in summer stock.

"Now I can make a movie in ten weeks," she said, "no songs, like a normal person. You do a movie in the daytime, and then you go home at night." On November 25, 1968, Columbia Pictures announced that Barbra would star in *Pussycat* and that the play, at Ray Stark's suggestion, was being rewritten to expand the character of Doris to that of a part-time folk singer. Stark called the revamped character a "folk hooker," but his idea was, thankfully, soon dropped; Barbra vehemently

refused to rely on her singing talents to embellish the role.

Longtime Streisand associate Herbert Ross was chosen to direct the film on the heels of *Goodbye, Mr. Chips,* his directorial debut, and Buck Henry, whose razor-sharp wit had enhanced screenplays for *The Graduate* and *Catch-22,* was set to write the script. Henry liked Manhoff's play, but he felt that the San Francisco locale should be changed to Manhattan to better suit his star's own background. "Lots of stuff in it was written for Barbra's rhythms," Henry said.

Since the play was an interracial love story, Ray Stark began looking for black actors to play opposite Streisand. Not surprisingly, his first choice was the only black male superstar at the time, Sidney Poitier. Streisand and Poitier were already personal and professional friends, having just formed First Artists Productions with Paul

Newman. In response to rumors that Poitier might be cast as Felix, Barbra joked, "Ray originally wanted to use Sidney for Nick Arnstein in *Funny Girl*, but we decided he looks too Jewish. So we went in another direction." For whatever reason, the interracial factor was dropped, and George Segal, a close friend of Buck Henry's, soon fell under close scrutiny.

Segal, a diversely talented actor who had first appeared off-Broadway with Henry in the satirical revue *The Premise*, later went on to star in such dramatic films as *Ship of Fools* and *Who's Afraid of Virginia Woolf?* (He received a Best Supporting Actor Oscar nomination in 1967 for the former.) His true forte was comedy, however, and after reading through the script with the producers, Segal was chosen to play Felix Sherman on July 7, 1969. He looked forward to the film, stating, "I like a tight, fast, funny script that's about somebody. The best comedies are about real people." By the end of August the film was completely cast, with irreverent comic Robert Klein signed to play Felix's pal Barney and Roz Kelly cast as Eleanor, Doris's friend and fellow hooker. It was the smallest, youngest cast of principals and (with the exception of Stark and Harry Stradling) production colleagues that had yet surrounded Barbra in Hollywood, and she loved it.

It surprised no one that Streisand once again requested that Stradling photograph the film. She was so confident in his abilities by this point that she was leery of entrusting her still-controversial looks to any other cinematographer. Principal photography on *The Owl and the Pussycat* began the

first week of October at soundstages Columbia rented on West Fifty-sixth Street in Manhattan, just north of the theater district. The shoot was destined—with only one sad exception—to become one of the least stressful of Barbra's career. "I couldn't wait to get to work every morning," she later said of the experience.

Doris and Felix, as unlikely a duo to ever fall in love during the course of a movie comedy, share some essential similarities. Both are basically sensitive, moral people who are deluding themselves about the realities of their respective lives. Felix is a would-be writer, supporting himself as a clerk in Doubleday's bookstore on Fifth Avenue. His natural intellectual personality is swamped by intol-

Director Herbert Ross, Barbra, and George Segal look serious as they prepare to shoot one of the film's most hilarious scenes.

erance and snobbism. Doris is a streetwise prostitute who claims to be a "model and an actress" and has been in a movie—that turns out to be pornographic. She justifies her profession by claiming that it's only part-time ("I may be a prostitute, but I am *not* promiscuous!"), but in reality her aggressive, vulgar personality conceals a rather shy, insecure young woman eager to improve her station in life.

Their story is a series of one-liners, frantic escapades, sexual jousts, and role reversals that ultimately brings them to the realization that in order to survive in these turbulent times, facing reality is the best and only answer. In a series of brilliantly played scenes, their relationship evolves from one of mutual disgust to passable interest to high-voltage lust to genuine love. In the amusing process, both characters strip away the illusions they have been harboring about their lives and ultimately decide to share an apartment and a future.

George Segal had heard the gossip charac-

terizing Barbra as difficult and temperamental, but he saw no such behavior. "She's fantastic!" he told the press. "I think there's Brando, and then there's Barbra. She has an unerring instinct; she's a natural phenomenon. She's the easiest person to work with; she's warm and even knows what she's doing!" Robert Klein agreed: "The comedy came naturally to Barbra," he told author James Spada. "She was much more adept at how to be funny; she seemed more sure of herself. . . . Her virtuosity really forced George to work hard at being funny. She was thinking *all the time* about how to do a particular thing, and she was completely thorough. Ultimately, though, I think George was quite effective with her. And, like him, I never, ever saw that side to her that I had heard a lot about. She was not only thoroughly professional, but she was very accommodating in making me feel at home."

Though gawking fans sometimes plagued such locations as Rikers restaurant and the trashy Club 45, where Doris's go-go-dancing career comes to a crashing end, the production encountered no real delays until Barbra stalled for time in her dressing room prior to filming the one part she had been dreading: a hilarious, fumbling lovemaking scene in which she had to appear topless. "Herbie, I can't," she pleaded to her director. "I've got goose bumps, and they'll show. What will my mother think of this?" Barbra also expressed doubts about the appeal of her figure. Buck Henry recalled: "Ross told her not to worry, she had a great body. They went into a closet, and she showed him why she thought she didn't have what it takes. Well, it happens that Barbra has a great figure, and Ross laughed and said, 'Well, you're nuts. You've got to trust me.'"

Finally, after further reassurances, Streisand agreed to do the scene, and to everyone's amusement, she requested a retake! When she saw the results in the finished picture, however, she asked that it be deleted. "I did [it] on condition that it wouldn't be used without my approval," she stated, "and I didn't like it. It's out and it stays out." By way of explanation, she said it distracted from the comic thrust of the scene, and she was probably right. It was still extremely rare at that time for a star of Streisand's magnitude to bare her breasts on-screen, and the moment, brief though it was, would surely have directed attention away from the comedy at hand. Though she was assured that the film containing her nudity would be destroyed, it wasn't. Barbra was horrified when, ten years later, frame blowups of her only topless screen appearance turned up in *High Society*. (She filed an injunction against distribution of the magazine, and several thousand were recalled, but not before a great many had been sold. They are now, of course, highly prized collector's items.)

The steady pace of the *Pussycat* filming came to a sudden standstill when, without warning, Harry Stradling, sixty-eight, exhausted from the long shooting schedule and the frigid New York winter, asked to be relieved from the film shortly before Christmas. Stradling flew home to California and released a statement saying that due to health problems he "would never [again] leave the L.A. soil." Negotiations were hastily conducted to replace Stradling, and Andrew Laszlo, a

"Who gave you permission to read my panties?" Doris's colorful evening wear became Barbra Streisand's most recognizable film costume.

Doris's disgruntled attitude is all wrong for go-go dancing.

young Hungarian cinematographer who had previously shot *The Night They Raided Minsky's,* was quickly summoned to finish the picture. Barbra was pleased with Laszlo's work and glad the filming was once again on track, but she was devastated when Harry Stradling died in Hollywood of a heart attack on the following February 14, just twelve hours after he learned of his Oscar nomination for *Hello, Dolly!*

As *Pussycat* production was drawing to an end, Barbra felt enthusiastic about the film, and her performance. She was handling the satiric material with finesse, and her line readings were so fresh and natural, she seemed to be improvising with Segal—and on several occasions they were. "As a writer," Buck Henry recalled, "I think in terms of the words meaning a great deal. . . . On the other hand, I am fond of improvisation. When it works it's sensational. . . . Barbra and George rehearsing would, now and then, lead me into a direction that would cause me to rework a scene, or there [were lines they] improvised that I put into the script." One scene that *was* scripted had Doris shout "Fuck off!" to a carload of harassing

punks, and thus Barbra Streisand became the first female superstar to utter the "F" word on-screen.

The film's final scenes (shot in the Sheep Meadow area of Central Park, where Barbra had performed her landmark free concert eighteen months earlier) prompted several colorful rumors. In the script, Felix forces Doris into the humiliating position of begging like a pet dog, and Doris goes along with his orders up to the moment when she suddenly begins crying and finally socks him in defiance. When asked how she was able to produce tears for the number of retakes required, Barbra allegedly responded with one of two replies: She was thinking about that evening's premiere of *Hello, Dolly!* and wept worrying about its possible failure; or, believing *Hello, Dolly!* would be a hit, she began to cry wondering if the public would accept her in *Pussycat* as a foul-mouthed prostitute. In yet another version, Streisand was reportedly unable to cry on cue until Herb Ross, needing to finish the scene before the sun set, reminded his star that she would surely look exhausted at the *Dolly!* opening just hours away if the scene wasn't wrapped quickly. The next take was supposedly a print. Whatever the case, these stories, later denied, made for provocative column items.

Filming was completed on January 19, 1970, and postproduction began several weeks later at the Columbia lot in Hollywood. The movie's soundtrack was composed by Richard Halligan and performed by Blood, Sweat and Tears, a popular rock band whose hit songs included "You've Made Me So Very Happy" and "Spinning Wheel." Stark and Ross felt that the sound of the film should be as contemporary as possible, reflecting the young-adult appeal of the story. Although Streisand had adamantly refused to sing on-screen, Stark had Martin Charnin write her a dramatic ballad, "The Best Thing You've Ever Done," in the hope that she would perform it on the soundtrack as musical background for a montage in the film. But Barbra refused: "I said there was no way I would sing. I was pushed around, made to feel like I was a bad girl or something. There was no reason for that." (She did, however, record the song, which was released as a single and eventually came to be included in her number-one 1973 album, *Barbra Streisand, Featuring "The Way We Were" and "All in Love Is Fair."*) In an unusual move, Columbia released an LP of *Pussycat*'s highlights that is unique in that large sections of dialogue

Doris's porno movie, Cycle Sluts, *is never seen in* The Owl and the Pussycat, *but Barbra had fun posing for a series of stills to convey its lurid meaning.*

from the movie were interspersed between the instrumental, horn-accented score. David Clayton-Thomas, lead singer of Blood, Sweat and Tears, performs the album's only vocal, a blues-tinged ballad, "You've Been Alone Too Long," played behind the film's closing credits. A highly specialized release, the soundtrack barely cracked the *Billboard* chart at 186.

Columbia executives were thrilled when they first viewed the final cut of *Pussycat* in late summer, 1970. Scheduled as their major Christmas release, the studio was counting on the film to be big at the box office, and they were encouraged by hugely successful sneak previews held in Hollywood and New York. The movie's advertising slogan, "The Owl and the Pussycat is no longer a story for children," was accompanied by a photo of Barbra dressed in an outlandish "modeling" outfit Doris wears as lounging pajamas. ("For whom do you model," asks Felix, "the Boston Strangler?") A sheer, low-cut, black getup with pink hands sewn over each breast cup and a rhinestone heart at the crotch, the costume drew one of the biggest laughs in the movie and has become, arguably, the most famous of Streisand's film career. Some newspapers, including the *New York Times*, refused to run the *Pussycat* ad unless the offending hands and heart were airbrushed out of the photo.

Nationally released on November 20, 1970, *The Owl and the Pussycat* had its world premiere in Manhattan. The mainly positive reviews joyously embraced Streisand's return to the free, daring, and natural performance style that had so energized her early stage and club performances. The film itself and George Segal's performance also received favorable notices, and *Pussycat* went on to become the year's most successful comedy, grossing over $11 million in the United States alone—quite a hefty take for that time. The success of the film confirmed that a new, frank, sexy era had dawned in terms of what audiences wanted to see in a romantic comedy. Though only six years had passed since Doris Day and Rock Hudson's will-she-or-won't-she scenarios had reigned at the box office, it seemed more like an eternity.

Miniskirted, go-go-booted, and pot smoking, Barbra's Doris, a "sexual Disneyland," was a cinematic progression to the independent, yet vulnerable, Streisand persona seen in most of her subsequent films. The theme of the dominant female as the romantic aggressor (first utilized in *Hello, Dolly!*) came to full force in *Pussycat*. Barbra was later to refine the species in *What's Up, Doc?* and most endearingly in *The Way We Were*. The dichotomy of emotions Doris displayed were important in many ways, and as a star, Streisand proved unequivocally that she needn't sing to captivate a movie audience.

REVIEWS

"In her first non-singing role, Miss Streisand emerges on her own, demonstrating the variety and depth of the dramatic talents that were indicated but unexploited in her musical roles. She has all the brass of a street urchin, the toughness of the survivor and the tawdriness of the tramp for the exterior Doris . . . but it is the interior Doris, with the sharp mind and the tender heart, that makes her characterization valid, that justifies the loud mouth and bravura behavior. In her performance, Miss Streisand . . . makes her role a delight—at last even for non-Barbra addicts."

NEW YORK

"George Segal gives a fine, subtle comic performance in a film that is anything but subtle, and opposite an all-stops-out display of fireworks by La Streisand. She doesn't sing, but she does every bit of shtick and business that writer Buck Henry and director Herb Ross could cram into one film; she is alternately crude, witty, bawdy, and hilarious, and so is the film."

WOMEN'S WEAR DAILY

"There she comes, right where she belongs, in a real New York street . . . the way girls used to come into our movies, and our fantasies, and it's about time we remembered that Streisand is the latest of our girls—our Normands, Lombards, Harlows, Blondells, Monroes. In The Owl and the Pussycat, Streisand is a splendid comic fantasy: our friendly neighborhood hooker with no learning, no money, no love, no nothing but her TV set, without which she would die of sleeplessness, her high-toned aliases, her mother wit—a mother of a mother wit—and the snappy rakish saintliness of all movie fantasy girls. . . . Streisand devotes the most amazing comic energy seen on the screen in a very long time."

NEWSWEEK

What's Up, Doc?

(1972)

A Warner Bros. Release of a Saticoy Picture

CAST

Barbra Streisand (*Judy Maxwell*); Ryan O'Neal (*Howard Bannister*); Kenneth Mars (*Hugh Simon*); Austin Pendleton (*Frederick Larrabee*); Sorrell Booke (*Harry*); Stefan Gierasch (*Fritz*); Mabel Albertson (*Mrs. Van Hoskins*); Michael Murphy (*Mr. Smith*); Graham Jarvis (*Bailiff*); Madeline Kahn (*Eunice Burns*); Liam Dunn (*Judge*); Phil Roth (*Mr. Jones*); John Hillerman (*Mr. Kaltenborn*); George Morfogen (*Rudy, the Headwaiter*); Randy Quaid (*Professor Hosquith*); M. Emmett Walsh (*Arresting Officer*); Eleanor Zee (*Banquet Receptionist*); Kevin O'Neal (*Delivery Boy*).

CREDITS

Producer and director: Peter Bogdanovich; associate producer: Paul Lewis; assistant director: Ray Gosnell; screenplay: Buck Henry, David Newman, Robert Benton; music arranger and conductor: Artie Butler; unit production manager: Fred Ahern; production designer: Polly Platt; photographer: Laszlo Kovacs; special effects: Robert Macdonald; set decorator: John Austin; art director: Herman A. Blumenthal; script supervisor: Hazel Hall; editor: Verna Fields; sound: Les Fresholtz; makeup supervisor: Don Cash; hairstylist: Lynda Gurasich; publicist: Carl Combs. Running time: 94 minutes.

The "youthening" of Barbra Streisand's screen image that had resulted from the success of *The Owl and the Pussycat* was bolstered by a parallel transformation of her musical profile. With the release of two hit rock-tinged pop albums within a seven-month span she had acquired countless new, younger fans. And just as Barbra found that singing songs by her contemporaries had invigorated her recording career, so, too, did she seek to collaborate with the best of the new breed of Hollywood filmmakers for her future movie projects. As much as she had enjoyed working with the "old guard," as personified by William Wyler and Vincente Minnelli, she was eager to put Dolly Levi, and all that she represented, firmly behind her.

Barbra's starring in this film and her subsequent alliance with the talented, young Peter Bogdanovich, however, came about ironically, even by Hollywood standards. In February 1971, Warner Bros. halted production on the Manhattan-based comedy *A Glimpse of Tiger* because its star, Elliott Gould, had allegedly lashed out violently at director Anthony Harvey (*The Lion in Winter*) and costar Kim Darby. Though he admitted to recreational use of marijuana and LSD, Gould claimed that his tantrum was strictly stress-induced. "I was very unstable," he admitted later, "but it wasn't drugs." The studio wasn't so sure. The project was canceled, effectively ending the upward trajectory of Gould's movie career.

Deeply concerned about her ex-husband, Barbra stepped in and asked Warner Bros. executive John Calley, whom she had briefly dated a year before, if she could help Elliott avoid a lawsuit. Calley quickly suggested that the *Tiger* script be retooled to enable Barbra to assume Gould's role as a con artist in the "comic fantasy" that addressed current social issues. Streisand liked the idea and felt director Peter Bogdanovich, thirty-one, would be an ideal choice to helm the project, for she greatly admired *The Last Picture Show*, his acclaimed new film. Bogdanovich, though thrilled at the prospect of working with Streisand on a big-budget studio release, convinced her to let him fashion an entirely new comedy for her, a wild romp in the style of the screwball comedies so popular in the 1930s and 1940s.

Barbra agreed on the condition that the film be ready to shoot by early summer and that it costar her handsome new lover of several months, Ryan O'Neal. The boyish blond actor had parlayed success on television's *Peyton Place* into movie stardom via the immensely popular tearjerker *Love Story*, released the year before. Warner Bros. was more than happy to approve O'Neal's casting, and Bogdanovich, serving as both producer and director, set about assembling his production team for the picture he would title *What's Up, Doc?*

Bogdanovich had difficulty explaining the movie's convoluted plot. "It's kind of a combination of a Feydeau farce—with much running in and out of rooms and slamming of doors—and a kind of screwball comedy," he offered. "It plays awfully fast." Against the background of a musicologist's convention in San Francisco, bright, eccentric college dropout Judy Maxwell (Streisand) avidly pursues Howard Bannister (O'Neal), a straitlaced academic attending the convention (with his neurotic fiancée) in the hope of landing a grant to fund his study of the musical qualities of igneous rocks. Frantic complications arise when several identical plaid suitcases (carrying everything from Judy's undies to state secrets to a fabulous jewel collection) get hopelessly mixed up among hotel thieves and federal agents. All ends happily, with Judy and Howard united in romance after a wild, multivehicle chase through several of San Francisco's most famous districts that culminates in everyone falling into the bay.

For Streisand's first film not derived from a Broadway play, screenwriters David Newman and Robert Benton concocted a madcap scenario that emerged as an unabashed tribute to the classic 1938 Howard Hawks–directed comedy *Bringing Up Baby*. The writers took less than two weeks to complete the first draft of the script. "Peter said he needed it fast," Newman recalled, "because he had a 'pay or play' deal with Streisand and O'Neal. If he didn't have a script ready to shoot by July, they were gone. So we flew out to Los Angeles and went into these intensive sessions with Peter, where we hashed out the story. Peter would talk to Howard Hawks every night, and he'd come in the next day and say, 'Howard thinks we should try such and such.'" Streisand was in constant contact with Bogdanovich about the plot as well. "Peter talked to her every night," Newman added. "He'd tell her the story so far; then, the next morning,

he'd say, 'Barbra loved this, she didn't like that, she thinks it would be funny if she got to do that.'"

To complement his two superstar leads, the director selected a gifted cast of character actors whose comic brilliance was apparent even during first script run-throughs. "Barbra really got twitchy about it because all those other people were going to be very good," says Buck Henry, who was brought in later for script revisions. Austin Pendleton, Mabel Albertson, Liam Dunn, Kenneth Mars, and Madeline Kahn, in her screen debut, promised to enliven every scene they were in. Having never appeared in a comedy, Ryan O'Neal couldn't help but feel intimidated, particularly by his leading lady. Visiting the set, publicist Steve Jaffe, a good friend of O'Neal, observed Ryan "dancing around like Muhammad Ali before a fight, just getting ready for a scene with Barbra. He was trying to act at his absolute peak. Not only because Barbra's so great and such a perfectionist but because he was in love with her. He wanted her to respect him. He wanted to be as good as he could be."

Admittedly, Bogdanovich liked being the star of his own productions, and Barbra didn't need to be venerated and adored by her director. She wanted a good, funny film, and she placed her trust in Bogdanovich to pull it off. Which isn't to say she didn't disagree with him. For one thing, their concepts of comedy were different. "Barbra has a great sense of truth," stated Irvin Kershner, who would direct her next film. "Even when she's funny, she's very real with her humor. It's not one-liners; it's not gags. It's the character saying what has to be said, which is what makes it funny—but not trying to *be* funny. . . ." Conversely, the essence of screwball comedy is characters and situations that don't make sense, with rapid-fire dialogue and visual gags; if one setup doesn't connect, the next surely will.

Barbra found Bogdanovich an opinionated, autocratic director. "He knows how he wants to do things and doesn't waste a lot of time. Even when he's wrong, it's the right way to do it. I gave up script approval, costume approval, everything to him." (The costume issue didn't amount to much, for Streisand had only a handful of wardrobe changes, all casual street fashions.)

Six weeks before the start of filming, Bogdanovich called in Buck Henry to rewrite the screenplay. "I didn't think I could do it [in that

time span], but Barbra was going to walk off, and so was Ryan, and they were right. The script was in no condition to shoot. Peter asked me, 'Can you do something about Barbra's part?' Well, I couldn't rewrite Barbra without rewriting Ryan, and I changed so much of Ryan that I caught her up a little short. There's a very long period in there where she doesn't say anything—the whole chase scene and the court scene and the stuff between Howard and [his fiancée]. She, understandably as a movie star, thought, Where am I? How did I get lost?"

What's Up, Doc? began shooting on location in San Francisco on August 16, 1971, and it soon became clear that filming the stunt-laden production would be much more expensive and time consuming than anticipated. "I have never been in a more difficult film," acknowledged Austin Pendleton. "Peter . . . wanted everybody to talk fast, fast, fast. We couldn't do it fast enough for him. And we had overlapping dialogue. The pressure was tremendous, because if you blew a line, the entire shot would be ruined, and everybody—not just you—would have to do the whole scene

Judy Maxwell is happy to offer proof that her heart is indeed racing at the start of the film's comical banquet scene.

again." The twelve-minute chase sequence alone took weeks of planning and over $1 million and a month to shoot. Doubles performed all of the high-risk stunts, one of which called for Barbra to furiously pedal a vendor's cart, with Ryan sitting atop, that was rolling backward down one of the city's steepest hills. "But for close-ups," Henry explained, "we had to have the cart moving down the hill at the same speed as the long shots, and Barbra had to do those. She wasn't too happy about that; it was stressful for her, and a bit frightening." As filming progressed, Barbra wasn't too happy with the whole enterprise. "This doesn't seem very funny to me," she complained to Bogdanovich. "It'll play funny, Barbra," he replied, "trust me." But she wasn't placated. "We're in a piece of shit, Ryan!" she confided to O'Neal. "This is not funny. . . . I know what's funny, and I'm telling you this movie isn't funny."

With the story evenly balanced among the large ensemble cast, Barbra found herself in the unusual position of having a lot of free time on her hands. She shopped and took in some of the typical tourist sights with friends and four-year-old Jason, a frequent visitor from Los Angeles. If she wasn't happy with how the production was evolving, she certainly seemed the happiest and most relaxed she'd ever been at work. She often went unrecognized on the street, especially when she wasn't with Ryan, and that in itself was a luxury she hadn't enjoyed in years.

By the time the production returned to Los Angeles, Barbra's misgivings about the film's potential had dissipated, though she still resisted Bogdanovich's attempts to mold her into a Hepburn/Lombard ideal. ("Are you giving me line readings?" she quizzed him on the set one day.) "She isn't always a hit with her studio bosses because she is a highly individualized person with an abundance of talent, a drive that won't stop, and enough eccentricities to make her bizarre but not grotesque," read her Warner Bros. publicity

89

Director Peter Bogdanovich has some last-minute tips
before Ryan O'Neal and Barbra film their playful love
scene.

biography. Working with a totally new crew, Barbra developed a reputation for being friendly, though not a back-slapping "pal," on the set. Austin Pendleton recalled that she would join the large cast for chats between scene setups. "We'd talk about acting, mostly. I think Barbra was a little in awe of us because we were New York stage actors. Barbra talked about a lot of things in her life." Pendleton was amused when Streisand mentioned her relationship with Pierre Trudeau. "I got the impression they still saw each other occasionally," the actor said, "and it was funny because she was so famous, most of us had already read about the things she was telling us. We wanted to say, 'Yeah, yeah, Barbra, we know all about that.' But she wasn't like some superstars who get bored the minute the subject isn't them. Barbra was interested in our lives and ideas and problems, too."

In order for the zany love story of *What's Up, Doc?* to work, there had to be genuine romantic chemistry between Barbra and Ryan, and early rushes indicated that there was plenty. (Offscreen affairs have never guaranteed that actors will give off sparks when they are coupled on-screen. For whatever reasons, the opposite is often the case. The grand, public passion of Elizabeth Taylor and Richard Burton, for instance, seldom ignited their movie love scenes.) "Ryan was probably the easiest actor I've ever had to work with," Barbra divulged, "and the most fun. Just terrific." Later, she offered a glimpse into their personal relationship. "Ryan and I had an argument on our first date. He won. I never felt better losing. . . . Ryan isn't afraid of my image; he respects my talent, but he's not in awe of my career. I guess that's what made me like him at first." Though the Streisand-O'Neal affair had been going strong for some time, gossips couldn't help but suggest that Barbra had thrown Ryan over in favor of her dynamic young director, who was married at the time to the film's production designer, Polly Platt. The rumors began because Bogdanovich, a hands-on filmmaker, was not

above giving Barbra a passionate hug or lingering kiss to show Ryan how he wanted it done. "Bogdanovich frequently calls her gorgeous," wrote one visiting journalist, "holds her hand, kisses her cheek, and once patted her fanny. Barbra responded to him with warm smiles and hugs." For all of her reservations about the kind of film he seemed to be making, Barbra never felt any animosity toward her director, whom she found personally charming. In fact, their easygoing relationship helped keep the complicated production on an even keel.

After the filming was completed, Barbra got together with arranger Artie Butler to discuss "You're the Top," the Cole Porter song Bogdanovich suggested she sing under the film's opening and closing credits. A composers' strike provided the director with the perfect justification

extension of talent than a reflection of ego. "When you get a call to work with somebody like Barbra, it's a joy. And along with the joy comes a lot of tedious work. But look at the end result: Years later I still get compliments on that arrangement. Frankly," he says, "I got into the music business to work with people of that caliber." Butler's dynamic arrangement set off Barbra's punchy vocal perfectly, and for the version behind the closing credits, Ryan O'Neal joined in with a singing performance that is more good-humored than musical.

What's Up, Doc! opened at Radio City Music Hall on March 9, 1972. Reviews depended on each critic's appreciation of screwball comedy more than on his or her appreciation of Barbra Streisand, but most hailed it as her most subdued, ingratiating performance yet. A G-rated family motion picture, it was the perfect feature for the Easter holidays. It was also one of the top-grossing films of 1972, outperforming *Funny Girl* by $2 million to become Streisand's biggest hit to date.

Because it displayed a contemporary—some would argue a homogenized—Barbra, which people were hearing more and more of on her records, the importance of its acceptance among young, heretofore nonfans cannot be overemphasized. For once she wasn't an imposing, larger-than-life figure; she was part of the fun. Slimmer than she had ever been on film and sporting long, flowing blond hair and a deep, flattering suntan, Streisand presented audiences with a youthful, sensuous, accessible image as Judy Maxwell. She and Ryan—also at his most sun-kissed and attractive—radiated sex appeal even as they tackled the kooky slapstick elements of the picture. In their final scene they got a huge laugh (at the expense of *Love Story*'s most famous line of dialogue) when Judy, batting her eyelashes at Howard, says, "Love means never having to say you're sorry," to which he responds, "That's the dumbest thing I ever heard."

to score his film with standards. (Barbra also sang a sexy though frustratingly short snippet of "As Time Goes By" as a prelude to Judy and Howard's first kiss.) According to Butler, "You're the Top" was recorded in front of a live studio orchestra, producing a memorable result. "When you're on a session and you have a singer of that caliber performing live, it's an added plus," he stated. "Because hearing her through the earphones makes you play differently; it's like lighting a match. You not only play the notes on the paper. You start playing the music; and there's a big difference.

"About a week later, I got six or seven phone calls from musicians on the session who thought it was one of the best sessions they'd done in years." Butler also had many late-night conversations with Barbra about which tracks to use for her vocals in the final cut. That process, he feels, was more an

The stars' fears of being upstaged by the supporting cast came close to being realized. Kenneth Mars is wonderful as Hugh Simon, Howard Bannister's slimy competitor. His name and obnoxious persona had been modeled after acerbic New York critic John Simon, a chronic Streisand nemesis. ("Meaner!" Barbra would laughingly yell at

Mars during rehearsals. "Make him meaner!") Mabel Albertson is delightful as the wealthy, outlandishly garbed Mrs. Van Hoskins, whose jewels are stolen, and Madeline Kahn, as Howard's possessive, adenoidal fiancée, Eunice, is nothing short of hilarious. Other cast members who would also go on to prominence included Randy Quaid, John Byner, John Hillerman, Sorrell Booke, and M. Emmett Walsh.

Since Barbra did not remember it as a particularly joyful picture to make, *Doc*'s success took her totally by surprise. "Barbra and I, having seen *What's Up, Doc?* separately, both thought that the comedy didn't work," said her longtime manager, Martin Erlichman. "We were in Vegas when Warner Bros. held three or four previews at Radio City, and Peter and several other people called to say, 'You've got to see it with six thousand people roaring with laughter. We've got a big, big hit!' Neither of us could believe it, [so] I got on a plane and flew to New York to see it for myself." Erlichman was happy to find that Bogdanovich hadn't been exaggerating. The film was a bona-fide audience pleaser. But Barbra never mellowed in her assessment of the picture. A year after it had played out, she said, "I hated it with a passion. What interests me is how so many people like it. I was embarrassed to do that film. I thought it was infantile humor and not one-sixteenth of the film that it was trying to emulate. . . . It was a disappointing experience." Although harsh, Barbra's opinion was right in that *What's Up, Doc?* lacks the cohesiveness and warm glamour of *Bringing Up Baby.* And despite his earnest efforts, Ryan O'Neal's comedic talent is limited, and protracted scenes of the bad guys chasing down the mixed-up suitcases get redundant. Overall, the film succeeds—and still holds up—as an enjoyable farce, peopled by zany, wonderfully acted characters, and it offers a relaxed, luminous Streisand presence that still appeals to her fans. Barbra's feelings about the film apparently never rankled Peter Bogdanovich, for the two have remained friends and colleagues.

Ryan and Barbra make one of their first public appearances at a screening of Ryan's film, The Wild Rovers, *at the Chinese Theatre in Hollywood in November of 1971. By the time* What's Up Doc? *opened four months later, their romance had cooled down.*

Barbra's lighthearted performance as Judy Maxwell remains one of her most popular.

REVIEWS

"Comedy, more than other genres, depends on the performances of the actors; and this film is blessed with an abundance of gems. Streisand, minus her Flatbush twang, is wacky, campy, and endearing—her best performance to date."

VILLAGER

"Nothing that happens in the movie—none of the chases or comic confusions—has the excitement of her singing [of "You're the Top"]. When a tiger pretends to be a pussycat, that's practically a form of Uncle Tomism. Yes, she's more easily acceptable in What's Up, Doc? than in her bigger roles, because she doesn't tap her full talent and there is an element of possible unpleasantness, of threat, in that red-hot talent—as there is in Liza Minnelli at full star strength—which produces unresolved feelings in us. It's easy to see that those people who haven't liked Streisand before could like her this time, because here her charm has no real drive. . . ."

NEW YORKER

Up the Sandbox

(1972)

A First Artists Presentation of a Barwood Film

CAST
Barbra Streisand (*Margaret*); David Selby (*Paul*); Ariane Heller (*Elizabeth*); Terry/Gary Smith (*Peter*); Jane Hoffman (*Mrs. Yussim*); John C. Becher (*Mr. Yussim*); Jacobo Morales (*Fidel Castro*); Paul Benedict (*Dr. Beineke*); George Irving (*Dr. Keglin*); Jane House (*Mrs. Keglin*).

CREDITS
Producers: Irwin Winkler, Robert Chartoff; associate producer: Martin Erlichman for Barwood Films; executive in charge of production: Hal Polaire; director: Irvin Kershner; screenplay: Paul Zindel (based on the novel by Anne Richardson Roiphe); production manager (New York): Jerry Shapiro; production manager (Kenya): Eva Monley; production assistant: Jeff Benjamin; production designer: Harry Horner; director of photography: Gordon Willis; set decorator: Robert De Vestel; hairstylist: Kaye Pownell; wardrobe designer: Albert Wolsky; makeup: Lee C. Harman; publicist: Harry Mines; casting: Cis Corman. Running time: 97 minutes.

Barbra Streisand's sixth film was a total departure from her previous list of comedies and musicals, and it remains one of the most unusual endeavors of her career. It also stands as a somewhat unsung landmark in terms of both its content and its contribution to Streisand's efforts to gain some control over her movie projects as she neared thirty. For the first picture produced through her Barwood Films company (and First Artists, the alliance she had coformed three years earlier), Barbra chose to dramatize the offbeat story of Margaret Reynolds, a young Manhattan housewife who uses fantasies to project herself into an exciting life beyond her Riverside Drive apartment. During a period when the times really *were* a changin' for millions of American women, this motion picture stood to

play a pivotal role in a career that was still building momentum.

Up the Sandbox was loosely based on the 1970 novel by Anne Richardson Roiphe, which received a good deal of attention and attracted favorable reviews. Producer-director Robert Altman and producer Irwin Winkler (whose previous credits included *They Shoot Horses, Don't They?*) competed for movie rights. Winkler was the high bidder at sixty thousand dollars. He sent the book to Barbra, who had just completed four films in a row and was close to committing to *What's Up, Doc?* "I read it and I thought *ecccch*," she later confessed. "I liked it well enough, but I'd just finished working, and I wasn't so crazy to start again. But then you're pulled together and you want to do something and it becomes *ahhhhh!*"

At a time when feminist icon Betty Friedan was proclaiming: "Something is very wrong with the way American women are trying to live their lives today. There is a strange discrepancy between the reality of our lives as women and the image with which we are trying to conform," the author of *Sandbox* was advocating more tolerance: "These days I feel a cultural pressure *not* to be absorbed in my child. I am made to feel my curiosity about the growth of my babies is somehow counterrevolutionary." As for Streisand, she recalled Voltaire's ironic view that "perhaps when we demand equality, we give up our superiority." Later, she was less flip: "There is something between radicals and the women who go around proselytizing for women staying at home. . . . *Up the Sandbox* isn't a women's-lib picture, but on the other hand, it's not designed to please antilib groups. We're against

Margaret Reynolds makes bath time fun for her infant son in the opening moments of Up the Sandbox.

polarization. We're saying a woman should feel it's right to stay wherever she can be fulfilled."

Margaret Reynolds's predictable, if often domestically chaotic, world is turned upside down when she discovers she is pregnant for the third time. As she postpones telling her husband—a respected professor—about her condition and as she contemplates the possibility of having an abortion, she finds herself wondering if her life as devoted wife and mother is all it could be. As part of this self-evaluation process, Margaret indulges in a series of outrageous fantasies in which, among other scenarios, she confronts Fidel Castro with a pro-feminist speech at a press conference (after which Castro reveals that he is, in fact, a woman); journeys to the wilds of Africa in search of a painless method of childbirth; shoves the face of her obnoxious mother into a cake at a family gathering; and becomes instantly and hugely pregnant at a pretentious cocktail party. Eventually Margaret decides to keep her baby, and tells her husband she's pregnant in the film's touching final scene.

Robert Chartoff–Irwin Winkler Productions announced a fall 1971 start for the film. For those who doubted Barbra's sincerity in her desire to submerse herself in such an ordinary role, eyebrows were raised with the signings of screenwriter Paul Zindel as screenwriter and director Irvin Kershner. Zindel was the Pulitzer Prize–winning author of *The Effect of Gamma Rays on Man-in-the-Moon Marigolds,* and Kershner, whose film *Loving,* with George Segal, had particularly impressed Barbra, had earned a reputation as a fine director with a sure touch for warm domestic scenes. Kershner got together with Streisand in San Francisco during the filming of *What's Up, Doc?* to discuss the script. "I was a bit afraid to tackle this movie. You hear so many stories about Barbra. I thought, We're going to have problems," he admitted after the fact. "But we didn't."

Due to previous commitments, production was rescheduled for the spring of 1972. Key scenes would be shot first on location in New York and Africa and then in Hollywood. With a screenplay beginning to take shape, the next task was casting. "We wanted everyone [except herself, of course] to be quite unknown, to be more like real people," Barbra pointed out. Actor David Selby, who gave a much-admired performance in *Sticks and Bones* on Broadway and who had starred in *Dark Shadows,* a Gothic TV soap opera, was chosen to play Margaret's husband, Paul. As happy as Selby was to be cast, he never got over feeling intimidated by the superstardom of his costar. "You can't blame him," Kershner said. "To suddenly play opposite Barbra Streisand and be new to the screen is pretty overwhelming. It affected his work, in fact; in [certain scenes] he had to try very hard to just be there on the screen with her. It was tough on him."

In March 1972, shortly before the opening of *What's Up Doc?,* small crowds of New Yorkers watched Barbra at work as *Up the Sandbox* commenced production. Locations varied from Pier 14 on the Hudson River to a small playground off 123rd Street and Riverside Drive, near Grant's Tomb. As often happens with out-of-sequence filming, the first of David Selby's scenes to be shot, at the Central Park carousel, were actually his last moments in the film. Howard Koch Jr. was a production assistant on the shoot, and it was his job to make sure the chronically tardy Streisand wouldn't hold up production when she was needed before the cameras. "I would go to her trailer, knock, and say, 'Barbra, they're ready for you,' and she'd stall and say, 'Just a minute.' And then I would remind her that she was one of the producers on the film and that it was her money that was being wasted. 'You're right!' she'd say, and fly out of the dressing room."

Filming in Africa was not without its inherent problems. First, the original location that had been selected near Mount Kenya was deemed too modern. For this particular fantasy, director Kershner was striving for a sense of "poetic reality," but like most growing, prospering African regions, the Kikuyu village was highly sophisticated. "It looked like the back lot of Universal," Kershner said. A new location was hastily scouted, and the filmmakers settled for an isolated Samburu community 1,540 miles north of Nairobi.

"At first, we were suspicious of them, and

Margaret and her husband, Paul, stage a mock battle prior to making love. In his first film role, David Selby found Streisand's stardom — but not Barbra herself — highly intimidating.

they were suspicious of us," Barbra said of the experience. "Do you know," she marveled, "that these women are not permitted to experience pleasure, nor are they permitted to show pain? They can't even scream when they have a baby. They seem happy, but wow! Who am I to say anything . . . to preach?" At the conclusion of shooting in Africa, the influence of another culture—and the money the film unit had pumped into the local economy—had begun to show its effect on the natives, who were by now many goats and shillings ahead of previous years. "It's funny," Barbra observed. "These people are used to walking five miles a day. But only yesterday [after three days with the American film crew] they asked for a bus to take them back to their villages."

The *Sandbox* company was based in Africa for nearly a month to film what would amount to less than eight minutes on the screen. Actor Paul Benedict remembered one moment when he and Barbra were waiting between takes. "Kershner and the camera crew were stationed about one hundred and fifty yards off, and Barbra and I were just sitting around. . . . The native women grew restless and started chanting in Samburu dialect. Barbra really got into the melody and began humming it. Then she picked up the words and sang along with the tribeswomen. During this performance, Kershner came up to us to discuss something, and Barbra stopped singing. When he left, she began again. I was so impressed with that because you knew she wasn't showing off; she just really appreciated the music and wanted to be a part of it."

Production on *Up the Sandbox* was finished in Hollywood on soundstages the company rented at 20th Century-Fox studios. *Sandbox* was brought in on time and under budget. Now began the tedious chore of examining what could be used and what scenes needed to be scored—and perhaps wondering if it was all worth it.

Billy Goldenberg, the composer also known for the score of *Play It Again, Sam* and *Queen of the Stardust Ballroom,* remembers times when Barbra would go home at around 2:30 A.M. from a late-night session and her mind was still on her work. She would phone Goldenberg: "Hum me the music for tomorrow," she usually requested, and he would proceed. Barbra was particularly concerned with the look of the movie. ("This is the first picture I've done over which I've had some control. That's why all those stories about my having so much power in the past are so ludicrous.") Both Barbra and Irvin Kershner worked closely with Gordon Willis, the cinematographer responsible for much of the look of *The Godfather* and *Annie Hall.* In a period heavily influenced by *Easy Rider* and other low-budget films, Barbra expressed a desire to get away from the visual excesses of her glossy Hollywood vehicles. "I wanted to get back to reality in doing this picture."

The look the filmmakers conceived was one of subtle, basic tones. *Up the Sandbox* was to be a portrayal of real life—at times dreary, sometimes moody, often fantastic. From the opening shots of Margaret bathing her children through her closing "I love you" to her husband, Kershner and Willis kept a tight rein on the "ordinary yet extraordinarily revealing moments." There were no special lenses, no close-ups carefully shot through gauze, no highlights on Barbra's eyes or hair lit from the back to give her an added glow. Instead, Willis used half-lights to balance her face against the harsh backgrounds, often letting the bright street- or daylight blindly obscure shape and form.

One sequence, an insufferable anniversary party for Margaret's parents, was photographed so innovatively as to make it the stylized highlight of the picture. In a moment of inspiration it was decided to film much of the proceedings as if for a home movie, complete with overlit rooms and people shooing away the camera, while others ham it up. The result is the most memorable family get-together since another Maggie and her husband, Brick, detonated the celebration in *Cat on a Hot Tin Roof.* Another powerful scene is a masterful collaboration of the most elemental cinematic arts, particularly editing and scoring. It begins at an abortion clinic where Margaret is still struggling with herself over whether or not to have a third child. A mystical feeling permeates the atmosphere as our heroine walks down the hall past the young, expectant mothers waiting in impersonal, sparsely furnished cubicles. She dreams her stalwart husband will come to rescue her from this brutal ending and fantasizes a struggle between him and the nurses with musical accompaniment from other scenes in the film. The scene ends as a heavenly choir sings and Margaret's stretcher lifts its wings and transports her into the neighborhood sandbox in which her children often play. (Five-year-old Jason Gould makes his film debut in this scene as one of the children cavorting near the sandbox.)

"I like making movies best of all," Barbra enthused, "even though there is very little continuity. You have to project ahead and backward, out of sequence. It's incredibly exciting and challenging. However, once the film is put together, it's there as a permanent performance. Years from now you can look back and say, 'Oh, so that's what I was doing then.' It does carry a kind of immortality with it."

Barbra's latest bid for immortality was previewed in San Francisco. Many moviegoers were expecting a comic follow-up to the light nonsense

While filming in Africa, Barbra donned local costumes and accessories for promotional photos.

*Irvin Kershner and Barbra confer
prior to filming one of the movie's fantasy vignettes in which Margaret
delivers a blistering impromptu speech
denouncing masochism at a Fidel
Castro press conference.*

liked it as a book," he said, "but it wasn't the kind of mate-rial I would choose for a film. There wasn't enough drama in the main story. All the drama was in the fantasies, which didn't work because you knew it wasn't really happening. I was unhappy going with it, but I had been warned by Barbra's agents not to tell her that I was unhappy with the story because she would just walk off the picture.

"Now, once we were work-ing and we got to know each other in a professional capacity, I revealed to her one day that the reason we were struggling every day and every night was because we never made the story work as well as it should. She said, 'Did you know this before we started?' I said, 'Of course I did.' 'Well, then, why did you start?' 'Because I was being pushed, and I was told that if I didn't start and made you aware of my doubts about the material, I'd lose you.' She said, 'That's ridiculous. We just would have kept working until we got it right.'"

they had loved just months before in *What's Up, Doc?* and their response to *Up the Sandbox* sur-faced in nervous laughter. People just didn't know what to make of it. "They're confused by the fan-tasies," Barbra noted, "because there's no clear-cut distinction between reality and fantasy." (In Roiphe's novel, the fantasies had been set apart by chapter.) "But that's the way it is in life. There's a fine edge between dreams and reality," Irvin Kershner added. "This movie should make you think long after you've left the theater. It's a comedy, but it's a *serious* comedy."

Publicly, star and director were promoting their movie, but months earlier, shortly after pro-duction had begun, Kershner was afraid to tell Barbra that they might be headed for trouble. "I

In an effort to clarify the picture prior to its release, Billy Goldenberg was asked to write a theme song. Performed with conviction by Barbra, "If I Close My Eyes" might not have made the story line any clearer, but it did have the potential to entice middle-of-the-road audiences who weren't quite sure about *Sandbox*. But for some unexplained reason it was never used. Columbia Records later released the single to coincide with the film's opening, but despite positive listener response, it disappeared, a victim of poor promo-tion. Still, Goldenberg's excellent musical score (often utilizing a child's toy piano to underline dramatic scenes) remained an integral part of the film.

Distributed through the auspices of National General Releasing, *Up the Sandbox* burst upon the holiday season with advertisements by artist Richard Amsel of Barbra depicted on the cover of *Time* magazine as "Dust Mop of the Year!" If the public wasn't sure how to welcome this strange Christmas greeting, the lawyers from *Time* were even less impressed. They got a court injunction restraining First Artists or National General from using the controversial artwork, and a new—much less stylish—poster was designed. However, no matter how the film was advertised, it failed to find a substantial audience despite praise from many critics, who hailed the thoughtful approach to its subject, its avant garde sensibility, and the naturalness of Streisand's performance.

Despite his misgivings, David Selby manages to hold his own with Barbra on-screen, though *Sandbox* did little to advance his career; a decade later he would achieve success as one of the ensemble cast of *Falcon Crest*.

As several reviews noted, *Sandbox* contains a Streisand performance that is unique. There is very little of her vulnerable housewife that reminds one of any of her other roles; the character is totally original. She would give performances in the future that perhaps drew on the subtlety acquired through Margaret Reynolds, but none would match its quiet integrity. "I believe I found something in her that I never saw on-screen before," Irvin Kershner has said. "I got this different visual quality. . . . She looks different in [this film]. Then, as I got to know her, I found that there were personality elements that I had never seen in any of her previous work, and I encouraged those elements. What came across, above all, was a softness and a sweetness and a femininity. Then, when we wanted to pull the plug and let . . . that strident thing out, the contrast was very pronounced. I think she has an enormous range. I think she could do anything."

What she could not do, unfortunately, was attract crowds to *Up the Sandbox*. "It was very discouraging," Barbra said of the film's disappointing reception. "I remember taking a friend to a theater in Westwood and there were four people there. It sure made me feel bad." A few years later, she was defiant: "I liked *Up the Sandbox.*

In the film's most bizarre fantasy, Castro attempts to seduce Margaret... so that he can reveal to her that he is really a woman.

That was my statement about what it meant to be a woman. It's what I wanted to say, and I'm glad I said it, even if it didn't make a nickel." In a 1996 interview with the *Los Angeles Times*, she named it (along with *Funny Girl, The Way We Were, Yentl,* and *The Prince of Tides*) one of the five favorite films of her career. *Up the Sandbox* is a strangely intriguing effort, filled with promise and possibilities—some carried out, others left unfulfilled. Much of the picture is vague, at times intentionally, so as to allow the audience to interpret for themselves. But it doesn't quite work. Still, as Barbra advocated, "it's a picture that has to be seen more than once to catch all the meanings and shadings."

David Selby and Barbra enjoy a lunch break with their movie children. (Photo courtesy of Richard Giammanco)

REVIEWS

"Barbra Streisand adds another accomplishment to her many with a superb display of acting. In this touching, funny, exhilarating, and mature movie set in New York, Miss Streisand creates a remarkable portrait of a wife and mother of two, who discovers she is pregnant at a time when she is concerned with the value of women—to men and to themselves. Streisand's Walter Mitty vignettes—working with black revolutionaries . . . or rebelling against an officious mother—are gems of humor and insight. This is a fine film and an important one in its treatment of female versus femininity."

CUE

"You admire her not for her acting—or singing—but for herself, which is what you feel she gives you in both. She has the class to be herself, and the impudent music of her speaking voice is proof that she knows it. The audacity of her self-creation is something we've had time to adjust to; we already know her mettle, and the dramatic urgency she can bring to roles. In Up the Sandbox, she shows a much deeper and warmer presence and a fully yielding quality. . . ."

NEW YORK

"Even with a few arid patches and fantasies that unwind a bit methodically at times, Barbra Streisand's sixth film is her sixth hit. Yes, think of it. An hour after seeing this new one, which is ripe, yeasty fun, it's hard not to think of this extraordinary woman, perfectly wedded to the camera with her instant Modigliani face and timing. She's the picture, true, but the teamwork is admirable. Nearly everything works and meshes . . . even when they're way out, the vignette musings generally miss blandness and strain because our heroine is a bright, likable girl, not a pinhead."

NEW YORK TIMES

The Way We Were

(1973)

A Columbia Pictures Release of a Rastar Productions Picture

CAST

Barbra Streisand (*Katie Morosky*); Robert Redford (*Hubbell Gardiner*); Bradford Dillman (*J.J.*); Lois Chiles (*Carol Ann*); Patrick O'Neal (*George Bissinger*); Viveca Lindfors (*Paula Reisner*); Allyn Ann McLerie (*Rhea Edwards*); Murray Hamilton (*Brooks Carpenter*); Herb Edleman (*Bill Verso*); James Woods (*Frankie McVeigh*); Diana Ewing (*Vicki Bissinger*); Sally Kirkland (*Pony Dunbar*); Marcia Mae Jones (*Peggy Vanderbilt*); Don Keefer (*Actor*); George Gaynes (*El Morocco Captain*); Susie Blakely (*Judianne*); Eric Boles (*Army Corporal*); Barbara Peterson (*Ash Blonde*); Roy Jensen (*Army Captain*); Brendan Kelly (*Rally Speaker*); Connie Forslund (*Jenny*); Robert Gerringer (*Dr. Short*); Suzanne Zenor (*Dumb Blonde*); Dan Seymour (*Guest*).

CREDITS

Producer: Ray Stark; associate producer: Richard Roth; director: Sydney Pollack; assistant director: Howard Koch Jr.; second assistant director: Jerry Ziesmer; screenplay: Arthur Laurents; music: Marvin Hamlisch (song "The Way We Were" composed by Marvin Hamlisch, lyrics by Marilyn and Alan Bergman, sung by Barbra Streisand); music editor: Ken Runyan; unit production manager: Russ Sanders; production designer: Stephen Grimes; costume designers: Dorothy Jeakins, Moss Mabry; director of photography: Harry Stradling Jr.; set decorator: William Kiernan; script supervisor: Betty Crosby; supervising film editor: Margaret Booth; makeup: Donald Cash Jr., Garry Liddiard; hairstyles: Kaye Pownell; unit publicist: Carol Shapiro. Running time: 118 minutes.

Predominantly Streisand, little for Redford. Good production, sluggish direction. Should open big, but weak legs seen. . . ." *Variety*'s review for *The Way We Were* missed it by a long shot. The film's "weak legs" walked circles around the competition. It single-handedly resuscitated a studio that had been in serious financial straits. It inspired a nostalgic look at "the way we never

really were" across the nation, influencing fashion, makeup, and hairstyles. Its title song became an instant standard. No less importantly, it established its reluctant male star as a romantic idol and, after years of flirting with such success, a superstar.

What seems even more amazing is how the film's quality and appeal have increased in the estimation of former cynics. An erstwhile "two-star, soppy tearjerker" would, within a few short years, become an acclaimed four-star classic and the ideal contemporary model for a movie romance. Premature predictions of doom and gloom—from *Time* magazine's description as "[an] ill-written, wretchedly performed and tediously directed film" to Pauline Kael's complaint about "a whining title-tune ballad [that] embarrasses the picture in advance"—could not begin to measure what the movie would inevitably mean to young adults coming of age during the 1970s. It has become their *Casablanca*. "It is hard not to be carried away by the film's lush romanticism," Howard Kissel wrote in *Women's Wear Daily*. "*The Way We Were* is the sort of film that makes you wish Hollywood were thriving again."

The comparison to *Casablanca*, an all-time movie favorite, is not without justification. Both productions were troubled from the outset. As with Robert Redford and *The Way We Were*, *Casablanca* propelled Humphrey Bogart onto the uppermost rung of male movie stardom—romantic leading man—but not before multiple screenwriters were consulted in an effort to give his character more depth. There was much infighting on the *Casablanca* set between the producer, director, and writers; Warner Bros. wasn't sure they weren't

throwing their money away on a "grade B turkey." When the film was released, the audience response was solid, but the reviews were mixed. No matter. It was a quintessential romance and the Best Picture of 1943. *The Way We Were* was received in much the same way.

Producer Ray Stark commissioned Arthur Laurents to write a story for Barbra Streisand. Laurents, a champion of Barbra's since *I Can Get It for You Wholesale*, delivered a fifty-page treatment—a poignant tale of a star-crossed love between Katie Morosky, a politically and socially committed Jewish girl, and Hubbell Gardiner, a glamorous jock and aspiring writer who couldn't care less about politics. Their turbulent relationship is set against the complex political landscape of America in the late 1930s through the early 1950s.

Sydney Pollack, of *They Shoot Horses, Don't They?* fame, was set to direct. Pollack's first reaction to the screenplay was that his friend Robert Redford *had* to play the role of Hubbell. To his surprise, he discovered that Redford had already passed on the project when it was submitted to him in treatment form. But neither the director nor Barbra could give up on him; both felt that Redford was the only one who could bring any kind of realism to this all-American version of Sir Lancelot. After Laurents completed a first draft of the screenplay, Pollack again showed it to his friend, but Redford still didn't understand what he saw in the project. "He didn't want to do *The Way We Were* in any way, shape or form," the director revealed to author James Spada. "He didn't like the script, he didn't like the character, he didn't like the concept of the film, he didn't think the politics and love story would mix. There was nothing about it he liked. And in fact, he kept saying to me, 'Pollack, you're crazy! What are you doing this for?' [That was] the longest running battle I've ever had with him."

Pollack still believed he had a shot. From Redford's then wife, Lola, he learned that the conflict extended into their home life. "I wish he would make up his mind already. He's driving me crazy," she told him. "He sits up at night and says, 'What should I do? I don't like it. Pollack is really turned on by it. I trust him. Maybe he sees something I don't see. . . .'" Pollack persisted in his campaign. "It had to be those two (together). They were so prototypical of what the story was about. I

couldn't see doing it with anyone else," he said. "I must say my greatest ally was Barbra, who felt the same way. I needed the strength that Redford brings on the screen, and Barbra understood that."

The picture's producer wasn't convinced that only Robert Redford could play the role. According to Marty Erlichman, "Ray Stark called Barbra and said, 'If we're going to get Redford, you're going to have to give up a lot of scenes.'" But Barbra wasn't worried about her screen time. "He's a valuable asset to the film," she replied. "I'd rather have fewer scenes than not have him in the picture." On June 10, 1972, Pollack received an ultimatum from Stark. Bored with what he considered to be a game on Redford's part, Stark gave the director an hour to get a commitment from Redford; otherwise, he would offer the role of Hubbell Gardiner to Ryan O'Neal. End of discussion. At 11:30 P.M. that Thursday evening, the producer got a call back from Pollack; Redford said yes.

"The reason I took it was that I wanted to work with Barbra and I felt it was a wonderful premise for a love story," he later told Spada. "The original script was written with more of a feel for the woman's role," he noted. "The question was: Could you bring a balance into things?" Alvin Sargent and David Rayfield were called in for script surgery—a move that would cause considerable resentment on Laurents's part—with instructions not to tamper with the story but to enrich it by giving both protagonists a viewpoint. According to Laurents, no less than twelve writers were brought in, including Francis Ford Coppola and Dalton Trumbo, before he was called to put everything back together again.

Sidney Pollack relates: "I spent enough time with Barbra prior to shooting to let her know where my head was . . . to listen to what her fears were . . . and to discuss what this picture was about, where we might have trouble, what was moving to me and what was moving to her. I think it's safe to say she trusted me." The director told Streisand biographers Donald Zec and Anthony Fowles that he never felt threatened by Barbra "because I was so impressed with the way she was thinking about the part. When I hear an actress talking to me with an understanding of a role that's so close to my own understanding, that makes me feel confident that we're not going to have a problem. And we didn't. The least of my problems was Barbra, funny enough."

Principal photography began on September 18 in Schenectady, New York, where Union College had been re-dressed to resemble an Ivy League campus, circa 1937. Seven hundred and fifty college students submitted to period haircuts and styles in order to sign on as movie extras. To many, the odd but intriguing chemistry between Streisand and Redford that would excite moviegoers a year later was immediately apparent in Schenectady and no less revealing than in their opposing acting styles. "Bob is a very instinctive actor," Pollack has expressed on several occasions. "He doesn't like to talk about a role a lot, and he doesn't like to rehearse a lot. However, he doesn't mind a number of takes as long as you give him something different to do; if you don't, he'll change the performance from take to take, anyway. Barbra, on the other hand, is very thorough and obsessive. She likes to talk about her role."

The director's job was to balance the two performances so that he gave Barbra enough time to warm up, but not too much, before Redford cooled off. It was a difficult task made a little easier because both actors were very taken by each other's work and therefore sympathetic to their mutual problem. "There was no friction," Pollack emphasized, "because it all got aired out. He would say, 'I understand, I understand. I'm just not used to doing this,' and she would say, 'I understand totally, and I don't want to do it *too* much. But I don't know where I am if I don't talk it out first.' Barbra wanted to go straight with this movie and not rely on what we normally expect of her—the timing, the gestures, the facial expressions. She didn't want to use any tricks. She and Redford fed each other. It's really a combination of two rare talents with charisma and acting ability as well."

There might have been another dynamic at play. "She was simply mesmerized by him," Arthur Laurents revealed, "because she found him so beautiful." Barbra called the actor "an intelligent, concerned human being." Sally Kirkland, who worked with the duo later in the shoot, felt that "there was almost a mystery about Streisand and Redford in the way they were together. It was almost like they held on to that mystery in order to keep the romantic sexual tension between them in the film."

At a 1978 seminar sponsored by the American Film Institute in Los Angeles, Sydney Pollack would illuminate how *his* rapport with his leading lady helped to coax her emotional potential to the surface. "In the first week of shooting, we came to a scene in a writing class where the professor reads a story written by [Hubbell]. The girl Barbra plays is heartbroken because she wants more than anything for her story to be picked. She runs out of class, down a path to a wastebasket, and tears her story to shreds. The camera rises to her face, and she's supposed to be crying. The assistant director came to me and said, 'I think she's a little uptight about this scene.' When we began rehearsing the shot, what I saw was an actress getting more and more upset in anticipation of a scene. She's supposed to cry and thinks she can't. Now, that's like a stew cooking; you just let it stew for a bit, then, if she can relax, the tears will come.

"Barbra went back to her starting position behind a big tree to get ready for the take. I said to [the A.D.], 'Okay, you wait here. I'm not going to say, "Roll it," and I'm not going to say, "Action." When I give you a wave, turn on the camera.' Now, I can't explain this exactly, but I walked up behind her and I put my arms around her. I just held her gently for about twenty seconds, and she started sobbing. I waved my hand . . . and pushed her off. She did the scene beautifully, in one take. And for the rest of the picture I didn't have to say or do much in similar scenes because once she knew she could do it, she did it [by herself]."

Sometimes Pollack dismissed the crew for an hour while the trio discussed the staging of a scene. James Woods recalled a moment when this camaraderie worked to his own advantage in terms of screen time. "I had a five-line part, and there was a scene where Streisand and Redford are in the library and she's looking at him and yearning for him. I said to the director, 'I should be in this scene. I'm her boyfriend.' He said, 'Get out of here.' So I went up to Barbra and said, 'Let me ask you a question. If you were sitting in the library and you were looking at Redford, that would be interesting. *But* if your boyfriend was sitting opposite you and you had to wait until he was looking down at his book to sort of steal a look at Redford, that would be twice as exciting, wouldn't it?' She said, 'You bet!' and if you notice, I did make it into the scene."

The cast and crew journeyed to Manhattan the first week in October for a hectic few days on location. Sally Kirkland was cast as Pony Dunbar, Katie's Communist-sympathizing friend. The

reason she was hired, she was told, was because "you're the kind of person Barbra would like, and that's important. We want to capture that on film." The reason she accepted the relatively small part (when she was playing important leads off-Broadway) was because "I absolutely adored Barbra Streisand." But Kirkland's connection with Barbra extends beyond a surface appreciation of her talent. First of all, both are native New Yorkers who sought creative and intellectual stimulation in Greenwich Village. As a birthday surprise, a friend had taken Sally to see a young performer at the Bon Soir; she was knocked out by her stage presence and a "voice that could break hearts."

Kirkland kept track of Streisand's progress, tuning in to see her on *Tonight* or *P.M. East*. "I thought that she was hysterically funny, and risky," she says. "She would always say outrageous things and take chances like I had never seen anyone take. As a 'kooky' personality, she presented herself in such a charming, loving, ballsy way. She had the guts to be a comedienne just [by] being a person. Sometimes when people see performers like Cyndi Lauper or Madonna they don't realize that Barbra started that, in a way. She had all this incredible character built on her. And she has continued to allow herself to be what I call a life actor. In other words, her life is the act."

The scene for which Kirkland was hired didn't make it into the final cut, but at the time, the filmmakers thought it was important. "The scenario was that we hadn't seen each other in a long time and she comes running down the street, grabs me in her arms, hugs me, kisses me, and blurts out some incredible, happy news about Hubbell. I was very nervous because it was my first Hollywood film. I remember I had these earrings on, and at the moment she hugged me, one of them fell off. Then I got flustered, and she tried to improvise it into the scene, but I think she burst out laughing. And it was one of those shots where Sydney Pollack and his cameraman were way up on this crane and there were all of these extras. It had to have cost a lot of money to reshoot. Anyway, afterwards she said, 'I like you!' and I'll

Redford and Streisand await a scene on the beach at Malibu.

never forget it because here I made this incredible faux pas and she just laughed. I think it reminded her of the kind of thing she would have done a few years earlier . . . and it endeared her to me because she was vulnerable enough to pick up on my vulnerability."

By October 11, the ensemble was back in Los Angeles, and Columbia was glad to have them where they could watchdog the production (already a few hundred thousand dollars over budget). The constant worrying over finances, added to previously voiced concerns about the script, made most of the production team feel as if they were doing time in prison. Sally Kirkland was brought to Hollywood to film a short scene in which she and Barbra are wartime switchboard operators. "And again it was 'Sally, how are you? What have you been doing?' She couldn't have been more warm," Kirkland adds. "She just stopped everything she was doing and behaved like a girlfriend. It was very sweet. All of these people complain about her rudeness or temper,

and I never got any of that in *The Way We Were.* What I got was that she was curious about me, really looked, really listened, and really wanted to know everything about me. She absorbs people; she takes them in. And she has one of the most insatiable curiosities I've ever seen in anyone."

Another recurring aspect of filming *The Way We Were* was the late-night telephone calls Barbra had become famous for. But Sydney Pollack didn't seem to mind. "She called out of compulsive worry," he said, "the way I'm a compulsive worrier. And I loved her for it. As a matter of fact, when she gave me a gift at the end of the picture, she wrote on it: 'For all those eleven o'clock phone calls.' She knew." *The Way We Were* wrapped on December 3, 1972.

On May 3, 1973, just as Barbra was about to begin the first sessions on her classical album, the principal cast of *The Way We Were* was recalled to shoot an additional sequence on a Bel Air estate. The faith of Columbia Pictures in their major release for the fall of 1973 was fading fast.

"The initial responses to [the film] in rough-cut [form] were not good," Sydney Pollack confirmed. "And then, in September, we went to San Francisco for a preview, and I did something I'd never done before. We scheduled two previews, one on a Friday night and one on Saturday. At the first, the film was going very well. Until we hit a spot in the third act where we just lost the audience completely. I went up to the projection booth with [editor] Margaret Booth, taking a razor blade with me . . . and made a cut of about eleven minutes. It was a whole sequence where [Katie] was being named as a Communist, which precipitated the breakup. The problem was that the breakup was inherent in the picture right from the beginning . . . so it wasn't necessary to [stop everything] for this new development. When we previewed it the next night, the audience absolutely loved the picture. All of a sudden everybody was ecstatic . . . and morale [at Columbia] turned around."

One could argue that the film's potential would have been even greater "if it had more meat on its bones," but it certainly wasn't for lack of trying. Throughout the production, Pollack tried to make politics "more organic" to the film, weighing the political dimensions versus the personal ones. (The Watergate scandal was occurring at the time, resulting in controversial events not unlike those of the era depicted in the film.) One thought Pollack had was to make the Redford character an informer. "The danger," he said, "was that the background would become so interesting to those of us making the film that people watching it would say, 'Oh, yes, this is all very interesting. But let's get back to "Is he going to kiss her?" or "Are they going to fall in love?" or "Are they going to get together?" That's what the film is about. I think it dealt very well with politics, but it's hardly the definitive film about McCarthyism [just as *Casablanca* is hardly the definitive film about World War II]. It was never intended to be. . . . What I basically like about the film is what attracted me in the first place.

Lois Chiles, Bradford Dillman, Robert Redford, Barbra, and Allyn McLerie in a tense scene set in a producer's lavish home where a bugging device is found unexpectedly.

entitled "The Sleeping Beauty Was a Man."

For many, the couple's first night together—with a drunken Hubbell making love to Katie as if on automatic pilot—was an all-too-familiar slice of contemporary relationships and a refreshing twist on the traditional scenarios of such love stories. Streisand's Katie Morosky was both aggressive and passive. She pushed Hubbell but downplayed her own talents; ironically, she respected his talent more than he did. It is her rediscovery of her real self near the end of the movie—when she and Hubbell recognize the way they are and stop traumatizing themselves with fantasies about the way they might have been—that makes their final meeting so poignant. The great love is still there; only now they see the futility of pining for something that cannot be. And it's the timelessness of those emotions that keeps the film from being dated.

In addition, *The Way We Were* reversed the sexual clichés. *She* could be the pursuer, the decision maker, the stronger partner, but always as a woman operating in the masculine world, not as a dominating *Mildred Pierce* stereotype. In analyzing the film with James Spada, Redford surmised that "[Barbra's] femininity brings out the masculinity in a man, and her masculinity brings out a man's femininity, vulnerability, romanticism . . . whatever you want to call it." Such an exchange of gender roles spoke volumes to 1973 audiences, who were struggling with various new sexual postures being thrust upon them by societal changes—an issue that apparently flew right over the heads of many critics.

In films like *Up the Sandbox* and *The Way*

When I read it, I cried, and I managed to get that on the screen."

On October 16, New York and Los Angeles had a chance to see exactly what Pollack, Streisand, and Redford had gotten on the screen. Much has been said about Redford's subsequent transformation into a Hollywood sex symbol, but not enough has been said about Streisand's acceptance in a similar vein. *The Way We Were* established Barbra as the perfect screen heroine of the 1970s: a liberated woman who was eager to be on equal footing with men but reluctant to give up the romantic traditions of the past. "Here we see Barbra Streisand at her most convincing. For if she is made to seem somewhat foolish as the political activist, she is absolutely marvelous as the modern woman poised between pride and desire," Catherine Hiller wrote in a *New York Times* article

Portrayed compellingly by Robert Redford and Barbra Streisand, Hubbell and Katie's bittersweet love story holds an endearing place in the hearts of millions of movie fans.

We Were, Barbra began to effectively develop this duality in her nature on-screen. Pauline Kael noted, "The tricky thing about the role of Katie Morosky is that Streisand must emphasize just that element in her own persona which repelled some people initially. Her fast sass is defensive and aggressive in the same breath. But it's part of her gradual conquest of the movie public that this won't put people off now."

Aside from Streisand's and Redford's outstanding performances, *The Way We Were* succeeded because its lovers are so recognizable to moviegoers, especially Americans. Pollack was right about their being "prototypical": Katie is the serious-minded daughter of European immigrants for whom everything is a struggle, while Hubbell is the privileged golden boy whose roots might be traced back to the Mayflower and by whom nothing is taken too seriously. And surely no other combination of actors, who were also major stars, could have brought these characters to such vivid life. "More than ever," James Spada has written, "in *The Way We Were*

Barbra Streisand was America's Everyperson, acting out on-screen what each audience member had at some time experienced: the longing for an unattainable love object. Many women and gay men certainly related to her lust for Hubbell, but millions of others, heterosexual men included, also identified with her. Who at some point hasn't felt unattractive, been mocked, or hurt by love?"

The film does miss the mark as a trenchant study of the paranoia of the Hollywood blacklisting phenomenon (though it was the first major release to even address the issue), but the decision to sacrifice some of the political components to the demands of the love story was a wise one. As symbolized by Katie's famous gesture of brushing Hubbell's hair away from his forehead when they start their relationship and again in the film's moving final moments (a visual equivalent perhaps of "Here's looking at you, kid"), the lush romanticism of *The Way We Were* continues to captivate audiences. There has long been talk of a sequel in which it has been suggested that Katie and Hubbell's daughter would reunite her parents against a backdrop of the campus unrest of the 1960s, but in 1998, Redford announced he would never agree to a sequel, no matter what the story line might be.

Negative reviews notwithstanding (and there were enough to suggest that several critics, as some would twenty-five years later in reviewing *Titanic*, took great pains to avoid being drawn in by the love story), *The Way We Were* garnered six nominations from the Academy of Motion Picture Arts and Sciences: Best Actress, Cinematography, Art Direction, Costume Design, Original Dramatic Score, and Original Song. (Redford was nominated that year for *The Sting*.) But only Marvin Hamlisch's score and song won. By any standards, Barbra had given the standout female performance of the year, but Glenda Jackson took home the award for her light comedy performance in *A Touch of Class*. The loss devastated Barbra, who was waiting backstage after rushing to the ceremonies from the set of *Funny Lady*. This time, she felt more than deserving of the acknowledgment: "Unlike the year I was up for *Funny Girl*, and there were five strong performances, this time I felt it was the best performance of the year." But such validation was not to be forthcoming. (She did, however, win her second David Di Donatello Award in Italy as Best Foreign Actress.)

Though the focus in *The Way We Were* was aimed squarely at the two leads, able supporting performances were delivered by Bradford Dillman as Hubbell's friend J.J.; Lois Chiles as the pretty deb Hubbell cheats on Katie with; Patrick O'Neal as a demanding movie producer; and Viveca Lindfors as Paula Reisner, a socialist screenwriter who encourages Katie to revive her political activism. The film was photographed beautifully by Harry Stradling Jr., who filmed Barbra with the same care and affection his father had in her first three pictures.

Box-office earnings for *The Way We Were* were strong throughout Thanksgiving and Christmas. Only three and a half months into its release, it was ranked number four among the top films of 1973. Its financial reputation looms even larger in people's memories, no doubt aided by the tremendous success of the title song. "I had to beg her to sing [it!]," Marvin Hamlisch said, laughing. "Everybody in the picture had to vote before she'd sing it. We all outvoted her." (Hamlisch and Marilyn and Alan Bergman composed two entirely different songs under the same title. The castoff was later sung by Barbra as "The Way We Weren't.") Ironically, "The Way We Were" went on to become the top single of 1974 and is, of course, one of the songs most identified with Barbra Streisand.

REVIEWS

"The Way We Were *is almost a milestone because it's a thoughtful, believable love story for adults. For once, the characters are sharply defined, and their relationship develops and deepens persuasively. . . . The differences that attract them will ultimately separate them; but there is real electricity between them. . . . Some of the electricity comes from the two stars; their chemistry keeps the movie engaging. Streisand is still too shrill at moments; but this is the most forceful, controlled acting she's ever done. Redford is superb. . . .*"

NEW YORK TIMES

"The Way We Were . . . *is everything a movie should be: a love story that is a mirror of the hearts of many. . . . Due to the casting, which is nothing short of masterful, the film is vastly superior to the Arthur Laurents novel on which it is based. [Laurents wrote the novel after completing the screenplay.] Barbra Streisand, as Katie, the ugly-duckling college student who majors in leftist causes and later, as the same Katie, now an attractive young matron who tries vainly to change her basic nature to please the college sweetheart she has married, gives the kind of dramatic performance of which Academy Award nominations are made. . . . The measure of the success of this brilliant motion picture is that it draws the viewer so deeply into its web of character and plot that one is so involved in the dreams and disappointments of its principals that one leaves the theater feeling as one often does when close to a couple who resorts to divorce—wondering 'Which one was right? Which one should I see in the future?' See both Katie and Hubbell again. In* The Way We Were. *It's worth it.*"

AFTER DARK

For Pete's Sake
(1974)

A Rastar Production for Columbia Pictures

CAST

Barbra Streisand (*Henrietta*); Michael Sarrazin (*Pete*); Estelle Parsons (*Helen*); William Redfield (*Fred*); Molly Picon (*Mrs. Cherry*); Louis Zorich (*Nick*); Vivian Bonnell (*Loretta*); Richard Ward (*Bernie*); Heywood Hale Broun (*Judge Hiller*).

CREDITS

Producers: Martin Erlichman, Stanley Shapiro; executive producer: Phil Feldman; director: Peter Yates; assistant director: Harry Caplan; screenplay: Stanley Shapiro, Maurice Richlin; music: Artie Butler ("For Pete's Sake [Don't Let Him Down]" composed by Artie Butler); lyrics: Mark Lindsay (performed by Barbra Streisand); production manager: Jim Di Gangi; production designer: Frank Thompson; cinematographer: Laszlo Kovacs; film editor: Frank P. Keller; sound: Don Parker; Miss Streisand's hairstyles: Jon Peters; casting: Jennifer Shull. Running time: 90 minutes.

I wish some of the film scripts that were written for Bette Davis would be written for me today," Barbra remarked to an English journalist in 1975. Not that she literally wanted to remake *All About Eve* or *The Letter*, but having a studio—which used to have a vested interest in its contract players—develop quality projects on any kind of recurrent basis would have been reassuring. With *Funny Girl, Hello, Dolly!* and *On a Clear Day*, Barbra predetermined her schedule for several years when she first came to Hollywood. Through the formation of First Artists and Barwood, she also got an early lead developing her own projects. By the time she elected to take a break from filming in 1970, she was already firmly entrenched within the system and aware that her next move was pretty much up to her. She was offered her pick of films—*Cabaret, Klute, The Exorcist, Alice Doesn't Live Here Anymore* among them—but none with the directors who would ultimately bring them to the screen. (And regarding *Alice Doesn't Live Here Anymore*, Barbra felt audiences wouldn't accept her playing a failed lounge singer.)

As screenplays stockpiled on her desk, another problem became evident. "Writers know that if they're going to write something on spec," Paramount Pictures production chief Robert Evans told the *New York Times*, "there are ten male stars and one woman they can put the picture together with." With the competition so fierce for the attention of one female star, promising new writers were naturally inclined to try their luck where the odds were better. It was a classic Catch-22 situation. Fewer scripts for women meant fewer visible female stars; fewer stars meant fewer roles for women. It wasn't, as one movie executive offered, "a short-range problem." It would take years to resolve.

Whether she was bankable or not, the trickle-down scenario also stifled Barbra's options. Manager Martin Erlichman didn't wait for things to get worse before seeking a number of tailor-made scripts for his client. One of the projects he acquired for Barwood Productions was *Freaky Friday*, a novel about a mother and daughter switching identities. (It was ultimately filmed with Barbara Harris and Jodie Foster.) In May 1973, Paramount announced that Marty would be producing *With or Without Roller Skates* for them later in the year. The black comedy revolved around the real-life adventures of a rather unorthodox nurse working in a veteran's hospital.

"Barbra and I met the nurse twice," Erlichman told the *New York Times*. "She is a fascinating woman, hilariously funny and very realistic about her running battle with hospital authorities over what she considers the rights of her patients." Before he was able to develop a script, however, Barbra told him she couldn't see herself doing the film. After the drama and turmoil of *Up the Sandbox* and *The Way We Were*, she was in the mood for lighter fare.

Undaunted, Marty went to screenwriter Stanley Shapiro, the author of fluffy comedies for Doris Day and Rock Hudson, with another idea of his, which Shapiro liked. For Barbra, he devised a domestic comedy about a young Brooklyn couple struggling to make ends meet. When the cabdriving husband needs three thousand dollars to invest in a "guaranteed" quick turnaround in the commodities market (which he needs to finance the completion of his education), his wife borrows from a loan shark. But when she is unable to repay on time, her "contract" is sold to various nefarious types that force her into prostitution, the delivery of explosive devices, and cattle rustling in exchange for payment. The script was known by the rather unpleasant title of *July Pork Bellies*. "It's the kind of part I've always wanted," Barbra joked about her most physical role. "An intelligent, refined, sophisticated woman of the world . . . a woman who always travels first-class."

In the interest of making the whole package stronger, Erlichman and Shapiro took it to Ray Stark. At that time, Stark was producing exclusively for Columbia Pictures, which was always in the market for a profitable Streisand vehicle. "I felt more secure that everything was being looked after, since it was my first picture as line producer," Marty says. "So Stanley and I coproduced it under Ray's auspices." The elements came together quickly. Barbra submitted a list of directors she'd like to work with, including Czechoslovakian émigré Milos Forman. "She has a great sense of humor, and she can really sell comedy on the screen," Forman said later. But at the time he didn't feel capable of tackling something so intrinsically American. Peter Yates's agent heard about the project and arranged for Yates to meet Barbra and Marty. Englishman Yates, then capturing industry attention with action pictures like *Bullitt* and *The Hot Rock*, impressed the pair with his ideas and was hired to direct.

Three actors were tested for the part of Barbra's husband: Michael Landon, James Farentino, and Michael Sarrazin. "It's very difficult to cast somebody in a film opposite Barbra," Yates told James Spada, "because unless you have a major star, you're going to have problems of balance. But no major star wanted to play it. . . . It was like the girl's part in almost any other film. Instead of the girl following two paces behind the guy, it was the other way around. So we had to find somebody who was a strong personality who could act . . . and get along with Barbra." The lanky, puppy-eyed Sarrazin got the role.

Originally, the producers planned to shoot most of the film in Brooklyn. But that idea began to lose validity as actual locations were being scouted. Principal photography commenced on September 24, 1973. Sites scheduled for the first two weeks of filming included Prospect Park, the Grand Army Plaza, Borough Hall, the Brooklyn Heights Promenade, the Brooklyn Bridge, the Court and Schermerhorn subway station, and assorted side streets. The atmosphere turned out to be more colorful than anyone had bargained for. Advance publicity had alerted New Yorkers that Barbra was gong to be filming on the streets of her hometown, and camera-toting citizenry lined the streets and sidewalks at every location. "They wanted to see her, and they wanted to touch her," assistant director Harry Caplan recalls.

It was difficult enough setting up shots that wouldn't reveal the crowds; dealing with the cat-calls was nearly impossible. "You get hoarse asking people not to interrupt a scene," Caplan remarks. The most intense situation occurred when Barbra was supposed to climb in and out of a manhole in her flight from a law-enforcing canine. "We were right out there on Fourth Avenue," noted the assistant director, "and because of the scene, we couldn't be too close to her once we turned the camera on (although there was someone in the manhole with her). The minute she lifted the lid and came out of the sewer and the director shouted, 'Cut!' the crowd would surge forward. The street was just full; traffic had stopped. . . . It wasn't always easy to get her back to her trailer. It was a frightening experience for her."

The reaction could be rather comical. "Hey, Barbra! Sing 'On a Clear Day' for us!" one cab-driver yelled as he drove by. But when the production paused to take some publicity photographs,

Barbra clowns around on a studio street dressed to look like downtown Brooklyn. Sitting on the camera boom are (left to right) *producer Martin Erlichman, director Peter Yates, and cinematographer Lazslo Kovacs.*

Stu Fleming, the second assistant director on the picture, remembers a couple of people hurling obscenities at Barbra. "I just remember this one crazy girl screaming, and Barbra was getting pissed, and I didn't blame her. . . . It was a hassle to film a picture [in Brooklyn], especially for Barbra." Regarding the shoot at the Court Street subway station, Fleming paints a memorable picture of Barbra hanging on to a strap inside the car. "I looked at her, and she had this faraway look in her eyes. 'Do you remember when you used to take the subway?' I said. 'Yeah,' she said, 'I hated it.' " (One of the reasons Streisand signed for the movie was "because I didn't want to be in L.A. any longer and I figured I'd go to New York and escape.")

Location filming wrapped up a week early. *For Pete's Sake*, as it was now called—in reference to Sarrazin's character—returned to the Burbank Studios, where Brooklyn could be safely re-created on Stage 18, the studio commissary, and the back lot. Barbra relaxed considerably, and Caplan, a veteran who had worked with everyone, from W. C. Fields to Elvis Presley, delighted in watching her educate herself to everything that was transpiring on the set. "When she saw something that she didn't understand, she wanted to know what it was [about] to its fullest extent, whether it was part of the camera or the special effects," he says. "She liked to know what every technician did, what their function was. . . . She'd go over to Laszlo Kovacs, the cinematographer, and ask to look in the camera. He was very good with her. 'What kind of lens is this? Why are the lights here?' He'd explain what kind of lighting he used on close-ups. She was always gathering information . . . but, of course, she had a different future lined up for herself . . . which many of us weren't aware of at the time."

"She does like to ask questions," director Yates stated. "I think some of her questions harass people because they are very pertinent. Unfortunately [for them], she does see things very clearly; she's not befuddled by the bureaucratic detail that sometimes gets in people's way when making movies. Now that she has a much larger knowledge of filmmaking, I think she is, in some

Barbra touches up her makeup on the set. The hairstyle is a wig designed by Streisand's future lover, manager, and producer, Jon Peters.

ways, easier to work with. On the other hand, she's obviously much more demanding because she would demand that everyone be as quick and imaginative as she is."

Caplan's nickname for Streisand was *"bala-bosta,"* the Yiddish word for the boss's wife, or "balaboss," because he did consider her "the boss." Caplan observed that Streisand's outside business concerns were enormous. "I must say that Barbra was pretty levelheaded about the whole thing. She didn't inflict any of her personal life or conditions on people working on the movie set. Nor did she allow it to affect her work. She's a very concentrated gal. Once she's on the set, she's there to work." When she wasn't needed on the set, she was on the phone or, on rare occasions, conducting a meeting. But, says Caplan, the only time this caused any tension was when there was a misunderstanding about time and the crew was ready before Barbra was. "[When] that [was] cleared up, *For Pete's Sake* was a fun set to work on," he reiterates. "I loved working with Barbra. I really did."

Peter Yates, making his first Hollywood film, found his star to be "far more friendly than her reputation would lead you to believe. . . . She was absolutely delightful. Mind you, we were making a film that was supposed to promote her; a proper old Hollywood star vehicle. And it's very difficult to quarrel with someone when you're trying to make them look as good as possible." One thing Barbra seemed to appreciate was that Yates wasn't at all intimidated by her. He told her the truth and didn't waste time beating around the bush. "I remember saying to her once after a take, 'That was absolutely terrible!' She collapsed laughing and said, 'No one's ever said that to me before, thank God!' I think she was really grateful. I mean that's what a director is for . . . to be used as a mirror."

Of course, the real news to emerge from *For Pete's Sake* didn't involve revelations about Barbra's star temperament (or lack thereof). More newsworthy was the Beverly Hills hairdresser who designed her closely cropped wig and stuck around

118

to redesign her personal as well as her professional life. Their first meeting, negotiated to accommodate two busy schedules, has been well documented. What hasn't been is Jon's perception of Barbra prior to that meeting. His first recollection of her was when a girlfriend dragged him to the Coconut Grove in 1963. "I didn't know who Barbra Streisand was," he says. "But when she came out, I was absolutely, magnetically, attracted to her. There was just something that she projected as she sang. I couldn't take my eyes off of her." Peters was eighteen. As he got involved in establishing his own business, he forgot about Barbra for the time being. Then his second wife, Lesley Ann Warren, took him to see her at the Hollywood Bowl in 1967. Warren was not only a Streisand admirer; she also knew Barbra slightly from New York and her short-lived stint as Elliott Gould's costar in *Drat! The Cat!* "She often talked about Barbra to me," Jon remembers.

Peters ingeniously turned his revived curiosity about Barbra into a sales tool for his beauty salon: He started telling patrons that he cut Barbra's hair (then short and all one length). His business went up 40 percent. "Many years later, I had opened salons in Beverly Hills and several other locations. I had invested in real estate . . . and I decided it was about time to leave the hairstyling business. One of the things I felt I needed to do before I quit was to set the record straight, so to speak. By then I had met three or four people who had worked with Barbra . . . and I told them, 'You know, I've always taken

credit for cutting this woman's hair; I feel a little guilty. I would really like to meet her and cut her hair for real. Please tell her I'll go anyplace, anywhere, anytime, to do her hair—for free.'"

"All he had to say was for free," Barbra joked later, but in reality, such offers are commonplace for celebrities. She never responded. Coincidentally, a year later, Barbra did require Jon Peters's services. She saw a hairdo she thought would be perfect for Henrietta Robbins, also

119

known as "Henry," the mixed-up heroine of *For Pete's Sake*. Upon inquiry, she discovered that the boyish style was created by Peters, and encouraged by Yates, she tracked down the hairstylist in London, where he was working on another project. The fateful meeting was set upon his return to Los Angeles.

The chemistry between the two was apparent from the beginning. "She told me she was doing . . . *For Pete's Sake* and said she wanted a new style for her hair," Jon recalled. "That was easy because I was good and I could do that for her. Then we started talking about the clothes she'd be wearing in the film. She showed me some pictures of them, and I said I didn't think much of them, 'I hate them, too,' she said. 'Okay, then let's go shopping,' I said. 'Great,' she said. Two days later, I picked her up in my car, and we went shopping. We bought the clothes together, and after that I used to go on the set with her. For four months we worked together, and we became closer and closer. First in a work sense, then in a total way. We started spending the odd night in one or the other of our houses. Then it just seemed to be the natural thing to do—to start being together all the time." By Christmas, 1973, they were. Two months later, they settled in Malibu.

Postproduction on *For Pete's Sake* was completed in the spring of 1974. Artie Butler was hired to write a musical score that would reflect the producers' vision of a "yellow and orange film . . . a madcap, utterly zany frolic." Butler also brought in Mark Lindsay (formerly of Paul Revere and the Raiders) to write the lyrics for a title tune to be performed by Barbra. The composer met with Streisand at M-G-M, where she was rehearsing within a backbreaking musical schedule for *Funny Lady.* "I wanted to write a much more contemporary song for the main title, but the producers needed to have 'For Pete's Sake' in there," he says. "I tried to explain to them that 'For Pete's Sake' wasn't a contemporary phrase to use in the title song, but they wanted it. I remember specifically playing the song for Barbra, and she said to me, 'I know the records you've made, and I know 'For Pete's Sake' shouldn't be there. I know it and you know it, right?' I said, 'Right.' She said, 'But we'll do it, right?' I said, 'Right.' I remember her saying it with a smile. . . . Working with her is many times a challenge and always a thrill."

For Pete's Sake was set to break nationwide on June 26, 1974. A trailer teasing audiences with comic bits from the movie had been screening with *The Way We Were* since Christmas. Columbia was intent on making *For Pete's Sake* the comedy hit of the summer. In June they launched a massive promotional effort along with an advertising campaign, which optimistically exploited the film as being in the vein of such classics as *The Awful Truth* and *Theodora Goes Wild* and the best of Chaplin, Keaton, and the Keystone Kops. "We expect this film will do as well as *What's Up, Doc?*" David Begelman, the studio's new president (and former agent of Barbra's), announced to exhibitors. With Streisand the sole name above the title, it was clear that this one was meant to be her picture all the way. After *The Way We Were*, there was no doubt that a huge audience would be waiting for the release of her next film. But how would they respond to it?

Amply supported by Columbia Pictures, *For Pete's Sake* established itself as a hit summer comedy, though not the blockbuster the studio had hoped for. That it was an unworthy follow-up to *The Way We Were* was voiced by critics and fans alike. Peter Yates subsequently found himself in the peculiar position of not being taken seriously for having directed one of Barbra's lesser films. "Not everybody can get up there and interest people the way a true superstar can, even in a bad film," he generalized later.

Aside from a handful of effective slapstick sequences, the humor of *For Pete's Sake* is often strained, and though her magnetic charm goes a long way toward making Henrietta an attractive, if not totally believable, character, the role offers no new challenge to Barbra's well-honed comic abilities, and Michael Sarrazin is asked only to be sweetly innocuous as Pete. Molly Picon is funny as a Jewish-mama-style madam, but Oscar winner Estelle Parsons is stereotypical as Pete's nagging sister-in-law. (Parsons's experience with Barbra contrasted greatly with that of costars from prior Streisand comedies. "She doesn't believe in sharing a picture," Parsons complained, "even a comedy, which has to be a team effort.")

"When I haven't followed my instincts it's been a mistake," Barbra said in 1972. One might suggest that her decision to make *For Pete's Sake* had less to do with her instincts than it did her desire—born of loyalty and friendship—to aid in Marty Erlichman's first attempt at hands-on film

production. Ironically, in making the picture, Barbra met the man who would soon take over many of the services Erlichman had been performing on her behalf since the earliest days of her career.

REVIEWS

"A lot of actresses could have played the dizzy dame in For Pete's Sake *(Stella Stevens comes to mind), but Streisand brings too much reality to the role. We begin to really care about her, because she contributes little quirks of characterization and personality to what's supposed to be in one dimension or it can't exist at all: the minute the people develop depth we find it curious that they'd be chasing cattle through Brooklyn or doing all the other zany things we're supposed to laugh at. . . . Streisand is a rare and original screen personality. Her success wasn't due to formula in the first place, and her future films won't work on that level, either."*

CHICAGO SUN-TIMES

"For Pete's Sake, a movie put together to honor its star, Barbra Streisand, is an often boisterously funny old-time farce. . . . Without apology, Stanley Shapiro and Maurice Richlin, who wrote the screenplay, and Peter Yates, who directed it, make use of the most ancient devices of farce: outlandish disguises, sudden reversals in fortune, pratfalls, wisecracks. Some of their material is fondly familiar; some is in raucously bad taste. . . . For Pete's Sake courts disaster, but most of the time manages to sidestep it."

NEW YORK TIMES

"Streisand's first pic since the hugely successful The Way We Were *contributes little to her advancement as a screen actress–comedienne, but diehard fans, and they are legion, will provide the Columbia release with a strong send-off in urban [markets].*

DAILY VARIETY

Funny Lady
(1975)

A Columbia Pictures Release of a Rastar Production of a Persky-Bright/Vista Feature

CAST

Barbra Streisand (*Fanny Brice*); James Caan (*Billy Rose*); Omar Sharif (*Nick Arnstein*); Roddy McDowall (*Bobby*); Ben Vereen (*Bert Robbins*); Carole Wells (*Norma Butler*); Larry Gates (*Bernard Baruch*); Heidi O'Rourke (*Eleanor Holm*); Samantha Huffaker (*Fran*); Matt Emery (*Buck Bolton*); Gene Troobnick (*Ned*); Royce Webber (*Adele*); Byron Webster (Crazy Quilt *Director*); Coleen Camp (*Billy's Girl*); Alana Collins (*Girl With Nick*).

CREDITS

Producer: Ray Stark; director: Herbert Ross; assistant director: Jack Roe; second assistant directors: Stu Fleming, Dodie Fawley; screenplay: Jay Presson Allen, Arnold Schulman (from a story by Arnold Schulman); music and lyrics to original songs: John Kander and Fred Ebb; director, musical numbers: Herbert Ross; assistant to Mr. Ross: Nora Kaye; music arranger and conductor: Peter Matz; music editor: William Saracino; unit production manager: Howard Pine; production designer: George Jenkins; costume designers: Ray Aghayan, Bob Mackie; cinematographer: James Wong Howe; special effects: Phil Cory; set decorator: Audrey Blasdel; special photographic effects: Albert Whitlock; film editor: Marion Rothman; sound: Jack Solomon; casting: Jennifer Schull.
Running time: 137 minutes.

You can't capitalize on something that's worked before," Barbra told producer Ray Stark early in 1973 when he presented her with Arnold Schulman's draft of *Funny Lady*, the long-discussed sequel to Streisand's award-winning debut film. "You'll have to drag me into court to do that picture!" (In 1968, he did file suit to get Barbra to honor the balance of her four-picture deal before committing to other projects. That action was dropped when she agreed to do *The Owl and the Pussycat*.)

Anytime a memorable character is created on-screen, there is the inevitable rush to repackage those elements into a new picture. Producer Stark knew there was a lot of mileage left in the Fanny Brice saga; he refused to give up on Barbra. "The *Funny Lady* project was going on and off, on and off, over many, many years," Marty Erlichman confirms, ". . . before Barbra finally committed to do it."

There were several reasons why she acquiesced. First, Barbra had maintained a relationship with director-choreographer Herbert Ross and his wife, Nora Kaye. *Funny Lady* would not only complete the cycle with him that had begun with *I Can Get It for You Wholesale* in 1962; it would also close the book on her nine-year-old commitment to Ray Stark. A rewrite by Jay Presson Allen, acclaimed for her masterful adaptations of *Cabaret* and *The Prime of Miss Jean Brodie,* produced "a very bright, literate and humorous" script that ignited a spark in Barbra. "For some time, Streisand has been the only bankable female because she alone plays gutsy roles, winners," Allen stated. "Even when she's getting the hell kicked out of her, you know she's going to get up again."

Irrespective of its origin, the continuation of Fanny Brice's story, culled from an oral history Brice dictated shortly before her death plus assorted books and tapes, accurately reflected Barbra's personal growth to date. Once again, fiction and reality came together to form an almost spiritual bond between the two women. Not wishing to be unduly influenced prior to *Funny Girl,* Barbra had not seen the Brice memoirs. When she did read them years later, she found a lot about

Fanny to identify with: a mutual love of white, an appreciation of beautifully made clothes and antiques, a knack for interior decorating, and some belated personal insight. "In the second part of Fanny's life, I feel she starts to discover herself . . . and finally lets go of her illusions and fantasies about men. She grows up," Barbra said. "[The story] bridges the kind of gap which she feels are negative qualities in her own personality—being open to somebody who is like her, namely Billy Rose, tough and yet gentle. Altogether, it's a most interesting framework for a film."

It seems no idle coincidence, then, that her own life had taken this direction recently. "He was a good whip for me, because he made me think, made me work harder to keep up with him," Fanny Brice had said about shorthand specialist turned lyricist turned producer Billy Rose, but the same sentiment no doubt applied to the Streisand –Jon Peters union. "I think I could say that besides everything else," Peters told British journalist Rosalie Shan, "she's the best friend I've got." Much of Funny Lady emphasized that Fanny and Billy were friends who could talk to each other and share experiences long before they became lovers.

In December 1973, Columbia officially announced that Streisand, Ross, and Stark would reunite for Funny Lady. Next on the agenda was casting a suitable male lead. Eleanor Holm, Rose's second wife, told columnist Shirley Eder that she was led to believe Al Pacino would be playing the man Fanny Brice once called "the Jewish Noël Coward." Robert Blake, the feisty star of television's Baretta, went to Barbra's home to talk about the film. She suggested reading a scene together; he insisted on reading the entire script. Two hours later, People magazine reported that Blake was offered the role. (Neither Barbra nor Marty Erlichman recall the conversation progressing that far.) Later in January, Rastar made a surprising selection: the actor who played the explosive Sonny Corleone in The Godfather, James Caan. Physically, Caan didn't come close to approximating the man, but he thought he could indeed capture the nervous energy and drive that made the fast-talking Rose a force to contend with in the "tinsel and cheesecloth world" of Broadway. "I'm ready for a musical," he said.

Barbra met Billy Rose in 1964, after her opening night in Funny Girl ("I hear I was married to you once. How was I?" she asked. "Great for the first five years," Rose responded), so she was aware that Stark and Ross were casting against type. But, she added, "it comes down to whom the audience wants me to kiss. Robert Blake, no. James Caan, yes." Omar Sharif was signed for a guest appearance as Nicky Arnstein. Roddy McDowall and Carole Wells would play two of Fanny's friends from the theater. Tony Award winner Ben Vereen took a leave of absence from Broadway's Pippin to accept his first featured role in a major film. He would portray Bert Robbins, a composite character suggested by dancers Bert Williams and Bill "Bojangles" Robinson. Taking no chances, the production company hired major talent for behind-the-scenes support: new songs by Cabaret's songwriting team of John Kander and Fred Ebb, with longtime Streisand associate Peter Matz composing the underscore; costumes by Ray Aghayan and Bob Mackie; and Vilmos Zsigmond as director of photography. "[Ray Stark] wasn't penny conscious when it came to putting it on the screen," Marty Erlichman says. Funny Lady, budgeted at $7.5 million, was to have a fourteen-week production schedule, including time in Atlantic City, Philadelphia, and New York City.

Rehearsals began on Stages 5 and 6 at M-G-M Studios several weeks in advance of the April 1 start date. Ross and production manager Howard Pine had devised an ingenious schedule whereby fourteen musical numbers could be filmed via multiple cameras in sixteen days, creating a cost savings of over $750,000. Cinematographer Zsigmond researched American musical theater of the 1930s in order to give audiences an opportunity to experience a realistic theatrical presentation. The final week of rehearsals, Ross brought in the production crew to block and light the major numbers as Barbra and Ben Vereen performed them with the dancers. M-G-M's unique theater soundstage, complete with proscenium and fly gallery, provided the setting; Zsigmond added to the atmosphere by keeping edges of the stage dark and allowing the audience to be obscured. But when dailies of the first number, a gospel-flavored "Great Day," came back, executives were dismayed that the footage was so dark. Over the strenuous objections of the director—and much to Barbra's surprise—Zsigmond was fired.

The next day, Ray Stark begged James Wong Howe to come out of retirement to shoot Funny

Fanny Brice sings "Blind Date" as her latest show closes in the middle of the Depression.

Lady. A two-time Academy Award winner, Howe's formidable credits stretched back to *The Thin Man* and included *The Rose Tattoo, Picnic,* and *Hud.* After impassioned pleadings from Stark, Howe agreed to photograph his first musical since *Yankee Doodle Dandy* in 1942. "I asked, 'When do I start?' " Howe told *American Cinematographer.* "They said, 'Seven-thirty tomorrow morning. . . .' If I hadn't had fifty-seven years of experience . . . I wouldn't have been able to jump into such a big project on twenty-four hours' notice . . . and without any preparation. . . . I was a bit nervous."

Howe passed his initiation easily, capturing in his richly textured and brilliantly colored work the M-G-M musical style that often eluded would-be imitators. Other numbers put on film during that three-week period included "So Long, Honey Lamb," "Blind Date," "I Found a Million Dollar Baby," "Clap, Hands, Here Comes Charlie" (two versions), "Am I Blue?," and "How Lucky Can You Get?" It was an exhausting schedule. A couple of

weeks after the company's return to the Burbank Studios, Howe took ill and was out of commission for ten days; Ernest Laszlo stepped in to take his place. When Howe rejoined the company, he endeared himself to Barbra by surprising her with delicacies from his kitchen. He would later describe her as "a smart gal . . . very honest and very hep. She came to me one day and said, 'Jimmy, you know they say I'm temperamental. I'm not really temperamental. I just want things to be right for me—and I know what's good for me and what's bad.' Well, I think that's a wonderful trait. She protects herself—and she should.

"When I was setting up to shoot my first close-up of her, I heard a voice say, 'What, no diffusion?' I turned around and said, 'No, Miss Streisand. I'm not using any diffusion, because this is a beautiful lens. It must have cost five or six thousand dollars, and it has wonderful resolution. I'm not going to ruin it by putting a $2.50 piece of glass in front of it. I'd rather get the effect with

James Caan and Barbra enjoyed a warm rapport on the set.

Streisand, disdainfully smoking while Caan . . . is solidly in character and remains so as a piece of tobacco gets stuck on the tip of her tongue. She carefully reaches up to pick it off just as Caan, in the passion of the promotion, grabs her hand to emphasize his point—and shoves her hand into his mouth. The entire company . . . explodes into laughter and from then on neither Caan nor Streisand can look at one another without giggling."

The opinionated leading man later confessed that "from that day on, I was yelling at her, putting her down, and calling her a spoiled rotten thing, and she would call me this or that. We'd carry on and we'd laugh. . . . I just remember giggling quite a bit." Caan reminisced about the scene in which both stars became drenched in talcum powder. "For some reason it was very important for Herb Ross to get this shot, and here [Barbra] came in this beautiful green spangled dress and made up just right. She said, 'I don't really think that Jimmy should hit me in the face with this powder. [It's] toxic, you know, and I'll get it in my lungs.' I could see that this big argument was going to start, so . . . I winked at Herb and said, 'Stay out of this.' I said, 'Barbra, I think you're right. Maybe I shouldn't hit you with the thing. Maybe you'll hit me and then I'll pick it up and I'll go to hit you with it and then I won't.' She said, 'Oh, that's terrific. That'll be great!' I said, 'Now, mind you—if you blink or back off when I start to raise my hand, I'm gonna whack you with it . . . 'cause it's only the idea that you're ready to accept it that'll stop me.' She said, 'Okay. I won't blink.'

"So . . . she hit me in the face with the powder. I picked it up and drew my hand back, and she just stood there. She did not blink. I hit her right square in the face with it. I'm telling you, I went to the floor laughing. I couldn't stop, and she looked at me. . . . I really felt bad for a minute because she was so shocked. She called me names. She said, 'You lied to me!' I was hysterical. And then she laughed, too." Barbra: "He had his fingers crossed so God shouldn't strike him dead, and then he let me have it." The first take was the only take.

Another bit had Fanny ordering Billy out of her dressing room. The backstage squabble was based on real life, though not Fanny's. "That scene was based on a fight I had with my producer Ray Stark during the making of *Funny Girl*," Barbra admitted to Dick Cavett. "We fight like hell," Stark

lights.' She didn't say anything else, and from then on we got along great."

Streisand and James Caan's first scene together was a confrontation at Billy Rose's Backstage Club. Neither star was feeling very hostile, but their acting did "strike sparks." On the sixth take, *Los Angeles Times* reporter Wayne Warga observed, "everything is going perfectly.

Fanny performs "I Found a Million Dollar Baby in a Five and Ten Cent Store."

admitted in 1975, "but they're all fights about creative opinions on which I can be right or wrong and she can be right or wrong. She's matured and become a lovely lady instead of a fiery, funny, kooky little girl." Barbra's approach to playing Stark's illustrious mother-in-law had matured as well. "This is more of a real acting job for me," she said, ". . . a character piece. I was very much true to Fanny Brice—to the lady who called everybody kid because she couldn't remember anyone's name." Barbra was also unafraid to reveal the harsher, demanding side of Brice that had only been hinted at in the first film. "I don't try to be liked," she said, "I don't know if she's likable, this character."

In terms of her *own* likability, Barbra was not unaware of the tension that can arise when she walks on a movie set, but its existence stymied her. "I really pride myself in professional behavior," she told Barbara Walters, "even though there have been times when a director has said something to me [that] made me feel very sensitive. Because

I'm aware that everybody is listening with such big ears. . . ."

On *Funny Lady,* Herbert Ross found himself pushing Barbra more than he ever thought he would need to. After the gratifying experience of *The Owl and the Pussycat,* he was unbridled in his enthusiasm for her talents. "I thought Barbra's possibilities were limitless," he said in 1976, "but *Funny Lady* was a curious experience. . . . It was a movie that was made virtually without her—she simply wasn't there in terms of commitment, and one of her greatest qualities is to make a thousand percent commitment." The director would later tone down his comments, but his disappointment was genuine.

Assistant director Jack Roe explains that "there's no doubt that once Barbra's on the set she gives a hundred percent to whatever she's doing; singing, acting. . . . She's obviously an extremely talented lady, and she's willing to try anything. But I think by the time she did *Funny Lady* she was

As the Crazy Quilt *revue opens on Broadway, Fanny belts out "Great Day."*

fairly wealthy and in love, and because she never really wanted to do the sequel, she probably didn't care as much about the film itself."

If Jon Peters was the problem (or "the distraction"), it was because getting involved with him was as intense a "project" as any record or movie Barbra chose to make. This relationship demanded a full-time commitment, and it was the first time since she arrived in Hollywood that her

major commitment didn't revolve around motion pictures. To her delight, Barbra was able to stay within Jon's reach when the eastern locations originally set for *Funny Lady* were nixed in favor of California sites.

First on the schedule was an elaborately choreographed shot of Barbra singing the "Let's Hear It for Me" finale as she took off in a 1937 biplane. "That was in the script from the beginning," Jack Roe says, "and she said flat out that she wasn't going to do it." Because of her great confidence in Herb Ross and her belief that Nelson Tyler—the aerial photographer who captured "Don't Rain on My Parade" so effectively on film—could get it all in a single take, Barbra agreed to one flight. But when the landing schedule at the Santa Monica airport unexpectedly backed up, "Barbra had to stay aloft for twenty minutes before they could get the clearance to come back down."

Later, she was able to laugh about the experience. "I nearly had a heart attack. I was so scared, but I knew I should do [the shot] myself," she said. "We went up, and the plane just kept going. The first thing I thought was, He's kidnapping me. Then I thought, The radio's dead, the guy can't land." Circling the coastal city, unable to communicate with the pilot in the open-cockpit plane, all Barbra could think was, Here I am risking my life for a movie! Back on the tarmac, the crew panicked as well when they realized that the plane wasn't returning to the field. Many anxious minutes later there was an only-in-Hollywood type ending. "The moment they touched down, you could hear Barbra screaming from one end of the runway," says Roe. "She was yelling at Herb. And I don't know how he did it, but he talked her into doing it again!"

The musical bridge of "Let's Hear It for Me" was visualized with Barbra driving Fanny's $85,000 Rolls-Royce in the hills near the Hollywood sign. The opening was shot a couple of weeks later, at the Beverly Hills Hotel. Other locations included the Olympic Swim Stadium, adjacent to the USC campus, the Columbia Pictures ranch, the Beverly Hills courthouse, the Malibu Pier (doubling for Atlantic City), the Pan Pacific auditorium (the art-deco entrance was re-dressed to resemble the NBC radio studio of the 1940s), the Los Angeles Theater (an ornate movie palace doubling as a legitimate theater), an Oakland train station (substituting for Cleveland), and finally the polo field at Will Rogers State Park. There Fanny would encounter Nick Arnstein for the first time since their divorce. Omar Sharif had not seen Barbra in years. "For the first two or three days, she seemed a little different to me," he stated. "But then I'm sure I appeared somewhat different to her, which is natural. [At the time of *Funny Girl*] she was married and had led a somewhat sheltered per-

sonal life. She had broadened considerably in the intervening years. I think it shows in her performing as well. . . . It was great fun to see and work with Barbra again."

Principal photography was completed on July 9, 1974. The wrap party took place that evening. Barbra made sure that none of the two hundred people on the cast and crew went without personal thank-you notes and gifts: James Caan received a sterling-silver rodeo belt buckle; James Wong Howe, an antique camera with a plaque on which Barbra had had inscribed, "Thank you for your talents, generosity and *cha siu bao*." For Ray Stark there was an acknowledgment of their long association. Across an antique mirror she scrawled "Paid in Full" in lipstick. The sentiment on the accompanying plaque was more endearing: "Even though I sometimes forget to say it, thank you, Ray. Love, Barbra."

Columbia began previewing *Funny Lady* early in 1975. The filmmakers were as yet unsure of how to end the film, and at least two different endings were shown to exhibitors. One version concluded with Fanny and Billy saying goodbye at a deserted train station. Another was a fictionalized reunion—shot months after principal photography was completed—between the two (in unconvincing "age" makeup), a year or so before Fanny's death. At the last minute, Peter Matz's underscore was augmented by an uncredited Marvin Hamlisch, who contributed a couple of "thematic" cues linking *Funny Girl* and *Funny Lady*. In the meantime, the film was running almost twenty minutes too long. Barbra had filmed several touching scenes detailing Fanny's relationship with her daughter, Fran, and her friends, but these moments—which would have defined Fanny outside of her relationship with Rose—were dropped, as were complete versions of the musical numbers "Am I Blue?" and "So Long, Honey Lamb." Even "Let's Hear It for Me" was truncated despite the effort it took to capture it on film.

Perhaps the most frustrating casualty of the editorial process was the Baby Snooks radio show. Few people had known the Fanny Brice of *Funny Girl*, but thousands of radio listeners came to love the Brice they heard in their homes every week. Snooks was Fanny's most identifiable success, and she got less than a minute in the final cut of *Funny Lady*.

The film premiered in March 1975, first in

Against her better judgment, Fanny agrees to see Nick Arnstein in California, where she is now playing Baby Snooks on the radio.

her heartbreaking romance with Nick Arnstein), *Funny Lady* opened strong over the Easter holiday and by year's end had ranked with *Shampoo* and *Tommy* as Columbia's top films of 1975, with a gross take of $39 million. And with a few notable exceptions—namely, Pauline Kael's seven-page tirade in the *New Yorker* that blamed Streisand for most of the film's shortcomings and managed to insult her fans in the same breath— the movie received fine reviews; many critics were so happy to welcome Barbra back into the musical-comedy realm after five years that *Funny Lady*'s considerable flaws and excesses were largely overlooked. In retrospect, it's difficult to grasp why the film cast such a spell over so many reviewers, particularly those who would attack subsequent, more worthy Streisand vehicles.

Directors were the stars of 1975's most important films: Robert Altman's *Nashville*, Stanley Kubrick's *Barry Lyndon*, Steven Spielberg's *Jaws*. Even *One Flew Over the Cuckoo's Nest* was Milos Forman's picture as much as Jack Nicholson's. It wasn't a good year for women in movies. Early in the year, 1974's Best Actress Ellen Burstyn urged Academy members not to vote for Best Actress in order to protest the dearth of women's roles. Of course, the category was not eliminated: The Academy knew they could always find five nominees of some distinction. Despite an acclaimed performance in a weak year, 1975's world film favorite was not to be among them. *Funny Lady* received four nominations (Cinematographer, Sound, Song, and Original Song Score) but took home no awards.

Washington, D.C., and later in New York City, where the presence of Barbra and Jon ignited a mob of fans and a menacing crush of photographers. The premiere in London on March 18 caused international comment. Encouraged by Jon to inquire why women (and not men) must wear gloves when meeting the queen, Barbra shocked some bystanders by being the one to speak first when presented to Queen Elizabeth II. While a palace spokesman later intimated that Barbra hadn't really broken any rules of protocol, the press had fun with yet another story.

Though it sorely lacked a distinguished song score and the two most appealing elements of its predecessor (Fanny's exciting rise to stardom and

Fanny Brice in costume for Baby Snooks, alongside Barbra playing the character in the film. Brice's most famous comic creation was all but ignored in Funny Lady.

REVIEWS

"Funny Lady *toys with the facts so much it sometimes resembles* Words and Music, *that fantasy biography of Rodgers and Hart. It makes you think Billy Rose was a jerk and Fanny Brice was a great lady. . . . Also, Rose gets credit in the film for songs by Arlen and Youmans, and there is no mention anywhere of Arnstein's son, William. (How did Fanny manage to dispose of one child along the way?) Eleanor Holm was paid a handsome sum to have her name slandered, but who cares?* Funny Lady *is so warm and funny and gorgeous you forgive it everything, including poetic license. It has restored my faith in movie musicals and my allegiance to Streisand. . . . Never has she been so dazzling, and in the final scenes she has so much gentility and poise that she actually seems to become Fanny Brice instead of merely playing her. The experience is pure enchantment."*

ENTERTAINMENT TODAY

"Barbra Streisand, like the picture, extends the characterization she launched so dazzlingly in Funny Girl. *She sings superbly and with, it seemed*

to me, more restraint on the remarkable dynamics of her voice, making for more subtlety but also more impact. The Brooklyn brashness just right for Funny Girl *has been let mellow. It is still there, but it is even easier to see as a defense against rejection—and as an ingredient of the Fanny Brice comedic persona. What I find most impressive and likable about the performance is the softened, bittersweet maturity that Streisand lets us see in Fanny Brice. You sense that Streisand understands the star as well as she understood the impetuous young hopeful."*

LOS ANGELES TIMES

"Every artist works on instinct, but when we talk about Barbra Streisand's working on instinct we mean something special: she's had so little experience in the theater she relies on instinct in a void. And her instinct has been playing her false lately. . . . There is danger now for any woman musical comedy star that she will begin to give her screaming fans what they want, not realizing how much malice and how much bad taste are mixed with their worship. . . ."

NEW YORKER

A Star Is Born

(1976)

A Warner Bros./First Artists Release

CAST

Barbra Streisand (*Esther Hoffman*); Kris Kristofferson (*John Norman Howard*); Gary Busey (*Bobby Ritchie*); Paul Mazursky (*Brian Wexler*); M. G. Kelly (*Baby Jesus*); Joanne Linville (*Freddie Lowenstein*); Oliver Clark (*Gary Danziger*); Vanetta Fields, Clydie King (*The Oreos*); Marta Heflin (*Quentin*); Sally Kirkland (*Nikki*); Mo (*Uncle Rudy*).

CREDITS

Executive producer: Barbra Streisand; producer: Jon Peters; director: Frank Pierson; assistant director: Stu Fleming; screenplay: John Gregory Dunne, Joan Didion, Frank Pierson (from a story by William Wellman, Robert Carson); choreographer: David Winters; musical concepts: Barbra Streisand; music supervision: Paul Williams; musical underscore: Roger Kellaway; musical conductor: Kenny Ascher; music and live recordings: Phil Ramone; production manager: Howard Pine; production designer: Polly Platt; cinematographer: Robert Surtees; special effects: Chuck Gasper; concert lighting: Jules Fisher; set decorator: Ruby Levitt; art director: William Hiney; film editor: Peter Zinner; sound mixer: Tom Overton; casting: Diane Crittenden.
Running time: 140 minutes.

On February 1, 1976, Barbra began filming her tenth—and most controversial—motion picture, a contemporary remake of a quintessential Hollywood story. The saga of this production's roller-coaster ride from printed page to movie screen and the ramifications it had on the lives of its principals has been reported, scrutinized, exaggerated, and frequently misrepresented. It's a story, in fact, that could easily fill a book of its own if told in its entirety.

The project originated with the married screenwriting team of Joan Didion and John Gregory Dunne during their Hawaiian vacation in July 1973. Tossing around ideas for a possible film, Dunne suggested "James Taylor and Carly Simon in a rock-and-roll version of *A Star Is Born*." The story of an alcoholic star's public fall from grace while his wife finds success in the spotlight had worked in 1937 for Fredric March and Janet Gaynor and in 1954 for Judy Garland and James Mason. (*What Price Hollywood?* [1932] is often referred to as the first telling of *A Star Is Born*, and though it did inspire its producer, David O. Selznick, to create the 1937 version, its story line is quite different.) A properly cast remake within the context of contemporary music could mean a licensing gold mine to those responsible.

Didion and Dunne pitched the idea to Warner Bros. Not only did the studio hold the remake rights; it was also a sister company to Warner/Elektra/Asylum Records, the home of both Simon and Taylor. Late in August 1973, the studio announced their intention of making the film, to be titled *Rainbow Road*.

Several months and one rewrite later, as various actors, directors, and singers paraded through the production office, the Dunnes became "thoroughly sick of the project" and contemplated moving on. In addition, Warners had second thoughts about the Simon and Taylor teaming. They feared the film was in danger of becoming a high-budget screen test, and they didn't like the idea of either Warren Beatty or Mike Nichols as director. Peter Bogdanovich passed on the project as a vehicle for Cybill Shepherd. Early in 1974 producer John Foreman and director Mark Rydell signed on. They hired Richard Perry to supervise the musical score.

Misgivings about the project itself continued. The script that Rydell called "frighteningly brilliant . . . a savage look at the rock world" Perry saw as not really capturing "the contemporary rock-pop milieu. Everything in it was clichéd." Others saw the story as too cold and cynical in an era that seemed to need romance more than ever. That conflict didn't help attract a strong female lead.

As the top female star at the box office (and certainly the top musical star), Barbra was offered *Rainbow Road* very early on. She turned it down. "I didn't want to do a remake, and that's the truth," she said then. Less than a year later, however, she was reluctantly drawn back into the project thanks to Jon Peters's interest in it. He felt the two of them should produce the film together; she wasn't so sure and challenged him to justify why the story should be retold. He described the film as being about two people "trapped by their money and success. The most important thing to them is communicating . . . wanting to have children, not the thousands of agents and managers and all that stuff that controls their lives. I just really loved the story." (Unfortunately, as rewrite followed rewrite, some of the key elements that had attracted Jon to the story became obscured.)

Peters also thought it was time for Barbra to update her screen image and play hipper characters than the wifely heroines of *The Way We Were* and *For Pete's Sake.* He saw her as "a young, hot, sexy woman—a little ball of fire. None of that had ever been conveyed on film." "People put me into a category—she plays *this* kind of role—just as the press puts me into a journalistic image they think people will pay to read about," Barbra said. "That whole Brooklyn-girl-makes-good thing is so boring to me, and based on the past. I've contributed to that, in a sense, by the roles I've played. But not anymore."

To prove he meant business, Peters eliminated his safety net; he sold his chain of hair salons. In the fall of 1974, after seriously rethinking what her involvement in such a production might be, Streisand signed to do the picture as part of her Warner Bros./First Artists contract. The film was given a comparatively low budget of $6 million; any overages were to be guaranteed by Barwood. A December 1974/January 1975 starting date was projected. Once Barbra committed, Jon says, she became the project's driving force.

One of the first changes Barbra insisted on was to own up to the movie's origin. Instead of ignoring the previous incarnations of *A Star Is Born,* as if *Rainbow Road* were a totally original concept, she wanted to invite audiences to compare the films and contemplate how much times had changed. "I wanted to explore relationships *today,* the role-playing today, as opposed to that of the 1930s and the 1950s," she explained. Streisand also visualized *A Star Is Born* as a singular opportunity to express some of her feelings about what it's like to be a celebrity performer—how frantic and chaotic and unreal that all-too-insular world can be, how hot the spotlight that strips away one's privacy. Criticism can burn hot, too, and simply by signing for the picture, Barbra set herself up for harsh reactions from fans of the Garland version, considered one of Judy's—and director George Cukor's—greatest triumphs.

As producers, writers, and even costars were consumed in the deceptive quicksand surrounding the production, the public attention focused on the Streisand-Peters relationship. "A lot of what people say is true," Jon stated in 1976. "I *am* riding on the wings of a star. . . . I never could have produced a movie like this without Barbra. . . . The theatrics of a hairdresser getting involved with a superstar play right into the Hollywood thing." But Barbra resented the insinuation that she had been hypnotized by this neophyte producer, characterized as "a modern-day Svengali." "I am a professional," she asserted in a 1975 interview with Barbara Walters. "I have integrity as an artist. Do people think that I would risk all that? People get angry at things that have not been done before. It's not that they're wrong; it's just that they're different. . . . Who's the Svengali? Maybe I'm his."

Jon admitted that producing Barbra's poorly reviewed *ButterFly* album had been a mixed blessing. "My instincts were good, but my abilities weren't. Barbra literally had to bail me out. . . . And then I learned what I could do and what I couldn't do. *A Star Is Born* was what I could do . . . or rather, I saw what it could be. I knew it could be a good movie because I knew how to put people together." Once Barbra and Jon became obsessed with the project, the problem became finding collaborators who shared their vision.

For several months, the project inspired a revolving door of talented names that led to further speculation that Barbra and her boyfriend

had gotten in way over their heads. Director Rydell left the project to make room for Jerry Schatzberg. Didion and Dunne finally departed. In their absence, a host of well-known names, from Buck Henry to Alvin Sargent and Jay Presson Allen, were bandied about, but Jon brought in young Jonathan Axelrod, who suggested switching the male and female leads so that Barbra would play a self-destructive Janis Joplin type. Hal Ashby and Arthur Hiller were approached about directing the picture, and Richard Perry, who had produced two of Barbra's most successful pop-rock albums, was approached by Peters to codirect. Finally, the gossip columns announced that Jon was not only contemplating directing the film himself but playing the lead as well. Both Barbra and Jon would later say that the idea lasted only "for about five minutes," but the public-relations damage had been done. "This movie is going to be the *Myra Breckenridge* of 1975," Axelrod said upon his leave-taking. Soon Richard Perry dropped out, and John Foreman was fired. Screenwriters Bob and Laurie Dillon came and went, as did suggestions that Sidney Lumet, Bob Fosse, Robert Altman, and Sydney Pollack might direct.

That spring, Streisand and Peters sat down for two hours with Elvis Presley in Las Vegas in a vain attempt to get him to reconsider the lead. (His name had surfaced earlier when Warner Bros. hoped to snag other notables, such as Cher or Diana Ross.) "He's always been underrated as an actor," Barbra said. "I think this could be a whole rebirth for him." What she didn't know was that the script hit a little too close to home. Peters had idolized Elvis. "But when we went up to see him," Jon recalled, ". . . it was real sad. He had this big stomach; he was dying, really. He was the character. He *was* John Norman." Members of Presley's inner circle have since stated that he wanted very much to do the picture and that they felt it might have saved him. But, for whatever reasons, his legendary, dictatorial manager, Col. Tom Parker, refused to even consider the idea.

After toying around with other costar possi-

In a scene that ended up on the cutting room floor, John Norman falls asleep as Esther plays her new composition, "Evergreen."

bilities (Brando, Jagger), Barbra and Jon agreed on singer-songwriter turned actor Kris Kristofferson (who had dated Streisand casually in 1971), whose "gentle craziness," they felt, was ideal for the role. "I'm flattered to even be considered . . . ," Kristofferson said, "[and] I'm really looking forward to working with her—just to see how she reacts to whatever I bring and whether I can cope [professionally] with somebody of that [magnitude.]"

Kristofferson's casting would add several important elements: Movie audiences would see an artist tortured by self-doubt, too weary to be truly cynical, too sensitive not to be in pain.

Moreover, Kristofferson was able to bring an even deeper understanding to the character, as he and John Norman both shared an increasingly dangerous dependence on alcohol. A further touch of reality was added to the mix when L.A. deejay Machine Gun Kelly signed to play an obnoxious radio personality and musician-actor Gary Busey—in one of his first featured parts—was cast as John Norman's roadie. Accepting a rare acting role, director Paul Mazursky agreed to portray a sympathetic record executive. Sally Kirkland would play a photographer, a part that was all but excised from the finished picture.

On August 6, 1975, the *Hollywood Reporter* announced that Frank Pierson had been signed to adapt the troubled *A Star Is Born* screenplay—and to direct. According to Pierson, he was approached by an executive at Warner Bros. to do a "fast rewrite," and in a moment of "mad ambition," he accepted the assignment on the condition that he direct as well. (Barbra: "But he never told *us* that until after we hired him as a writer.") His job, he was told, was to make sure he didn't get fired. Pierson had some nice writing credits—*Cool Hand Luke, Dog Day Afternoon*—but with the exception of one low-budget feature film, his directorial credentials were in television. "With all due respect, Barbra really should have directed the film," Jon says. "She ended up directing it, anyway. But she was frightened of taking the responsibility."

With the addition of Streisand's favorite new record producer, Rupert Holmes, to the musical team, work began to progress on the score. Having things back on track gave Barbra a chance to concentrate on her side of the picture. She took guitar lessons and attended rock concerts. She also observed classes at the West Coast branch of the Actors Studio, where she agreed to perform a scene from *Romeo and Juliet* with Sally Kirkland for Lee Strasberg. "When it came to her private moment in front of the mirror," Kirkland recalled, "which was this moment when Juliet was totally alone and discovering herself as a woman, I know she achieved what she had been working toward. The beauty, the love, the tears of joy. Lee talked quite a bit about that moment in his critique. He was very gentle with her. Of all the Juliets he had seen, he told her, she brought in this wholly original and creative way to do the role, which he never would have thought would have worked, but it did. 'It's a poetic, vulnerable, romantic, classical part of you that deserves to be seen by the world,' he said." Unfortunately, the demands of *A Star Is Born* kept Barbra from pursuing further involvement with Strasberg's studio.

After contributing a handful of new songs, Rupert Holmes left the production and was replaced by Paul Williams. Concerned that she would not have enough songs to fill out the broad tapestry of the score, Barbra sought help from outside sources, including Kenny Loggins and Marilyn and Alan Bergman, and she wrote several songs herself. A one-song experiment in composi-

tion turned into a joyously prolific period for her. "Night after night she'd sit alone in our living room until one, two, three o'clock in the morning plucking away on her guitar," Jon recalled. During one such nocturnal session, "Evergreen" was born.

During another particularly late night, as Leon Russell and Barbra were going over song ideas, Russell watched Barbra fool around with a classical motif she wrote on the piano. When asked about it, she tried to pass the tune off as nothing special, but Russell disagreed. It could be a terrific beginning for a song, he urged, and he started singing a countermelody to her accompaniment. The fruit of their collaboration was "Lost Inside of You," a song that solved a problem for the filmmakers. "We couldn't come up with a way to get the two characters together in their first love scene," Streisand said. "It's always the most difficult thing: How does the love thing happen? How do you all of a sudden start to kiss?"

"Songs began to emerge," marveled Pierson. "Barbra reshapes them, attacking the lyrics with a logician's mind. She insists on precision and simplicity, on lyrics meaning exactly what they say and saying what they mean. It's an education." Under the pressure of a final, absolute deadline from Warner Bros., the musical supervisor seldom appreciated the lesson. Arranger Ian Freebairn-Smith remembers some tension concerning "Evergreen." "Paul [Williams] wrote the lyrics and sent them to [Barbra], and [she] sent them back with a note saying, 'That's going to be a wonderful lyric when it's finished.' They're both very strong egos, Paul and Barbra, and it really made Paul angry to have anybody say that to him. He isn't used to having someone tell him his lyric isn't finished when he believes it is." (Ultimately, Williams, who has publicly admitted to being under the influence of alcohol and drugs during the production of *A Star Is Born*, was criticized for some of the lyrics he contributed to the score, most especially for "Evergreen.") "It was a very difficult time," Williams told *Billboard* magazine. "But I like to have creative control over *my* projects, so I understood her."

A gifted songwriter ("Help Me Make It Through the Night," "Bobby McGee"), Kristofferson had also been invited to contribute something to the song score but declined. Unfortunately, however, he wasn't comfortable with the songs and the Springsteenesque sound Williams and (musical

At the Sun Devil Stadium at Arizona State University, Barbra placates the crowd during a tension-filled day of shooting.

conductor) Kenny Ascher had created for him. He also howled complaints when Barbra and Jon attempted to doll up his band in a dated, flashy wardrobe. "I'm not rock 'n' roll," he objected, "but that look sure as hell ain't . . . and I'm not trusting my career to the judgment of a Vegas singer and her hairdresser!"

By the time production commenced in February 1976 in Pasadena, a serious problem threatened the film's delicate equilibrium: the collaboration between producer-star and writer-director was becoming one of constant struggle. Tired and underweight as filming began, Barbra was in danger of spreading herself too thin. She relied on Pierson to follow through on what they agreed on,

only to find camera setups completely changed around the next morning (and not always coordinated with the production designer, lighting director, or cameraman). The dual sets of instructions were counterproductive, wearing down a baffled cast and crew. "Tuthfully," Jon Peters states, "when I made the deal with Frank, [I said,] 'The only way you can direct this is if you partner with Barbra—that means a partnership. You collaborate, you communicate, and the result of that work is what you see on the screen.' But he didn't do that. The minute he got control he was like a child. He became a tyrant. Ultimately, a lot of his stuff was no good. I wanted to fire him [after the second day]—I did, in fact. But everybody, including

Esther Hoffman becomes a star singing "I Believe in Love" with her backup singers, played by Clydie King and Vanetta Fields. (Both singers had performed similar duties for Barbra offscreen as well.)

Warner Bros., felt there had been too much bad publicity and it would kill the movie." In fact, the bad publicity would continue unabated until the premiere, and beyond.

The majority of *A Star Is Born*'s sixty-day production was spent on location. Following Pasadena, the crew traveled to sites in the heart of Hollywood. A gorgeous mansion in Beverly Hills was stripped of its furnishings to become John Norman's "million-dollar slum," and the Biltmore Hotel in downtown Los Angeles served as a backdrop for the tumultuous Grammy Award sequence. In March the production moved to Arizona; three and a half weeks would be spent in the Phoenix area and another ten days outside

Tucson, where Warner Bros. had constructed John and Esther's eighty-thousand-dollar adobe hideaway.

Because of the intense interest in the movie, the studio had convinced Barbra and Jon to allow a three-day press junket revolving around a concert on March 20 at Arizona University's Sun Devil Stadium that Peters and veteran concert promoter Bill Graham were staging. To fill the stadium with a crowd that would serve as a backdrop for the filming of a scene in which Esther attends a John Norman Howard concert, Graham booked Santana and lesser-known bands, including Montrose and the L.A. Jets. (Peter Frampton bowed out at the last minute.) With a ticket price of only $3.50

Future director Barbra Streisand with director Frank Pierson and (wearing the white hat) *director-actor Paul Mazursky.*

(a percentage of which went to the March of Dimes), more than seventy thousand rock fans would materialize to hear the music and watch Streisand and Kristofferson make a movie.

That Friday, 150 members of the press were ushered into the stadium, where they were seated at circular dining tables on the fifty-yard line. Drinks flowed freely. Predictably drawn to what they perceived to be a potentially volatile situation, the press was not disappointed. The intense scrutiny, last-minute preparations for the concert to be staged the next day, and oppressive heat enflamed the atmosphere. Before Streisand, Kristofferson, and Pierson joined the press con-

ference, they rehearsed some of the action on stages set up for the concert. Frustrated and irritated as he attempted to serve two masters, Kristofferson blew up. "Who's the director?" he demanded in exasperation. A volley of sarcastic, threatening comments followed, culminated by Jon Peters's offer to slug it out—after the production was completed—and his insistence that Kris apologize to Barbra. The entire argument was picked up by a nearby mike and recorded by a salivating press corps. "As soon as I realized what was going on," assistant director Stu Fleming remembered, "I grabbed the mike and pulled it away from them."

The concert went surprisingly well considering that the vast audience had to sit through the numerous false starts and delays that inevitably accompany filmmaking. When the missteps and heat conspired to rile the crowd, Barbra would take the stage and sing, although she hadn't been scheduled to do so. She soothed the stoned, overheated mob with "The Way We Were," and she was heartened by their overwhelmingly positive response to "Evergreen" at its first public airing.

Most of the indoor concerts were filmed at Grady Gamage Auditorium in Phoenix. Fans had flown in from all over the country and Canada to watch what turned into a full day of filming. Their patience was rewarded by an exceedingly accommodating Stresiand, who joked with the audience, posed for pictures, and capped the day off with forceful performances of "Woman in the Moon," "I Believe in Love," and the emotional rocker that closes the film, "With One More Look at You/Watch Closely Now." In order to achieve the most effective visual design for each, Barbra worked closely with cinematographer Robert Surtees and lighting director Jules Fisher over several days preceding the event.

Filming concluded in mid-April on location in the San Fernando Valley. By the end of the summer, editor Peter Zinner and Barbra had assembled a rough three-and-a-half-hour cut of the movie. Upon viewing the footage, a Warner Bros. executive would certify the film a hit; there was no more grumbling about "Barbra and Jon's home movie." Eventually, the Barwood production of A Star Is Born was pared down to an economical 140 minutes. In November, the studio began sneak previews of the picture. Executives were ecstatic over the preview reactions but hardly overjoyed with Frank Pierson's tell-all article, which was published that month in New York and New West magazines. As with all deceptively clever exposés, "My Battles With Barbra and Jon" contained enough inverted truths to confuse even the most knowledgeable reader. In an apparent attempt to distance himself from what he felt would be the potential "embarrassment" of A Star Is Born, the director made public the private confidences of many coworkers as well as those of the controversial couple at the heart of the project. For the time being, the article was to become the definitive statement on an egomaniacal star and her equally power-hungry lover, instigating a new wave of hostility in the media. Reports that Star would be the year's most publicized bomb were being counterbalanced, however, by positive audience reactions to a final group of previews.

A Star Is Born had its gaudy premiere—replete with fireworks timed to go off upon Barbra and Jon's arrival—at the Village Theater in Los Angeles on December 18, 1976. In attendance were an assortment of Streisand supporters, from William Wyler to Ryan O'Neal. "The public statements have gotten out of hand," offered Frank Pierson, the man who had made the most damaging of them. "The impression is that Barbra and I differed on everything. It was actually ten to fifteen percent. We both cared strongly. . . . I think Barbra is a brilliant editor. She made me look better than I've ever looked in a movie. . . ." Kris Kristofferson told Geraldo Rivera at the New York premiere. "I'm afraid there's a tendency to knock her . . . and then give credit for everything that's good to me or Frank . . . and I feel terrible about [that] because she's a great filmmaker." Beyond the professional vindication, Kristofferson would have a personal reason for rallying behind the film; it inspired him to quit drinking. "It's the first time I was ever able to look at myself through [my wife's] eyes," he said. "And I think more than the bad I saw, I think that the good I saw affected me. It gave me enough confidence to think it was worth straightening up the act."

Encouraged by the positive word of mouth and glowing Hollywood notices, Barbra was devastated by many of the East Coast and national reviews—the most personalized and vicious of her career. She found tremendous support, however, from the reaction of the moviegoing public. Young and old, they were flocking to theaters, even during blizzards, in unheard-of numbers, curious to see the "earthier" Streisand the film promised to deliver. By this time, striking posters for the film featuring Barbra and Kris in a dramatic clinch, photographed by Francesco Scavullo, had been unavoidable in major cities for weeks, "Evergreen" was well on it way to the number-one spot on the radio, and despite the abundance of scathing reviews, audiences were eager to see one of their favorite pop singers within a contemporary musical setting for the first time in her movie career. And, of course, Kris Kristofferson fans were turning out as well. Others undoubtedly came to see if all the negative publicity had been true.

Strangely enough, the film became a battleground for admirers as well as detractors. Much of this had to do with the schizophrenic way Streisand was perceived by her followers at the time. For some, the gawky singer who delighted the cult in small bistros with exotic songs and shocked others on TV talk shows was their heroine. Her initial success only reinforced what they believed from the beginning—that she was a real find. *Their* find. As Barbra honed her craft, mass acceptance followed, but many fervently held on to the past. *Funny Girl*'s success in Hollywood was fine with them at first, but she wasn't supposed to *stay* in Hollywood. And the longer she did, the more she began to appeal to a broader base of fans, the greater the danger of her "specialness" wearing off for those early supporters. It was an inevitable separation of ways, but no less disheartening for those who simply wanted someone to follow in Judy Garland's stead. Many in this contingent preferred the elegant, demanding diva of *Funny Lady* to the frizzy-haired, braless, pop-singing Esther Hoffman of *A Star Is Born*. Other fans, however, were more accepting—indeed encouraging—of Barbra's desire to expand and refine her image as an entertainer and as a woman.

Part of the "Streisand mystique" is a genius for exploiting what the public thinks it knows about her. In *A Star Is Born* the audience tapped into some of Streisand's powerful emotions: the pain she might have felt about her star eclipsing Elliott Gould's (when she wanted so much for *him*); her terror of performing in front of a hostile audience; her desire to be taken seriously as a contemporary musical force; her need to have her thoughtful opinions respected; her feelings about the highs and lows of her relationship with Jon; even her delayed anger over the death of her father. As an actress, singer, and contributor to the film, she brought an immediacy to it that was hard to simply write into the script. Audiences could believe what was happening because they knew it had, in all likelihood, happened to Barbra. If, as Sally Kirkland observed, "[Barbra's] life is the act," much of that act was nakedly visible in *A Star Is Born,* and millions of young moviegoers—many seeing their first Streisand picture—responded enthusiastically, just as their older siblings (or parents) had to *Funny Girl*.

Critics were eager to tear *A Star Is Born* to pieces for being too much, too little, too stupid, too glossy, too tame. Its successes were mentioned grudgingly, if at all; few were willing to admit that what they observed to be the film's flaws were incurred by its bravery and that it was possible that the music, the romantic chemistry between Barbra and Kris, and the story's contemporary sensibility combined to create box-office magic. Produced for several hundred thousand dollars less than the financially disappointing 1954 version, the picture grossed $9.5 million its first nine days of release. Exhibitors were ecstatic. What made them even happier was that the film held up eight, ten, twelve weeks after its opening.

At awards time, *Star* took home five Golden Globes (Best Musical, Best Actress, Best Actor, Best Original Score, and Best Song). In its predictably superior way, however, the Academy delegated most of its recognition to nominations in the technical area: Best Cinematography, Sound, Original Song, and Original Song Score and/or Its Adaptation. "Evergreen", which Barbra performed on the Oscar telecast on March 28, 1977, proved to be the only winner among the nominees.

By then, even the industry snub didn't seem to matter. Aside from the film's success at the box office, what was important was that the experience woke Barbra up to her own creative potential. "*A Star Is Born* was the beginning of Barbra's examining her own power," Jon says. "It was a discovery period for her. And she started to realize that she could do it; she could take control of her life. I was the tool, in a way. The halfback. I was the one who ran interference for her, because there were a lot of changes she wanted to make, but she couldn't always articulate [them]. . . . I remember Jane Fonda calling her up after she saw the film and saying, 'Congratulations. Not only for the movie, but you are leading the way for all of us.' . . . In retrospect, I have to say that the most creative experience I've had in my life to date is *A Star Is Born*."

The passage of time has done little to ameliorate the film's inconsistencies. The superficial depiction of the "rock-and-roll lifestyle" and the script's feminist underpinnings have, like some of the hairstyles and costumes, dated badly. However, the sexual chemistry between the costars remains potent, and in terms of Streisand's musical performances, "Evergreen" lives up to its name, and the concert sequences still deliver a charismatic punch.

REVIEWS

"... a controversial, wonderfully excessive and often truly touching version of this sentimental classic. Ms. Streisand's magical presence spreads over the cinematic landscape like an iridescent mist. Sometimes she enchants, sometimes she disenchants ... [the] romantic moments are wondrous to see. When she connects, Streisand has an unholy allure, and Kris is probably the gentlest, sexiest man on screen in a decade. Let's just say that Barbra and Jon have made a fascinating, if imperfect, movie that's destined to be gold at the box office."

COSMOPOLITAN

"If there's anything worse than the noise and stench that rises from that record album, it's the movie itself. It's an unsalvagable disaster... . Every aspect of the classic story has been thrashed, along with the dialogue ... this is why Hollywood is in the toilet. What the hell does Barbra Streisand know about directing or editing a movie? Nobody at the studio ever saw any rushes or had any idea what was going on until the film was finished.... The result is a junk heap of boring ineptitude."

NEW YORK DAILY NEWS

"Let's not mince any words, okay? A Star Is Born is a great, big, thundering hit—and a highly satisfying movie to boot. Barbra Streisand simply doesn't know the meaning of the word fear, or else, she's so sure of her massive talent that she's willing to gamble and possibly make a fool of herself. The lady has guts. Whatever it is she does, it works. The finest compliment I can offer is that, without her, there would be no A Star Is Born. She's totally fascinating to watch, unforgettable and, again, probably the bravest soul at work in films today."

PHILADELPHIA DAILY NEWS

Recording the soundtrack album.

143

The Main Event
(1979)

A Warner Bros./First Artists Release

CAST

Barbra Streisand (*Hillary Kramer*); Ryan O'Neal (*Eddie "Kid Natural" Scanlon*); Paul Sand (*David*); Whitman Mayo (*Percy*); Patti D'Arbanville (*Donna*); Chu Chu Malave (*Luis*); Richard Lawson (*Hector Mantilla*); James Gregory (*Leo Gough*).

CREDITS

Producers: Jon Peters, Barbra Streisand; executive producers: Howard Rosenman, Renee Missel; director: Howard Zieff; assistant directors: Gary Daigler, Pat Kehoe; screenplay: Gail Parent, Andrew Smith; music supervisor: Gary LeMel; music: Michael Melvoin ("The Main Event" written by Paul Jabara, Bruce Roberts; "Fight" written by Paul Jabara, Bob Esty; medley performed by Barbra Streisand, produced by Bob Esty); music editor: William Saracino; production designer: Charles Rosen; cinematographer: Mario Tosi; film editor: Edward Warschilka; casting: Diane Crittenden, Karen Rea. Running time: 112 minutes.

The box-office success of *A Star Is Born* was the end of the battle but not the war for Streisand and Peters. Jon produced a series of financially—and sometimes even critically—successful films, including *Eyes of Laura Mars*. But the hairdresser jokes didn't stop for years to come, and they were only negated by perseverance and hard work.

While Jon planned his filmmaking future, Barbra, depleted from three years' work on *Star*, looked forward to a year's vacation, disrupted only by the demands of her hotter-than-ever recording career. The discussions about how to follow up on the film didn't stop, however. There was *Loveland*, a contemporary musical to be produced at Universal; a remake of the M-G-M classic *The Women*, with Diane Keaton and Raquel Welch

mentioned as costars; *Dead: A Love Story*, the true story of convicted murderess Ruth Snyder; *Fancy Hardware*, about "an ERA lady of the '20s"; and Paramount wanted her back for *Foul Play*. None of the projects were sufficiently developed for Barbra to make a commitment, and after a while she wondered if she ever would.

"What am I doing? Why am I not working?" she asked Sydney Pollack rhetorically. "What am I saving myself for? . . . So, every picture won't be great. . . . I just sit and wait and wait and wait—for what? For Chekhov to come along? For Shakespeare to come along? I'm getting older, and there are a million things I want to do. *What* am I saving myself for?" Indeed, Barbra had often said publicly that she yearned to play "the classics," the time-honored heroines she had first discovered as a youngster newly bewitched by the theater. But no one was offering her a chance to play Medea. Although strong roles for women had become slightly more available by the late seventies, they were still scarce, particularly for a superstar who was considered as much a conglomerate as an actress. And conglomerates must, for the most part, create their own business.

She and Jon had hoped to get their next coproduction in front of the cameras by the spring of 1978. Spring came and went without a starting date, but Barwood did have at least two prospects in development. One was *Yentl, the Yeshiva Boy*. The other was a comedy about the world of boxing written by Gail Parent (best known for her satirical work on the cult television comedy *Mary Hartman, Mary Hartman*) and Andrew Smith, who once boxed under the name Kid Natural. The project

"Kid Natural" meets the "Lady from Beverly Hills."

originated at M-G-M two years earlier, but rewrites and casting setbacks had forced *Knockout* into a turnaround; M-G-M dropped it. Producer Renee Missel sent a script to agent Sue Mengers, who liked the story enough to suggest it as a possibility for Barbra's next feature. Barwood bought the screenplay. After a succession of writers, Parent and Smith were called back in to refocus the script, which centered on Hillary Kramer, a sophisticated businesswoman who loses her perfume empire and is left with only one asset—a contract with an over-the-hill boxer whom she forces to fight again in the hope of recouping some of her losses. Predictably, Hillary and the Kid wind up a love match after countless verbal—and even physical—skirmishes in and out of the boxing ring.

Ryan O'Neal, who had recently bowed out of M-G-M's remake of *The Champ* due to a dispute with director Franco Zeffirelli, was the only actor considered for the role of the former boxer turned driving instructor in *The Main Event*, as the script was retitled. He had been offered the part when it was still attached to M-G-M, and Goldie Hawn and Diana Ross were looking at the female lead. A former Golden Glove boxer, O'Neal was one of the few stars who could hold his own in the ring as well as on-screen, and Barbra was adamant that she would do the film only if he agreed to do it as well. "Because, Ryan, if you don't want to do the part," she told him over the phone, "I don't want to make the picture." "If you're in it," the actor responded, "I'll do it." O'Neal, who hadn't had a solid hit in five years, was set to play Eddie "Kid Natural" Scanlon in April 1978.

After years of observing movie technicians at work and formulating her own ideas about film-making—topped off by the experience of producing *A Star Is Born*—directing was certainly

something on Barbra's mind. Patrick Kehoe, one of the assistant directors on *The Main Event,* says that Barbra mentioned to him that the original plan was for her to helm the comedy. Only after she decided that there wasn't enough time to prepare—and perhaps realizing that the property wasn't worthy of the effort—did she assign another director. "I suppose she felt she couldn't prepare as an actress and also as a director in the time that was available," says Kehoe.

Howard Zieff, whose direction of the battle-of-the-sexes comedy *House Calls* Barbra admired, was hired. Streisand envisioned making a film that was reminiscent of the harder-edged comedies of the late 1930s and 1940s. As with *What's Up, Doc?* she screened many of those cinema classics for the writers. "[Barbra] wanted them to see that we wanted more than just laughs," Jon said. "We wanted it to be funny and real." An important part of that realism was the casting of secondary roles. Jeff Goldblum was going to play David, Hillary's mournful ex-husband and lawyer, but on film he looked too young to have been married to Barbra, so the part went to comic actor Paul Sand, who, perhaps intentionally, reminded some observers of Elliott Gould. Whitman Mayo signed on as the Kid's trainer, Percy; James Gregory would portray crusty fight promoter Leo Gough; and Patti D'Arbanville won the role of the Kid's spandex-clad girlfriend, Donna.

Comfortably budgeted at $7 million, *The Main Event* was scheduled to begin production on October 2, 1978. As the starting date approached, the screenplay still hadn't been firmed; it was thought that keeping the story open for change might further improve its character and tone. Parent and Smith remained on standby throughout filming, often rewriting entire scenes in marathon sessions at Barbra's house the night before or on the set while the crews prepared the next shot. "Barbra wasn't just lounging around like some old-time movie star, saying, 'Write me something clever,'" said Smith. "She was *there* with us, improvising and suggesting lines."

147

Filming began on location at the famed Main Street gym in one of the grimier neighborhoods of downtown Los Angeles and moved on to an equally physical atmosphere at Gilda's, a posh exercise salon in Beverly Hills. Zieff and company kept the production out on location as much as possible. A house on the beach at Malibu provided a backdrop for a disaster of a fund-raising party for the Kid, and a residential neighborhood gained an unusual tenant when the crew constructed the boxing glove–shaped Knockout Driving Academy on one quiet street. There Hillary and the Kid had an opportunity to act out their aggression-attraction. "Men and women are always fighting, so why not physicalize it?" Barbra contemplated. "We had to figure out a setup for it, so we figured we'd have them pose for publicity pictures—the two of them in boxing gloves." Demonstrating the punch toward the camera, Barbra would describe the sequence to Zieff as "a sexual dance . . . man and woman stalking each other."

During its ten-week schedule, *The Main Event* production crew went into the studio to film a couple of scenes at the Hollywood General lot. The rest of the time, they took advantage of good weather in a variety of Southern California locations. They also shot eight days at Cedar Lake, near Big Bear in the San Bernardino mountains, two hours east of Los Angeles, where a picturesque early snowfall forced them to do a quick rewrite on the training-camp scenes.

Back in Hollywood, tensions escalated somewhat as Barbra tried to funnel her ideas through a by-now-reluctant collaborator. "Howard knew it was a hybridized kind of direction, that Barbra's opinions counted for a great deal and one couldn't dismiss it," assistant director Kehoe says. But in that acknowledgment there may have been a feeling that his position as director had been neutralized. Ryan O'Neal contrasted the experience with his past teaming with Barbra. "In *What's Up, Doc?* we did what we were told. Peter Bogdanovich ran the show," he told Rex Reed. "This time we tried all kinds of things. [Barbra] played the Bogdanovich role. Howard Zieff was under lots of pressure; I think he held up pretty well."

Well aware that she wasn't working with a world-class script, Barbra encouraged suggestions from anyone that might improve a scene. Actor Richard Lawson, who portrayed the Kid's boxing nemesis, Hector Mantilla, recalled improvising a scene with sportscaster Brent Musberger. "The lines were basically there," he said, "but the imitation Barbra did of my accent was improvisational. The scene took on a life of its own. It was written as a straight interview, but the whole aspect of her falling asleep and Ryan waking her up and of her calling Musberger 'Brett' and 'Burt'—all of that was total improvisation."

Assistant director Pat Kehoe, who later worked with Steven Spielberg on *The Color Purple,* joined the production at this stage. He feels that the mood on the set "wasn't tension so much as a kind of benign exasperation that this was the way it was gonna be. There were a couple of heads operating the body, which happens in film with unfortunate frequency. . . . Barbra, from my brief experience with her, was an extremely professional person. She's a perfectionist and has some interesting ideas. She's like Spielberg, in a way. If she has an idea a few minutes before the start of the shot, she'll articulate the idea with maybe a thorough knowledge of what the ramifications of enunciating the idea might be in terms of what you have to do to make it work. . . . If she's aggressive, she's aggressive in a very understated kind of way. At least she was on that picture. . . . She was the shining star . . . one of the glimmering highlights of my brief association with that picture. Because, I'll tell you, the rest of it was pretty ragtag."

The three major fight sequences were shot at the Olympic Auditorium in mid-December 1978. Streisand and O'Neal found working together again to be a special kind of shorthand. "It's so good to have somebody who understands the plot and understands your character as well as her own," Ryan said. "This was not an easy part for me to play." O'Neal had lost approximately forty pounds and boxed over 150 rounds with former champ Joe Torres and Hedgemon Lewis, a boxer O'Neal was sponsoring, in preparation for the role. With as many as five cameras going simultaneously to capture the action, O'Neal boxed his way through his final scenes.

Or so he thought. After principal photography had been completed, Barbra decided there was one scene left to film. Not everyone agreed with her, so she went back and shot it herself. "I just didn't think the relationship had solidified," she explained. "It didn't culminate in something more tangible than just going to bed with each other the night before, which is a very funny scene, but one

Barbra enjoys a few punches between scenes at the Main Street Gym in downtown Los Angeles.

has to confront the other person sooner or later." The morning-after scene, though lacking in subtlety in its depiction of expected male and female role-playing, became an audience favorite.

After the holidays, Zieff commenced work on his cut of the film. "Barbra always has final say on her movies," he said in 1979. "I was optimistic that my final cut would be good enough to prevail. As it turned out, I was right." A year and a half later, however, after the reviews had criticized some of the nonsensical plotting, the director would state that although Streisand was initially "very charming and seductive . . . she just took over the editing and cut the film to her own purpose." Reviews of Zieff's 1981 hit, *Private Benjamin,* would note the

very same structural problems: inconsistencies in character and a disappointing finale.

Barbra was discouraged from singing a ballad for the film's title song and was steered instead to songwriters Bob Esty, Paul Jabara, and Bruce Roberts, who had among them written disco hits for Donna Summer and Cher. Barbra vacillated about the resulting composition, "The Main Event/Fight," until she was convinced by her twelve-year-old son, who loved the song, to record her first dance-style single in years. (Barbra did record a ballad version of the song for the film's soundtrack album.) Esty makes note of the one time he saw something close to "the Streisand I had heard about. . . . We were at Todd-AO looking

149

Hillary signs away her perfume empire as her ex-husband stands behind her.

at the rough cut of the movie, and I said, 'Gee, it's a shame that after all this work it's going to be in mono.' And she said, 'What do you mean mono?' And I said, 'Well, the movie's in mono,' and she freaked out. It was explained to her that at the first meetings they had regarding the technical end of the movie it was decided, since it wasn't a musical, they were going to do it in mono because it was cheaper. She was appalled. They said, 'Don't worry, don't worry. [The song is] going to be released as a record, and people can play it all they want in stereo. It'll be on the radio in stereo.' And she was appeased, but she [felt] that the song had better be stereo if she was going to bother singing it. She was very involved in the scoring aspect and was very particular about what went into the movie."

Supported by an $8 million advertising campaign that included a provocative Scavullo-shot poster featuring Barbra and Ryan nose to nose in sexy boxing attire, *The Main Event* hit eleven hundred theaters nationwide on June 22, 1979. Critically, it was a split decision, but financially the

comedy established itself as a champ—bolstered by the success of Barbra's recording of the title song, which hit number three on *Billboard*'s singles chart.

Although it served its purpose as a summer hit, *The Main Event* proved largely unsatisfying, even for many Streisand devotees. Perhaps because several scenes were written, rewritten, or improvised at the last minute, there is a general inconsistency to the picture that is often more exasperating than humorous. In particular, Hillary Kramer—even allowing for the fish-out-of-water conceit—is rife with wildly varying character traits; efficiently commanding as a perfume tycoon, she is reduced to bubbleheaded incompetence when placed in the prizefighting arena. In addition, although she flaunts a finely toned figure, Barbra often looks frowzy or hard in the film, a result perhaps of the strain of the production. (Oddly, such had not been the case with *A Star Is Born*, in which she had photographed radiantly despite the overwhelming pressures she was facing.) Of course,

her performance is not completely devoid of charm or comic expertise, and she and Ryan have a pleasing on-screen chemistry, but the effervescence of their *What's Up, Doc?* teaming is lacking.

The Main Event completed Barbra's three-picture commitment to First Artists. By 1979, the production company had diversified its interests, establishing a music-publishing company and a television production arm, negotiating to buy a hotel in Atlantic City and a casino in London, and purchasing a sportswear company. But while all three original partners expressed an interest in continuing their affiliation, First Artists had seemingly lost interest in its stars. Steve McQueen sued the company in 1976 when it failed to give a go-ahead to one of his productions. Dustin Hoffman lost control of both his films in 1978 and was forced to file suit. Barwood subsequently disassociated itself from First Artists and reassigned several projects then in development to Jon Peters.

REVIEWS

"Though she has proved her ability to handle dramatic roles in films such as The Way We Were *and* A Star Is Born, *Miss Streisand's real métier is comedy. Given material suited to her particular brand of Jewish humor (similar in its self-mockery to Woody Allen's), she can keep an audience rolling in the aisles for hours. And the material provided her here is the best she's had since* The Owl and the Pussycat. *As for Mr. O'Neal, the film has given him the chance to cast aside the gee-whiz, wet-behind-the-ears image that has plagued so many of his performances, and reveal himself as an actor of range with undeniable comic gifts."*

BALTIMORE SUN

"Almost as mysterious as Streisand's attraction to such a lackluster script is the overall dimness of the movie. It is one of the tackiest looking major films in years, from Streisand's wardrobe to the uniformly dull locations and the cheap looking sets. . . . It's time for Streisand to get back to work with an important director on worthy material. Her popularity may prevent The Main Event *from meeting the dire box-office fate it deserves, but it cannot long insulate her from the withering blasts of such fourth rate work."*

PITTSBURGH POST GAZETTE

151

All Night Long
(1981)

A Universal Pictures Release

CAST

Gene Hackman (*George Dupler*); Barbra Streisand (*Cheryl Gibbons*); Diane Ladd (*Helen Dupler*); Dennis Quaid (*Freddie Dupler*); Kevin Dobson (*Bobby Gibbons*); William Daniels (*Richard H. Copleston*); Terry Kiser (*Ultra-Save Day Manager*); Vernee Watson (*Emily*); Chris Mulkey (*Russell Munk*).

CREDITS

Producers: Leonard Goldberg, Jerry Weintraub; associate producers: Terrance A. Donnelly, Fran Roy; director: Jean-Claude Tramont; assistant director: Terrence Donnelly; screenplay: W. D. Richter; music: Ira Newborn, Richard Hazzard ("Carelessly Tossed" composed by Alan Lindgren; "Cheryl's Theme" composed by Dave Grusin); production designer: Peter Jamison; unit production managers: Robert L. Brown, Hap Weyman; costume designer: Albert Wolsky; cinematography: Philip Lathrop; set decorator: Linda Spheeris; film editor: Marion Rothman; casting: Anita Dann. Running time: 88 minutes.

Any discussion of *The Main Event* and *All Night Long* inevitably becomes intertwined with Barbra's preproduction work on *Yentl*. It was during *The Main Event* that her resolve to film the Isaac Bashevis Singer short story was fortified and found realistic dimensions. Moreover, without her eternal commitment to *Yentl*, in all likelihood she would not have made *All Night Long*.

Even as *The Main Event* was playing in theaters around the country, the talk in Hollywood was that production on "Barbra's Folly" would start the following March. Barbra's seemingly endless research for *Yentl* led her to ask Rusty Lemorande, Jon Peters's executive in charge of creative development, to accompany her on a tour of eastern Europe in late 1979. "She wanted to make sure

[her vision of *Yentl*'s locales] could really exist on-screen," he says. A last-minute change in schedule kept her in Los Angeles, but Lemorande went to Europe and took countless photos of authentic locations in Hungary, Austria, Czechoslovakia, Romania, Poland, and Yugoslavia.

But it was just the tip of the iceberg in terms of her research. There were countless museums to visit; rabbis, historians, and scholars to consult; books from around the world to read. *Yentl* went into "hiatus" to allow further development. Barbra's advisers became concerned that she not allow herself to remain off movie screens as long as her previous sabbaticals. "You shouldn't be out of the system that long," they warned her. But where in Hollywood does one find a ready-made project for one hardworking, albeit highly idiosyncratic, actress?

"STREISAND REPLACES LISA EICHHORN IN 'NIGHT': MENGERS IN SHADOWS." The announcement in the trade papers on May 13, 1980, surprised even the most well connected Hollywood insiders, who knew that long before Barbra's involvement *All Night Long* suffered a series of creative and financial problems. Its checkered past began in 1978 when director Jean-Claude Tramont sold 20th Century-Fox on the idea of doing a film about dissidents—which, in turn, became a story about people who work at night. Tramont turned to W. D. Richter to write the screenplay. Richter delineated a charming, offbeat tale of a middle-aged "man in revolt" who quits his job of twenty years after being demoted to manager of an all-night drugstore; he becomes an inventor and leaves his wife for a younger woman, who had

been his son's lover. "What interested me was this man Dupler, going from suburbia to the city to find out what was important to him," Tramont told *Rolling Stone.* "It's as if now living in the city is seen as living on the fringe." Both the director and writer concurred in their selection of Gene Hackman as George Dupler. A script was forwarded to him via his agent, Sue Mengers, who also happened to be Mrs. Tramont. Anxious to get her number-one client back in front of the camera, Mengers sent a copy of the screenplay to Barbra. There were two female leads in the cast, neither of which seemed suited to Streisand. Barbra passed.

A few months later, *All Night Long* (then known as *Night People*) went into turnaround at Fox and was eventually picked up by producers Leonard Goldberg and Jerry Weintraub, who had recently aligned themselves with Universal Pictures. *Night People* was budgeted at $3.5 million. According to William Goldman in *Adventures in the Screen Trade*, "Universal didn't like it, felt they couldn't sell it, didn't want to do it. But [because of their deal with Goldberg and Weintraub], they were not in a position to pass."

Hackman's casting was announced in December 1980. The actor, returning from a self-imposed two-year hiatus ("I got tired of doing lousy pictures for the money," he said), loved the script and was more than willing to take a gamble on a small film. He offered to work on the picture for less than his usual salary if he could negotiate a percentage of the gross. Whatever they felt about the film's prospects, Universal had no intention of giving up its points in the picture; they paid Hackman his usual salary. The budget was now approximately $4.5 million. Lisa Eichhorn, the young actress who captured Richard Gere's heart in *Yanks*, was signed to portray Cheryl Gibbons, the "other woman" in George's life. Diane Ladd, Kevin Dobson, Dennis Quaid, and William Daniels completed the talented ensemble. French star Annie Giradot consented to a cameo appearance.

Filming began on April 14, 1980. "Three weeks into production, I parted ways with Tak Fujimoto, whose cinematography in *Melvin and Howard* I admired tremendously," the Belgian-born Tramont revealed the following year. "He had very definite ideas about giving the film a grittier look. Philip Lathrop, a craftsman of the old school . . . gave me equally 'realistic' images that were still saturated with color. I think of America as saturated with color."

Scarcely a week later, Lisa Eichhorn found herself a casualty as well. No official explanation would be forthcoming regarding what prompted her firing. *Daily Variety* reported that "inside sources indicate there was substantial friction between Tramont and Eichhorn." Tramont told journalists in 1981 that the actress simply wasn't working out, and since she had just begun shooting her scenes that week, it seemed better to correct the error before more confusion ensued. "The part was too much of a stretch for Lisa," he stated in the *Los Angeles Herald Examiner.* "It's no reflection on her acting ability."

Voicing the same kind of criticism that Barbra first encountered in Hollywood, the *Los Angeles Times* would uncover one source who insisted, "Lisa was very difficult on the set, objecting to things like camera angles as if she were . . . a star like Streisand." Another anonymous voice said Eichhorn's role "had an earthiness to it. Lisa is very ethereal; she has metaphysical qualities to her, and her part had to be more forthright." Costar Hackman refused to join the chorus of put-downs. "[Lisa's] got enough problems," he told columnist Marilyn Beck, "and I've been fired myself [on *The Graduate*]. I know how it hurts."

Eichhorn didn't wait long to tell her side of the story. "What happened to me on *All Night Long* came as such a shock. I'd already done three and a half weeks' work on the film when, out of the blue, the director called and said, 'I don't think it's working. You're just not funny. We've got someone else.' I'd never been fired before, so I called my lawyer and agent and asked: Can they do that? They assured me they could. And then I found out I'd been replaced by Barbra Streisand. I'd been so afraid it would be one of my peers, which would have just devastated me.

"I was in tears. It was so awful. But I did ask to see the dailies—something I hadn't done when we were making the film. They arranged that, and quite honestly I thought it was some of the best work I'd ever done."

Rumors flew fast and furiously. Was Streisand, recently named the National Association of Theater Owners' "Star of the Decade," approached before Eichhorn was let go? Did she usurp a role before Eichhorn's release was considered? Was she doing her friends a favor by jumping in to "save" an endangered production? Or was the surprise casting the behind-the-scenes work of Mengers, whose agency (ICM) represented Streisand, Hackman, *and* Tramont? William Goldman would later speculate that the news of Barbra's new interest in the role was simply too important for producer Goldberg to suppress. He had to tell Universal. "Now they love the picture," he wrote. "The sales force loves it, the advertising people are in ecstasy, fabulous." Such a scenario, while not implausible, would be virtually impossible to confirm. In May 1980, most of the blame was being laid in Eichhorn's lap.

"As far as I'm concerned, there were no problems on the picture. I loved working with Gene Hackman, and I got on well with Jean-Claude Tramont," Eichhorn insisted. "I read somewhere that I was supposed to have walked out because of 'artistic differences.' That's not true. When I got to New York . . . I read in a newspaper that I'd kept walking off the set and asking about camera angles. When I got to London, I read that I'd been conceited, temperamental, and difficult. The further away I went from Los Angeles, the worse I seemed to get." How much the firing had to do with Eichhorn's subsequent fade into acting obscurity is anyone's guess. (Over a decade later, in one of her only public statements about the picture, Barbra offered no insight into the Eichhorn controversy: "I made *All Night Long* because I was writing *Yentl* and I was so lonely in this room writing. I needed to act, so I took this job because it was for six weeks.")

Of equal importance in the entertainment business was the number of precedents *All Night Long* would set in Barbra's career. First, she insisted on second billing for her first supporting role in a motion picture. "It's mostly my film," said Hackman. "She has five or six good scenes, and that's it. It would be unfair to audiences to bill her in such a way that suggests this is Barbra's movie. It's about my character, not hers." In addition, Barbra's salary ($4 million plus 15 percent of the gross for twenty-four days' work) would set a new level for female stars. She'd made more money before, but never for a project she hadn't developed herself.

Production on *All Night Long* shut down temporarily to allow the actors and director time to rehearse and work through the new script. Richter's story had already been fleshed out to fea-

ture the female role more prominently. The producers anticipated further modification "but nothing substantial." Barbra intended to play Cheryl Gibbons as written. Hackman, who had known her ever since his lean days in New York with roommates Dustin Hoffman and Robert Duvall, wasn't afraid that Streisand would take over the picture. "My opinion was asked about her joining the cast. I gave my okay, and I'm sure everything will be fine," he said. Most of the rewrite focused on the third act, where George and Cheryl come to a final realization about themselves, their lives, and their complicated relationship.

As the screenplay was examined to accommodate the addition of a new actress, Hackman's "financial arrangements" were also renegotiated. The nice, small film was now catapulted into the $10–$12 million range. (That figure also included Eichhorn's $250,000 payoff and the retainer salaries paid to the crew during shutdown.)

Principal photography resumed June 9 when Barbra reported for her first day and night of work on location in South Pasadena. Despite the saturation of hurt feelings over the production's initial problems, filming with the revised cast progressed smoothly. Barbra had very quickly—and very completely—acquainted herself with every facet of her character. Academy Award–winning costume designer Albert Wolsky, who also worked with her on *Up the Sandbox,* remembered her single-minded approach to the role. Accordingly, he designed clothes that Cheryl, not his star, would wear. "[Cheryl's] a woman with strawberry blond hair that's always too done, fingernails that are always too brightly polished, clothes that are always a little too tight, a little too young," Wolsky noted. "The clothes are not expensive, but Barbra doesn't care about that. If she loves it, she doesn't care if it costs two dollars or two thousand dollars."

Draped in lavender velour and gold chains, smoking lavender-tinted cigarettes and speaking in a childish whisper, Barbra seemed to enjoy her brief respite as a working actress. (Five years after the fact, she told an amusing story about donning Cheryl's overaccessorized wardrobe and blond wig during preproduction and, hoping to go unnoticed, casually strolling into the Palomino, a popular country-western bar in North Hollywood. She wished to observe the social atmosphere in which her character would feel most comfortable. For all of her tacky camouflage, though, she was recog-

Gene Hackman and Barbra laugh it up amid the disarray of the Ultra-Save Drugstore. During filming at this South Pasadena location, one confused local resident wandered on to the set and attempted to purchase something from the shelves.

nized instantly, leading her to fret that the crowd would now think Barbra Streisand has terrible taste on top of everything else they might have heard about her.)

Richter's surreal, suburban temptress was just the kind of acting stretch she had been pining for: someone totally different from the stereotypical, self-possessed Streisand character. Certainly Cheryl couldn't have been less like Hillary Kramer or the upcoming, androgynous Yentl. The outgoing, ever-congenial tootsie also appeared to have a positive effect on Barbra's on-set demeanor. Relieved of outside production obligations, she enjoyed remaining on the set (even when she wasn't needed) to visit with friends or socialize with the crew—while Hackman fought his way through the movie. "As soon as I [returned to Hollywood], I realized why I left," he said. "I like this film, but the waiting around has already driven me crazy."

Dennis Quaid, who played Hackman's affable but somewhat thickheaded son (and Cheryl's paramour), Freddie, admitted he wasn't much of a Streisand fan prior to *All Night Long*. "I was dreading working with her because I'd heard stories about how difficult she is to work with," he admitted. "I was really surprised, because she was helpful on the set." Kevin Dobson, essaying the role of Bobby, Cheryl's dominating fireman-husband, likewise told the press that he witnessed "nothing but the utmost professionalism" from Barbra. The actor, who once worked as an extra on *Funny Girl* and *The French Connection* (the film that won Hackman his Oscar), found his *All Night Long* experience very rewarding. "[Barbra's] a doll. She's been really delightful. I've had such rapport with her . . . to the point where we sit down together and create, talk about the part and how to make it better. Let me tell you, she's all right."

The producer and director had determined

George encourages Cheryl to drop her glitzy facade and find the confidence to simply be herself.

that the entire picture was to be shot on location. Most was filmed in a vacant supermarket building that had been realistically converted into a twenty-four-hour Ultra-Save drugstore, replete with $750,000 worth of merchandise. After hours, the filmmakers also took over the Salt Shaker, a family restaurant conveniently located across the street. A remodeled tract house one hour north of Hollywood, in Valencia, became Bobby and Cheryl's indistinct home. There the principals struggled to look comfortable in the sweltering 106-degree heat. George's loft was re-created in downtown Los Angeles.

As the final days of principal photography approached in July, there was a great deal of concern that the picture be finished before an impending actors' strike. The only remaining scenes on Barbra's schedule were set to be shot at a Van Nuys fire station. On July 18, as Hackman discussed his role with Tramont, a bemused Streisand took a tour of the station. The fire pole was of particular interest to her. Firemen supervising the shoot had been very strict about not letting others slide down the pole, but Barbra was being asked to by the script. "Is it safe? How do you do it?" she asked one fireman. Looking down the pole from her second-floor perch, she obviously wasn't crazy about the idea. "Uh-uh. Not me. I don't think I could do it," she said. "I have a weak stomach." She got a reprieve.

At midnight on July 20, negotiations between producers and the Screen Actors Guild broke down, and a walkout was officially declared. "Conspicuously hard hit by the strike is Universal's reported $14 million Barbra Streisand starrer, *All Night Long*," *Daily Variety* reported. The film itself was due to wrap in four days, but Barbra only had one day left. Although small independent productions were signing interim waivers to allow their films to continue shooting, there was no chance of that with *All Night Long* completely tied up at one of the major studios. Additionally, since the most heated strike arguments revolved around residuals on the projected revenues for home video, cable, and pay television and

Universal, as the biggest supplier of television product, was contesting what they perceived to be excessive payments, there wasn't much hope that the matter would be settled quickly. Time, in fact, was on the side of the studios. With sufficient product in their libraries, they could afford to hold out; the actors might not be able to.

Suddenly, all of Barbra's plans were threatened as well. The delay allowed her to return her attention to finishing the *Yentl* script, but with her outstanding commitment requiring that she stay in Los Angeles, it put *Yentl*'s January/February 1981 starting date in serious jeopardy. Goldberg and Weintraub's plans to get *All Night Long* out in time for Oscar consideration also proved futile, and especially agonizing for Gene Hackman.

Following settlement of the strike in late October, Barbra finally slid down the fire pole and out of the film. Unfortunately, neither she nor the producers were able to shake their troubles off with as much ease. At the end of the year, a poorly edited teaser trailer actually drew boos and snickers at local theaters. Scattered previews throughout the country indicated that the movie was too long at 100 minutes and the elements of the comedy needed to be refocused. "These days, American anger is tinged with bitterness," the director bemoaned. "At our sneak previews, the audience I thought would react strongest to George Dupler's revolt—men over twenty-five—seemed to resent the movie!"

Universal's strategy to compensate for this didn't show much faith in the charming, unpretentious European-style film Tramont and Co. had attempted to make. *All Night Long* was, against everyone's wishes, touted as a zany Streisand comedy; the promotional angle shifted from Hackman to the peripheral, secondary lead. "It didn't fall into any kind of particular category they had any expertise in," Hackman said later. So Universal repackaged it as something they could comfortably exploit. The type of audience that might attend *All Night Long* was never properly addressed. Future advertising of the film would feature artwork of Barbra on the fire pole—with her skirt flying à la Marilyn Monroe in *The Seven Year Itch*—slyly evading the grasp of Hackman, Dobson, and Quaid. "She's got a way with men, and she's getting away with it . . . *All Night Long*," read the copy. Television commercials also misled audiences with a glimpse of Cheryl singing (purposefully off-key) and composing "Carelessly Tossed," a goofy county-and-western song.

The movie opened on March 6, 1981. (March was a traditionally slow moviegoing period.) Regardless of the soft competition, the film was advertised, Gene Hackman remembered, in a tiny box in the theatrical section of the *New York Times*. Ironically, just as Barbra was enjoying her greatest recording success with her *Guilty* album, she was enduring her lowest ebb as an actress. Although the movie appeared to open strongly, a distressing pattern emerged at the box office: Patrons were asking for their money back. "For most pictures, we'll have a full house and maybe one person will ask for his money back," one theater usher explained to the *New York Times*. "For this movie, there will hardly be anyone in the theater, and five or six of them will ask." *All Night Long* wasn't failing because of audience indifference but because deceptive advertising had led them to expect something the film could not deliver. "I don't think the film worked on a lot of different levels," Dennis Quaid offered, echoing the feelings of many. "In the timing of it, in the relationships. . . . It seemed long to me. It only ran an hour and a half, but it seemed like two hours and ten minutes."

Barbra bore the brunt of the criticism. "Many critics already dismiss Streisand out of hand as an overachiever whose arrogance is only equaled by the length of her boarding-room reach," the *Los Angeles Times*'s Patricia Goldstone wrote in 1979. "But that's too easy. She's entitled to more serious consideration because of her power, her phenomenal audience and the flashes of talent evident in even her worst films." Although the journalist was writing about her disappointment in *The Main Event,* her observations are valid for most of Barbra's films. This time, reviewers complained that the chemistry between Streisand and Hackman was nonexistent, that her performance was too subdued. "In most of her pictures, she's criticized for overpowering the screen," Tramont defended. "In *All Night Long* she's criticized for not overpowering the screen." Some questioned the director-star relationship. How did Tramont, a man known for writing one film (*Ash Wednesday*) and directing another (*Focal Point,* which was never released in the United States), secure this assignment? Surely the only reason Barbra did the film was due to her tie with Tramont's wife—and her agent—Sue Mengers. "My wife and I have been together for eleven years," the director said, sighing. "If she had the ability to force Barbra to do a picture with me, I wish she had used it sooner."

But there was plenty of praise, too. Supporters (Pauline Kael, Rex Reed) as well as detractors (Vincent Canby, Michael Sragow) felt that Streisand had created a rather touching, vulnerable portrait of a vague, insecure sexpot. Canby gave Barbra an offhanded compliment for playing the role with comparative modesty. "The film is

worth seeing if only to witness this ordinarily take-over kid subordinate that overwhelming public personality to the demands of a movie which, unfortunately, isn't worth the sacrifice. (Did I say sacrifice . . .)," he wrote in the *New York Times*.

With Universal's failure to capitalize on the art-film crowd, which might have embraced *All Night Long*, it was hoped that the film might recapture some of its market when it was released abroad. The movie had its European premiere at the 1982 Deauville Film Festival, and response was decidedly mixed. Shortly thereafter, it opened in London, supported by the same disastrous advertising campaign. The movie disappeared within a week. Its worldwide box office was negligible.

"Barbra called me [later] and said, 'You were well out of it, kid,' " Lisa Eichhorn told the *London Sunday Times*. "I wanted to tell her that with me it would have been a different film." It is virtually certain, however, it wouldn't have been a more commercial one. "Nobody bats a home run every time," Jon Peters said. "Barbra took a gamble, and it didn't pay off." However, one shouldn't assume that *All Night Long* was a waste of time for anyone. Back in the mainstream once again, Gene Hackman would get several more chances to explore the restless frustration of a man in his prime unable to express the full range of his talents or emotions in films like *Under Fire* and *Twice in a Lifetime*. Barbra's understated work as Cheryl Gibbons reconnected her with dramatic work in such past films as *Up the Sandbox* and *The Way We Were*. Her keen observations on the set

of *All Night Long* made the ensemble acting in *Yentl* that much easier.

It also spelled the end of Barbra's thirteen-year professional association with Sue Mengers. While a handful of insiders would speculate that her exit had to do with a dispute over ICM's entitlement to a commission—implying not only that Barbra didn't pay ICM, which she did, but that she did the film strictly as "a favor"—the stronger sentiment indicated a parting of the ways over the impending *Yentl*. By 1981 it was no secret that

Director Jean-Claude Tramont watches Gene and Barbra rehearse the film's tender love scene. "The timing may be wrong for this film," Tramont later admitted in an interview.

Barbra was absolutely determined to realize that vision despite concerned advice that it wasn't in her best interest. Those who didn't actively support that decision soon fell by the wayside, albeit temporarily.

REVIEWS

"All Night Long is one of the best, most unusual, comedies to come along in years. It has some of the same lyric buoyancy as the great romantic comedies of the '30's: it also has a serious subtext—a melancholia—that's more eloquent than many a more high-minded film. The movie keeps you in a state of gleeful, heightened expectation because, even though the middle-age-man's-blues material is familiar, the way it's been done isn't. . . . After her bombastic, emptily narcissistic performances in movies like A Star Is Born and The Main Event, this new, toned-down Streisand is a blessing. She makes us aware of how good she can be in the 'normal' range."

LOS ANGELES HERALD-EXAMINER

"I've been arguing for years that Barbra Streisand would be one of the greatest comediennes of all time if she'd just accept strong direction and not play it safe by controlling every detail of her films. Maybe I was wrong. Surely it wasn't Streisand's idea to play her character as a quiet, vacant-minded nonentity. Here's one of the most powerful personalities in movie history, and she doesn't have a single scene where she lets loose. . . . The result is a complete waste of her time."

CHICAGO SUN-TIMES

"There were times I couldn't tell whether Streisand was uncomfortable with the confused, frightened character she was playing or trying to indicate Cheryl's discomfort with herself. It's a Marilyn Monroe flower-child, crazy-lady role, and there was a certain amount of discomfort in it for us when Monroe did it, too—but a different kind of discomfort. The character came out of Monroe; with Streisand, it isn't clear what it comes out of. She's a thin-faced, waiflike question mark walking through the movie, and you can't quite grasp why George Dupler, who is very bright, would respond to Cheryl's bleached-blond tackiness."

NEW YORKER

160

Yentl
(1983)

A Barwood Film Released Through United Artists/M-G-M

CAST

Barbra Streisand (*Yentl/Anshel*); Mandy Patinkin (*Avigdor*);
Amy Irving (*Hadass*); Nehemiah Persoff (*Papa, Reb
Mendel*); Steven Hill (*Reb Alter Vishkower*); Allan Corduner
(*Shimmele*); Ruth Goring (*Esther Rachel Vishkower*); David
DeKeyser (*Rabbi Zalman*).

CREDITS

Producer and director: Barbra Streisand; executive
producer: Larry DeWaay; coproducer: Rusty Lemorande;
assistant director: Steve Lanning; Screenplay: Jack
Rosenthal, Barbra Streisand; (based on the short story,
"Yentl, the Yeshiva Boy" by Isaac Bashevis Singer);
wedding-dance choreography: Gillian Lynne; Music: Michel
Legrand; music orchestrated and conducted by Michel
Legrand; music editors: Robin Clark, George Brand; Lyrics:
Alan and Marilyn Bergman; production design: Roy Walker;
costume designer: Judy Moorcroft; cinematography: David
Watkin; camera operator: Peter MacDonald; set decorator:
Tassa Davies; art director: Leslie Tomkins; script supervisor:
Barrie Melrose; film editor: Terry Rawlings; sound engineer:
Tim Blackhan; location managers: Jim Brennan, William
Lang; casting: Cis Corman.
Running time: 134 minutes.

In the history of Hollywood, *Yentl* must surely
come close to holding the record for longest
gestation period. Early in 1968 producer
Valentine Sherry had a copy of the short story
"Yentl, the Yeshiva Boy" delivered to Barbra, as he
thought it would make a good movie. "I made a
commitment to *Yentl* when I read the first four
words of the story," Barbra recalled. They were
four highly evocative words for her: "After her
father's death. . . ." Isaac Bashevis Singer's story
itself was about a young girl in turn-of-the-century
Poland who disguises herself as a boy in order to
enter a scholarly world forbidden to women.

Streisand immediately purchased the motion-picture rights from Sherry for her newly formed
Barwood Films.

For years, Barbra's obsession with *Yentl*
became one of Hollywood's inside jokes. An exasperated David Begelman approached his client at
a party. "You've been after us a long time to
change your image because you're tired of playing
the little Jewish girl from Brooklyn," said the
agent. "Now you want to play a Jewish boy?"
Barbra was hurt. "It's just a one-liner, and it has
no bearing on whether or not you should do the
film," Marty Erlichman assured her.

At that time, Barbra saw *Yentl* mainly as a
provocative acting vehicle. Fifteen years and
twelve movies later, she had become the film's
obsessed auteur. The intervening years had seen
the project go through many permutations as
Barbra struggled with deep-seated, mixed emotions: she was as determined as a lioness to make
the film as she envisioned it, yet she was terrified
of taking the official control that would be necessary to guarantee the fulfillment of that dream. Jon
Peters vividly recalls the moment when Barbra
announced that her decision to direct and star in
Yentl was irrevocable. It occurred during the location filming for *The Main Event* at Big Bear. "We
were standing there in the snow, and she said, 'I
hate this movie! I'm going to do *Yentl!*' and I said,
'You're not going to do it! You're not going to ruin
your life and mine! We're going to do something
else together.' I was a little domineering, I guess,
and I remember her looking at me and saying,
'Just because you said that, I'm going to do the
movie *no matter what!*'" Jon had inadvertently

given her the challenge that would carry her through the next five years of planning and executing the production.

Despite his initial opposition to the project, Peters didn't hesitate to surround Barbra with people who shared her enthusiasm for *Yentl*. Peters's associate Rusty Lemorande: "Because I was a great admirer of hers, I took it upon myself to explore more fully the projects that I knew she was passionate about. There were two: *Yentl, the Yeshiva Boy* and *Third Time Lucky*. I responded strongly to both. I thought they were both well suited to my particular image of Barbra as a star. And Jon was quite pleased to find that kind of support for her."

Support was also found in Eric Peskow and Mike Medavoy, partners in Orion Pictures, *Yentl's* home from November 1979 until the end of 1980. After a series of scripts (including drafts by Isaac Singer and playwright Leah Napolin) proved unacceptable to Streisand, Medavoy suggested that she try writing it herself. "In all honesty," says Lemorande, "I don't think Barbra was prepared to recognize herself as a writer. In fact, she didn't put any authorship on the very first drafts that she contributed to. She wrote out of necessity. . . . I got a tremendous lesson in writing by being sort of at the knee of this process, where she and I did a draft and then I would find it being critiqued by the likes of Paddy Chayevsky, Elaine May. . . . A lot of people were constantly giving her encouragement and opinions when she asked for them; Barbra is certainly a believer in 'Let's hear an idea and *then* decide.' But it goes both ways; they'd ask her [for opinions] as well."

During 1980 she began exploring the musical terrain with Michel Legrand and Alan and Marilyn Bergman. (It was the Bergmans who first suggested that the story be musicalized.) "The four of us were like children playing," Marilyn noted. "We videotaped the first musical performance in our living room. One day, a choreographer visited Barbra at our house just as we were blocking out the wedding scene. We gave her a costume, and she instantly became part of the videotape."

Barbra's extraordinary salary for *All Night Long* reaped some charitable benefits as well as monetary ones. In 1980 she gave fifty thousand dollars of her *All Night Long* fee to establish the Streisand Chair of Cardiology at UCLA's School of Medicine. Another fifty thousand dollars was donated to create the Streisand Center for Jewish Cultural Arts at the Hillel Center on that university's campus. UCLA rabbis Chaim Seidler-Feller and Laura Geller were thus happy to discuss *Yentl's* theological and spiritual ideas with Streisand. "There's no doubt Barbra does view this [film] as a contribution to Jewish life," said Seidler-Feller. "She does want to make some sort of Jewish statement in an industry where there are many Jews reluctant to express their Jewishness, and I find that admirable."

During the strike-imposed hiatus in the *All Night Long* filming, Barbra and Rusty Lemorande made several trips to eastern Europe. In Czechoslovakia they shot super 8 mm footage of Barbra in costume as her male alter ego, Anshel, walking down the streets of Prague. "I always wanted to try everything out and see what the black costume looked like against the color of the walls, against the textures, the cobblestones, the light . . . the air." The tests would also help formulate many of Barbra's ideas about art direction and cinematography. On the way back to the United States, she stopped in Amsterdam, where Paul Verhoeven took her to see the Rembrandts and Brueghels at Rijak.

Upon his return, Lemorande was asked to prepare three separate budgets for the film: one with Los Angeles as the home base, with the villages of Yanev and Bashev being constructed either on the lot or at one of the studio ranches in Malibu Canyon; a second for Lake Placid, in New York; and a third for London and Czechoslovakia. "Jon Peters fought very hard to have it shot here," Lemorande recalled, "because he knew that it if weren't [based in New York or Los Angeles], he'd have trouble producing the film, because Barbra would want him over there exclusively. And even though she knew it was right aesthetically, Barbra was hesitant to film abroad. She had to be convinced that there wasn't a reason to do this . . . in her own backyard, so to speak."

On November 19, 1980, after endless discussion about location filming, Barwood turned the budget in to Orion; the company had previously indicated a cost ceiling of $13 million. That day, Vincent Canby's devastating review of *Heaven's Gate* was published in the *New York Times*. Suddenly, the studios didn't want to hear anything about movies being given budgets over $10 million, especially to novice directors operating in a foreign location. Such "unchecked power" did not make good business sense. When Jon Peters pulled out of Orion (to head PolyGram Pictures with partner Peter Guber), *Yentl* followed like an orphan child. It didn't stay there for long. "For personal reasons, we decided not to work together on this film," Barbra confided to the *Los Angeles Times.* "It was a time in my life when I needed to really be independent, both personally and professionally. I thought to myself: I have to make this picture, and I have to also be the producer." At the same time, Rusty Lemorande's status changed from executive producer to Barbra's coproducer.

Streisand gathered up her super 8 mm footage and the audiocassettes of the score and commenced pitching her labor of love to other companies. Studios formerly quite happily associated with Barbra on some of her biggest successes couldn't see past their checkbooks to give her a green light. Warner Bros., despite Barbra's impressive successes on that lot, wasn't interested; similarly, Columbia felt that the project wasn't commercial enough. Paramount passed. "It's a wonderful shaker-upper," she told the BBC, "a leveler of ego. It really puts you in your place. They say you're a 'bankable star' or whatever—so surely they'll put on something you passionately believe in. Then, when it comes time to do it, they say, 'Well . . . no,' even though I'm singing! I remember having to go into an executive's office to play them my tapes and explain the story. I felt like I was eighteen years old again and auditioning for a Broadway show. Would they like it? Would they invest some money? I had to prove myself all over again."

One of the main obstacles Streisand had to overcome was a deeply entrenched resistance to the hiring of a female director, particularly a neophyte. At the time, there were virtually none responsible for major studio releases in the United States. It hadn't always been so. In the freewheeling Hollywood of the late teens and early twenties, such women as Lois Webber were writing and directing with regularity. By the thirties, however, when the studio system's patriarchy became absolute, only Dorothy Arzner was allowed in the director's chair. She was known for guiding vehicles for Joan Crawford, Katharine Hepburn, and Rosalind Russell, but her career behind the camera was essentially over by 1943. Star-turned director Ida Lupino directed five films of varying quality beginning in 1950, but her 1966 effort, *The*

Trouble With Angels—though successful—would be her last. In the years since, women had all but disappeared from the ranks of the Directors Guild.

While Streisand was battling to get *Yentl* up and running, other actors, including Dyan Cannon, Lee Grant, and Betty Thomas, were moving into the directing arena, though with small projects and often with financial support from organizations such as the American Film Institute. And Marth Coolidge was on the brink of a breakthrough with *Valley Girl.* But, as of 1981, no female director in Hollywood history had ever tackled a project equal in scope to *Yentl.*

Late in March 1981, industry trades reported that Streisand was meeting with Norbert Auerbach and Steven Bach of United Artists. "She wants me to play her father," production executive Auerbach revealed to *Daily Variety's* Army Archerd somewhat prematurely. Bach and his staff believed *Yentl* to be risky, but Auerbach was sold on Barbra. "When she went in to play her tapes," says Lemorande, "she would hum over it if she knew that really got you charged. She knew what she was doing; [she was] putting on the disguise of being just a singer in the hopes of getting to be something else" (a ploy Yentl/Anshel would surely understand).

After visiting her at the Malibu ranch, even Bach was won over. "Like Auerbach, I fell in love," he wrote in his book *Final Cut.* "She is intelligent, professional, obsessive-compulsive, a perfectionist with a touch of parsimony, and far more attractive offscreen than on." On March 31, *Daily Variety* announced that a deal was in the offing. Ironically, the studio that had spawned *Heaven's Gate*—and ultimately quashed a number of big-budgeted Hollywood pictures—picked up *Yentl.* Equally dramatic was the fact that, after a shuffle of studio management, the agents who bought Singer's short story for Barbra in 1968 (David Begelman and Freddie Fields) were now her compatriots at the M-G-M/UA Entertainment Co.

That didn't mean, however, that Barbra didn't have to make important concessions to the studio. "I have to give up everything," she said, "I didn't get paid for writing, I got paid scale for directing. . . . I got paid much less as an actress than I did in my last film, and then I had to give back half of my salary if we went over budget." (She had already invested over $500,000 of her

Yentl takes the first step to disguise herself as a boy in order to study the Talmud. "I had a crack made in the mirror," Barbra said, "that would divide my face in half. Male and female."

own money in the project.) In exchange for a $14.5 million guaranteed budget, she also had to give up "all of my so-called power," including the director's treasured approval of final cut. Admittedly at the studio's mercy, it appeared that she would retain creative control only under the most perfect of conditions: with the film on schedule, under budget, and the director's cut certified as the accepted cut by the studio. But Streisand was poised to put her vision to the test. "Nothing mattered to me except getting this movie made," she reiterated.

An agreement was formally announced on June 22, 1981. The "as-yet-untitled" production was scheduled to be shot entirely on location in Czechoslovakia. Having to endure yet another strike—this time by the Writers Guild—Barbra returned to England to get a collaborator to help polish the screenplay. One was found in Jack Rosenthal, the writer of *The Bar Mitzvah Boy*, a popular play on London's West End. The balance of 1981 was spent assembling key members of the cast and crew. Avigdor, the romantic male lead, proved to be the most challenging because the choices were so diverse. Richard Gere's name had been introduced as early as December 1979. Gere agreed to do the picture if Barbra simply acted in it, ". . . or he'd let me direct if I didn't act." The possibility of adding Gere's raw sexuality to the lusty but brooding role of Avigdor intrigued production executives, but not enough to sweeten the deal by investing more money in the film. Other suggestions included Michael Douglas, Kevin Kline, John Shea, and even Christopher Walken. In December, Barwood and UA jointly announced that Mandy Patinkin would take the role.

Barbra saw the darkly handsome, intense actor onstage in *Evita* and in Milos Forman's *Ragtime*. They met several times throughout 1981 to discuss the script, but Patinkin held back from making a commitment without certain changes. "I thought [the character] wasn't serious enough," he told *USA Today*, "that he didn't have enough weight. We went back and forth, but the bottom line is [Barbra] was absolutely open to whatever feelings I had." The actor would further state that "almost every single thing from that initial meeting that I had any question about was satisfactorily changed by the time we shot it. So I was quite taken with how approachable and how caring she was about the piece . . . about its authenticity, on every level."

Amy Irving's experience with Barbra went a little farther back. "I used to see her (occasionally) when I was living with Steven Spielberg," she said in 1983. "Once, we spent an entire day at her ranch while she was pitching *Yentl* to him." Irritated at the time that Barbra focused most of her attention on Spielberg and couldn't remember her name, Amy soon put the incident out of her mind. "Now I realize that was evidence of Barbra's tunnel vision," she explained. "When she zeroes in on something, she can think of nothing else."

Actually, the actress Streisand and Lemorande originally thought could best project Hadass's wide-eyed innocence was Carol Kane (among other things, the star of *Hester Street*). When sentiment began to lean toward a younger leading lady, Irving was sent a copy of the screenplay. But the actress thought the character was more in line with the roles she played almost ten years earlier. "Just another sweet young thing," she thought. "I can do that standing on my head, and it's boring." She declined.

"My agent was astounded," Amy admitted. "'How dare you turn down a chance to work with Barbra Streisand! At least meet her and let her explain what she's doing.'" A meeting was arranged in which Barbra took the opportunity to describe her own feelings about Hadass. "That was more stimulating to me," Irving recalled. "I just didn't read the script well. . . . I was also very attracted by Barbra because she was so dedicated. . . . It was obvious she wasn't doing it for fame or fortune. It was something inside of her that she had to realize, and when someone asks you to help them realize their dream, you know the focus of the work is going to be something exciting."

Likewise, Nehemiah Persoff was a second choice, and another fortuitous one. (Morris Carnovsky, originally cast as Yentl's father in England, had a heart attack during a reading and passed away some time later.) Persoff, a veteran character actor, was signed after Barbra and her friend, casting director (and now Barwood producer) Cis Corman, saw his charming performance in a one-man show based on the tales of Sholem Aleichem. Once production got under way, Persoff would come to believe, as did Steven Hill (Hadass's father), that he was being entrusted with passing on the image of the Jew of that period.

He was also entrusted with the responsibility of bringing to life a rather vague, idealized character, one who only existed in Yentl's memory in the short story. Once in London, Persoff would have a pivotal conversation with Barbra regarding his role. "She was very bright and very smart about it because she didn't make me feel that I was being directed. . . . . She really told me about herself and about her relationship with her father, about her years of growing up and her frustrations. She wanted to find her father on a personal level, and she wanted a person she could relate to as a daughter."

The names behind the camera began to fall into place. Larry DeWaay, a production associate of director Norman Jewison's, signed on as executive producer. Director of photography David Watkin and editor Terry Rawlings (both Academy Award winners for their work on *Chariots of Fire*), production designer Roy Walker (another Oscar winner), and costumer Judy Moorcroft joined the talented ensemble.

Having been consumed herself with research for years, Barbra expected the other members of the cast and crew to also do their share. "She judged people by the amount of research they did," said Lemorande. Just prior to filming, Barbra gave Mandy Patinkin a seven-volume set entitled

Avigdor gives the virginal Yentl some sorely needed advice on love and sex.

The Legends of the Jews; Amy Irving received books about how to keep a kosher kitchen, how to prepare fish, how to bake bread. Individually, Persoff and Patinkin continued their education by attending local yeshivas.

After the year-end holidays, most of the principals journeyed to London to complete the final phase of preproduction. That first step, Lemorande ventures, is what constituted the real act of courage for everyone. "The giving up of family life and isolating yourself in a foreign culture—whether it was London or Prague, it wasn't New York or Beverly Hills." For Barbra it also meant putting in long

hours while trying to provide continuing support for her sixteen-year-old son. Additionally, her leave-taking caused her mother some anxiety: "You can't make a movie in Czechoslovakia," Diana fretted. "There's a war in Poland, and they haven't got fresh vegetables there."

One relationship that didn't make it through the production was her romantic involvement with Jon Peters. "By the time we had been together for eight years," Barbra told *People* magazine, "our relationship had reached a turning point. We were butting horns because I was passionately involved in *Yentl* and neglecting him. We had also been too dependent on each other. And you come to resent dependency. We needed to be apart."

"I don't think Barbra chose between me and the film," Jon insists. "I think she chose the film, and I think it was time for us to separate."

Two weeks prior to principal photography, the cast reported to Lee International Studios, outside London, for rehearsals. Filming began on April 14, 1982, ten days before Barbra's fortieth birthday. The production schedule called for four weeks at Lee, ten to twelve weeks on location in Czechoslovakia, and then a return to London.

"When I arrived on the set that first day," Barbra recalled, "this propman shook my hand with a sweaty palm. I said, 'Are you nervous?' and he said, 'A little,' and I said, 'Well, feel my hand. No one's more nervous than I am. If you make a mistake, it's fine, because I'll be the one making most of the mistakes.' . . . I had dreaded that first day. But when the time actually came for the first shot, I suddenly realized, Oh, I know how to do this. I just have to trust my instincts."

The affectionate support of the crew (they had presented Streisand with a custom-made, personalized director's chair on the first day of shooting) warmed her heart. "I found the experience very humbling," she recalled. "I was very moved by it. That power is very humbling. And I found myself being very soft-spoken, feeling even more feminine than I have ever felt. More motherly, more nurturing, more loving. I had patience I never dreamed I would have. I never wanted people to feel that I was so powerful. . . . As the director and producer, I could set the stage for the atmosphere I wanted on the . . . set, and that was that anyone could come up to me and give me a suggestion. Because if they can make it better, then I'm gonna use anything they can offer to me."

To her own surprise, even the financial constraints inherent in the project fueled her inspiration. "You have to create this scene, but you have X amount of time. That's life. Life is a compromise. Life is imperfection. So my so-called perfectionism is quite realistic. And one wouldn't want everything perfect because it is too sterile, too inhuman. It's the striving for perfection that interests me."

Her assumption of so many crucial roles on the film intrigued her coworkers. "If I needed something from the producer," said Mandy, "I would talk to her in a different way than I would with the director about a scene. Sometimes I'd be talking to the director, but I'd really be talking to the actress. . . . It was wild." Streisand's dedication, concentration, and stamina endeared her to the crew. But some aspects of it also worried them. With her typical day beginning at 6:00 A.M. and ending at 2:00 A.M. the next morning, many expressed concern that she would run out of energy. "Yet she never flagged, and [she] looks wonderful in the film," Patinkin added. "Some mysterious power sustained her." "I don't know how I survived it," Barbra admitted. "It was so overwhelming, I was sick every morning on the way to work."

In order to dispel the usual trouble-on-the-set rumors, the crew sent a letter to the *London Times* and several other publications describing how easy they found Barbra to work with. "She has captivated us all with her dedicated professionalism," they wrote. The letter caught her by surprise and touched her deeply. "[It] is one of my most treasured possessions," she said at the time, and years later she often brings it to the attention of journalists assigned to interview her.

Streisand and Amy Irving seemed to have a particularly trusting, responsive relationship. "She'd fix my hair ribbons," Irving recalled, "brush an eyelash off my cheek, paint my lips to match the color of the fruit on the table, I was like her little doll that she could dress up." Filming one of *Yentl*'s most famous scenes—Hadass's seduction of Anshel—brought out a new dimension in Barbra's "little doll." "In rehearsal," Irving stated, "we never actually kissed. When it came time to shoot the scene, [Barbra] said, 'Well, we'll do some takes with the kiss and some without it.' " After the first take with the kiss, it was obvious there was no need to shoot an alternative. "I had asked [Amy] to be very maidenly before that scene, and she did it beautifully," Streisand recalled. "But in the bedroom, when she comes on erotically, I asked her to let all her sexiness out, and wow! Did she let it out."

In July, *Yentl* moved behind the Iron Curtain to the tiny village of Roztyly, about two and a half hours outside Prague. Location filming had been delayed several days due to unseasonably heavy rains. In spite of the unexpected weather conditions, however, Roy Walker had magically created the entire village of Yanev out of an area that had formerly contained a few wooden houses on a pig

Yentl's *director, star, cowriter, and coproducer checks a setup on location in Czechoslovakia.*

Yentl bids a heartfelt farewell to her devoted "wife," Hadass.

farm. The British crew was joined during these weeks by a Czech unit under the supervision of Karel Skop of the Barrandon Film Studios.

She was a new director in a strange new environment, and yet, on the outside, Barbra hardly seemed to be fazed by it all. "There were flies in that village as big as beetles," Jon Peters noted, "but they never bothered her. She just swatted them." Rusty Lemorande concurred: "She was an American woman directing her first film in . . . an eastern European culture, yet she was able to react as the situation required. My admiration for Barbra grew enormously." Local residents, acting as extras, were filled with admiration as well when Barbra made sure the on-set buffet table

was stocked with fresh vegetables and other imported provisions she thought might not be available in the area.

From Roztyly, the company moved on to the old Jewish quarter of Zatec, which was used for the exterior of Bashev, the town where Avigdor and Anshel study. Next, they moved back to Prague. Among the locations chosen there by Streisand and Walker was the famous Charles Bridge, the oldest standing in that capital city. Normally it was restricted to foot traffic, but Barwood got permission to close it for a couple of days and bring on a few carts and horses. The resulting moments on-screen proved to be among *Yentl's* visual highlights.

Out of costume, Barbra enjoys a hug from Mandy Patinkin. (Photo courtesy of Richard Giammanco)

For Barbra, the experience of shooting in Czechoslovakia was physically grueling but exhilarating—directing, acting, singing, watching the budget, maintaining a happy set, learning lines, having wardrobe fittings at 11:00 P.M. when everyone else had finished for the day. Lacking the extra time to spend on her vanity reaped wonders in terms of her understated characterization of the young boy, Anshel. "*Yentl* was a stretch for her because there was no way she could fall back on past mannerisms," Marty Erlichman says. "Barbra the director was smart enough to know that Barbra the actress couldn't do that." As a result, Streisand delivers a marvelously fresh and subtle performance in *Yentl*—the kind of work many critics had often claimed a strong director would bring out in her.

By September 1982 the production team was ready to return to its Lee International Studio base. With all of the dialogue scenes and material involving other actors out of the way, all that remained for Barbra to do was Yentl's first soliloquy as Anshel, the prayerlike "Papa, Can You Hear Me?" which was shot on a soundstage, and the rousing finale, "Piece of Sky," which was filmed on a freighter of the period outside Liverpool. After returning to London, the filmmakers discovered that the footage had been damaged, so they had to reshoot. Production officially wrapped in late October, though for the next nine months

171

Streisand continued commuting back and forth between London and Los Angeles to oversee countless postproduction and recording details.

Barbra's most poignant—and misinterpreted—battle to protect her vision didn't involve the film's editing or scoring, however. It concerned a completion-bond agreement that had been foisted upon her a day before commencement of principal photography. United Artists insisted that she take out a policy protecting them against any cost overages. Barbra had no choice but to acquiesce, and the $700,000 premium was deducted from *Yentl*'s budget. Scarcely 11 percent over budget (typical for movies shot on location) when she brought the film in, the completion-bond company demanded that Barbra finish dubbing the picture in six weeks even though it wasn't due to be released for a year. "It was all about money," she clarified. "I did anything to get it done so that they couldn't take [the film] away from me."

Unfortunately, the ultimatum started rumors in the press that Streisand had lost control of her dream project, a charge United Artists was quick to dispel. "I want to make it clear that Ms. Streisand is, has been, and always will be the credited producer . . . retaining full artistic control," said M-G-M/UA vice chairman Frank Yablans. "I've never dealt with a person more responsible in terms of cost than Barbra was on this film. Every dime ultimately ended up on the screen."

Promotion was the next phase that preoccupied Streisand. Although *Yentl* had been in the planning stages first, two hit films about male-female role-playing managed to precede it to the screen in 1982: *Tootsie* and *Victor/Victoria*. Barbra wanted to sell her film simply as "a film with music." All jokes about *Tootsie on the Roof* aside, the studio considered changing the title to something deemed less ethnic. One executive wanted to call it *A Secret Dream*, while *Masquerade* was suggested as an alternative. But *Yentl*, to Barbra's delight, prevailed. United Artists took advantage of its extra lead time and did additional testing on the finished film. The results showed that young women were the biggest potential audience for the film. "They accept the way I look," Barbra observed. "Younger boys and older men have some trouble believing [in the fantasy]."

As the days drew near the film's November 16, 1983, world premiere at the Cinerama Dome in Hollywood and as Amy Irving was telling the press, "Everything Barbra Streisand has done before *Yentl* has been a rehearsal," Barbra became extremely anxious. "Don't worry even if you fall flat on your face with *Yentl*," Rusty Lemorande reassured her, "and I have every faith that you won't. Don't ever think that people will start to reconsider the brilliance of *Funny Girl, What's Up, Doc?* or *The Way We Were*. Nothing will ever tarnish those films; your stock is safe."

Steven Spielberg's response following a screening of the film was even more encouraging. Dubbing her work one of the most dynamic directorial debuts since Orson Welles and *Citizen Kane*, the director would tell the *Los Angeles Herald-Examiner* that he was struck by the generosity of her direction. "I think she tried to put everyone ahead of her in her list of priorities. It's selfless directing. . . . I have a feeling that all this comes from her experience not as an actress being directed and watching other directors work but from her autonomy as a musician and vocalist. If you listen to her songs, they're impeccable on every level. That's Barbra directing herself."

Much would be made of the movie's dedication: "To my father—and to all our fathers." Jon Peters felt *Yentl* represented Barbra's chance "to say Kaddish for her own father. She created him on film so she could love him and say goodbye to him. . . . I cried when I saw the movie. I sobbed, actually. I wish I had produced it." Sydney Pollack's response to the film was admiring as well. "It would be polished for a twentieth film, but particularly so for a first film. I was terribly impressed with it."

On November 18, 1983, *Yentl* opened in thirteen showcase theaters across the nation; the exclusive engagements produced excellent word of mouth. Two weeks before Christmas, the motion picture received its general release. It was to become the number-three performer at the box office that season (below *Sudden Impact* and *Terms of Endearment*). With domestic film rentals of $19,630,000—a better showing than *Funny Lady*, a certified hit—*Yentl* eventually became the sixth-ranking title on Barbra's all-time list. The film proved to be a hit in Taiwan; it broke records in Finland and Norway. Barbra noted with pride that her film was doing better box office in Texas than in Brooklyn. But *Yentl* was greeted with mixed reviews: Vincent Canby in the *New York Times* characterized the score as "one long, dreadful song," while Richard Corliss in his review for *Time* called it "the most romantic and sophisticated original movie score since *Gigi.*"

Yentl was welcomed warmly, however, by many of the most prestigious critics—some of whom had loathed Barbra's most recent releases—and it landed on the year-end Top Ten lists of the National Board of Review and *Time* magazine, among several others. Streisand was disappointed when Isaac Bashevis Singer wrote a lengthy essay in the *New York Times* criticizing the picture ("Yentl was no feminist," he grumbled), but she was heartened by the flood of subsequent supportive letters to the paper, including an eloquent response by Mrs. Walter Matthau.

Encouraged when *Yentl* was awarded Golden Globes for Best Picture (in the musical or comedy category) and Best Direction, Barbra was crushed when the film failed to receive Academy Award nominations except for its musical score and Amy Irving's performance. The obvious Oscar snub became a cause célèbre among many journalists and a rallying cry for Streisand fans. In the long run, Barbra received more publicity and support as a result of the oversight than she might have had the picture taken home an armful of Oscars. But the refusal of the industry to recognize her for what she—and many others—considered the most heartfelt effort of her career was a blow from which she was slow to recover.

REVIEWS

"*To put it succinctly and at once, Barbra Streisand's* Yentl *is a triumph—a personal one for Streisand as producer, director, co-author, and star, but also a triumphant piece of filmmaking. . . . At long last, with backing from United Artists, she has realized her dream. Magnificently. One finds, not surprisingly, traces of other directors she has worked with; but the concept, particularly the integration of the Alan and Marilyn Bergman lyrics into the progression of the storyline, is uniquely her own. And she makes it work seamlessly, effortlessly. Streisand is the only character who sings in the movie; and the songs become a projection of her inner feelings. . . . The device itself, like the soliloquies in Shakespeare's plays, is so perfectly attuned to the psychological needs of the character that it becomes not only acceptable but fascinating in its own right. . . . Streisand's performance alone could carry the picture, a star vehicle if ever there was one. Happily, she's too great an artist to let it go at that. As director, she has elicited outstanding performances from her entire cast.*"

HOLLYWOOD REPORTER

"*It would constitute a Hollywood scandal if Streisand were denied an Oscar nomination for her direction of* Yentl, *which could also place her in the running for acting, producing, and screenwriting awards.*"

WASHINGTON POST

"*Her voice remains a glory and now Miss Streisand has scored in her debut as a director. Rarely have I experienced such attention to detail, so haunting a sense of place, so unerring a sense of people in a first film. Yentl's setting will seem strange to many, but isn't that the goal of the best directors: to take us where we've never been? To make the unfamiliar familiar? As Coppola and Scorcese have shown us the Italians, as David Lean has shown us the British . . . so Barbra Streisand, through this universal love story, admits us to a world now gone—a world apart—making it our own. . . . Speaking very personally, Yentl has already become, for me, a moving motion picture—a cherished film.*"

THE TODAY SHOW

*N*uts

(1987)

A Barwood Films/Martin Ritt Production Released Through Warner Bros.

CAST

Barbra Streisand (*Claudia Draper*); Richard Dreyfuss (*Aaron Levinsky*); Maureen Stapleton (*Rose Kirk*); Karl Malden (*Arthur Kirk*); Eli Wallach (*Dr. Herbert A. Morrison*); Robert Webber (*Francis MacMillan*); James Whitmore (*Judge Stanley Murdoch*); Leslie Nielsen (*Allen Green*); William Prince (*Clarence Middelton*); Dakin Matthews (*First Judge*); Paul Benjamin (*Harry Harrison*); Warren Manzi (*Saul Kreiglitz*); Elizabeth Hoffman (*Dr. Johnson*); Castulo Guerra (*Dr. Arantes*); Stacy Bergman (16-year-old *Claudia*); Hayley Taylor-Block (eleven-year-old *Claudia*).

CREDITS

Producer: Barbra Streisand; executive producers: Teri Schwartz, Cis Corman; director: Martin Ritt; first assistant director: Aldric La'Auli Porter; second assistant director: Martina Ritt; screenplay: Tom Topor, Darryl Poniscan, Alvin Sargent (based on the play by Tom Topor); music: Barbra Streisand; music arranger and conductor: Jeremy Lubbock; unit production manager: George Goodman; production designer: Joel Schiller; costume designer: Joe Tomkins; costumer for Ms. Streisand: Shirlee Strahm; director of photography: Andrzej Bartkowiak; set decorator: Anne McCulley; art director: Eric Orbon; editor: Sidney Levin; casting: Marion Doughtery.
Running time: 116 minutes.

When it opened off-off-Broadway at the WPA Theater in the 1979–1980 season, *Nuts* received enough critical praise to warrant a move to Broadway, where it ran for three months at the Biltmore Theater. Playwright Tom Topor had spent twelve years as a reporter for the *New York Post,* and his experience covering stories in police stations, courtrooms, hospitals, and psychiatric wards led him to concoct a riveting drama hailed for its unflinching portrait of Claudia Draper, an intelligent but turbulently trou-

bled, high-priced prostitute who must struggle heroically within New York City's legal system to prove her sanity so that she may be allowed to stand trial for killing a client who tried to strangle her in a maniacal rage. During the course of the play—and Claudia's competency hearing—it is revealed that her stepfather not only sexually abused her for several years starting at age eleven but paid Claudia for his transgressions. Outspoken and truthful to the point of embarrassment, Claudia, with the help of a court-appointed attorney, declares war on the legal system, prison psychiatrists, and her well-heeled parents, who strive to have her judged insane rather than face a possibly scandalous manslaughter trial. "It'll look better to the neighbors to send cupcakes to a hospital rather than a prison," Barbra would later observe.

On December 26, 1981, columnist Marilyn Beck reported that Streisand was interested in playing Claudia in the film version of the play, but Mark Rydell, who was set to direct for Universal Pictures, didn't want to wait for her to become available. "She wanted me to delay production until she finishes *Yentl,*" Rydell told Beck, "and that won't be for way over a year. I intend to be shooting *Nuts* this summer." Shortly thereafter, Rydell, red-hot after guiding Bette Midler through a remarkable film debut in *The Rose* and coaxing Oscar-winning performances from Henry Fonda and Katharine Hepburn in *On Golden Pond,* briefly considered Midler as a possibility for Claudia. Twenty-six-year-old Debra Winger also seemed to have a corner on the role following her strong showing in *Urban Cowboy.*

As Barbra became embroiled in the produc-

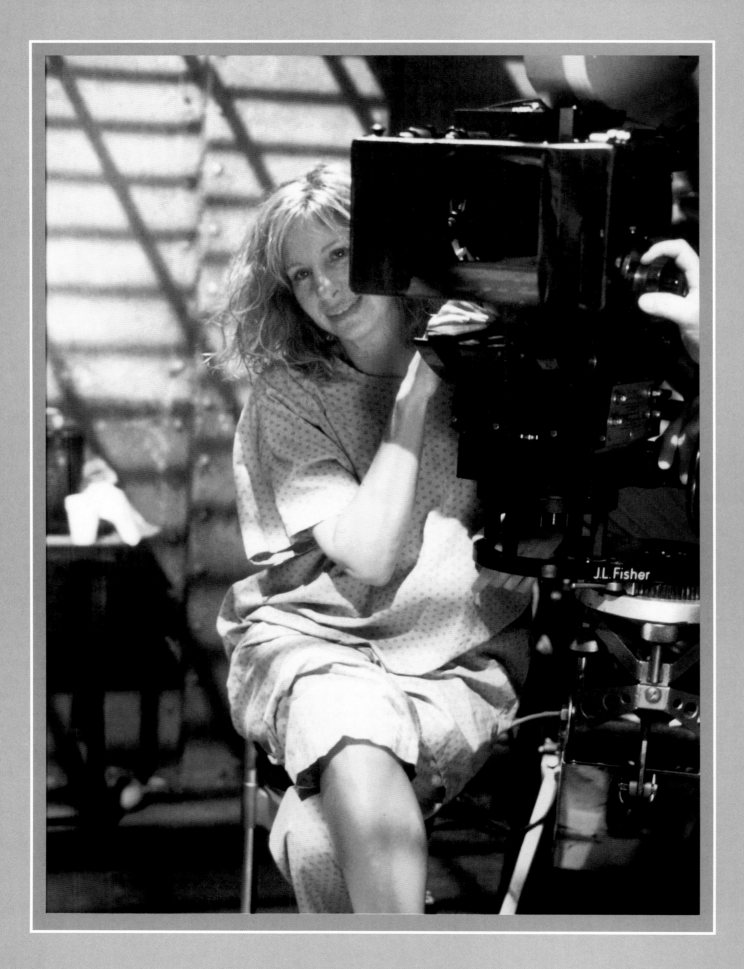

Barbra Streisand, as Claudia, and her fellow prisoners await arraignment.

tion of *Yentl, Nuts* embarked on a rocky road to the screen. "Part of the original deal," playwright Topor said, "was that I would do the first-draft screenplay and [Universal] would buy the movie rights." When Rydell saw the script, he asked for "a few little changes. . . . I did draft after draft after draft. I don't know, it was endless. Next thing I know, I was off the picture. In a way Mark was right . . . it's the director who makes the picture. Mark's emphasis was far more on incest. My emphasis was far more on power." When Rydell's projected 1982 starting date came and went, he took a hiatus from *Nuts* to direct *The River*. Meanwhile, Winger reached a career peak with acclaimed performances in *An Officer and a Gentlemen* and *Terms of Endearment,* but in the process she acquired a reputation as a trouble-maker. By January 1983 she was out of the *Nuts* equation, and eighteen months later, Universal dropped its option on the property. "Someone over there thought it was too hot to handle,"

Rydell told *Daily Variety.* "It's very raw, and I guess they got scared." Almost immediately, Warner Bros. acquired *Nuts* for less than $600,000. It was no coincidence that Barbra, now free of her *Yentl* duties, had reactivated her interest in the project and Warners had signed a releasing deal with Barwood.

Rydell then made a serious gaffe that brought the project to another standstill. Prior to leaving for a Hawaiian vacation, he secretly turned the script over to two accomplished writers at the same time. When *Ordinary People* scenarist Alvin Sargent found out that Darryl Poniscan (*Cinderella Liberty*) was also working on the script, he left a terse message on Rydell's answering machine: "After Hawaii, go directly to hell." One of Barbra's first chores on the production was to convince Poniscan and Sargent to return and collaborate on the *Nuts* screenplay. At times, Streisand's struggle to keep the project on track mirrored Claudia's battle to prove her sanity.

Warners officially announced the production on September 30, 1985, and projected a January 1986 starting date. Barbra would receive a $5 million fee for her acting, and she would—along with associates Cis Corman and Teri Schwartz—produce the film. By March 1986, Rydell was off the picture. The studio had been concerned for some time about his inability to rein in what threatened to become an out-of-control budget. Refusing to adjust the budget or take a salary cut, Rydell walked off the project he had nurtured on and off for five years. "We have nothing but respect for Mark's talent and success as a filmmaker," a typical studio press release stated. "We wish him every success in the future." Rydell issued his own statement: "If I have any regrets, it is that I will not be able to work with Barbra Streisand, an immense talent with whom I have enjoyed an excellent working relationship."

There was immediate speculation that Streisand had forced Rydell off the picture in order to direct it herself—something Warners had, in fact, asked her to do. However, realizing she was confronting the most serious, demanding performance of her career, Barbra didn't feel she could do Claudia justice if she took on the directing chores as well. Which is not to say that she didn't expect to work in a collaborative atmosphere in which her opinions would be considered. "She tried to become the mediator between Mark and Warner Bros.," said Marty Erlichman, who had recently reassumed his chores as Streisand's manager. "When Barbra found that there was no way she was going to convince Warners to take him back . . . she said she would like an actor's director. And they selected Marty Ritt" (but only after the studio offered the job to Alan Pakula for $2 million behind Barbra's back—a move she, as the film's producer, deeply resented).

A respected veteran, Ritt had pulled Oscar-winning performances from Patricia Neal in *Hud* and Sally Field in *Norma Rae*. "I always wanted to work with Marty," Barbra told Gene Shalit. "He read the script and he liked it, and he came to see me, and he said to me, 'I'd like to do this movie. There's only one thing. I don't know if you could play the part.' And I said, 'What?!' And I thought, He said the right thing. He got my hair up, you know, my challenging bones ready, and I said, 'Good. You're the one. It's a match.'" Ritt's initial questioning of whether Barbra was ideally suited

to play Claudia Draper was later echoed in some reviews, even from critics who admired the performance.

Aside from the acting challenge it presented, *Nuts* held other attractions for Barbra. If she had utilized *Yentl* as a means to create a loving father and bid him a fond farewell, she saw *Nuts* as an opportunity to symbolically exorcise the pain she still harbored over the emotional abuse she had suffered at the hands of her stepfather, Louis Kind. "I find these films are kind of cathartic," she told the British press. "One is given a chance to express certain feelings, and they get easier . . . to live with."

Often criticized for bluntness that the uninitiated find rude, and a lack of patience for ineptitude, Streisand also admits to a passion for "not being lied *to* or lied about." For these qualities and others, she felt a strong kinship with Claudia Draper. "She speaks the truth, and she gets into trouble," she said. "I identify with her. . . I do say what I feel a lot of the time, and it gets me into trouble. I have *opinions*. I think that I'm a nice person, I don't hurt people, but I do like to say what I think, and you get crucified for that, like she does in this movie."

To gain a better understanding of Claudia's deep-seated psychological quirks, Barbra met with a number of therapists and psychologists. She observed numerous patients in mental-health facilities at UCLA, at Elmhurst Hospital in Elmhurst, New York, and at Manhattan's renowned Bellevue Hospital. "I went to see schizophrenics at hospitals," she told Shalit. "I felt totally comfortable with them, with their directness, with a kind of lack of social etiquette, you know, a kind of honesty that was just so engaging."

In a press item that she has neither denied nor confirmed, London's *Daily Mirror* claimed that Barbra's research also took her to a Hollywood brothel to talk with some of the pricier call girls, quizzing them about their lifestyles, their rates, and their wealthier clients. "Hey, I really like that Barbra Streisand look-alike," one man on the premises said. "How much does she charge for the afternoon?" "Barbra roared with laughter when the madam told her that her services were in demand," the tabloid asserted. "She said, 'Of course, I refused the invitation, but it just shows what can happen when a girl is really acting the part.'"

With Ritt in place, the next hurdle became

the casting of Aaron Levinsky, the court-appointed public defender who comes to Claudia's aid and in the process discovers her tortured family history. Several top name actors, including Richard Gere and Robert Duvall, were considered for the role, but on April 14, 1986, Richard Dreyfuss became the unanimous choice of Streisand and Ritt. An Academy Award winner for his portrait of a self-absorbed stage actor in 1977's *Goodbye Girl,* Dreyfuss had survived a publicized cocaine habit and was enjoying a comeback in the hugely successful comedy *Down and Out in Beverly Hills.* In less than a week, however, Dreyfuss opted to sign for *Tin Men,* opposite Danny DeVito, scheduled to begin production on July 2. "He is deciding to take a feature in which [he] will be the star," Ritt said. "We have to start the search for an actor all over again."

Barbra had known Dustin Hoffman since her earliest days in Manhattan, when they were both eager, determined drama students. When Hoffman suddenly became available following the collapse of a film he was scheduled to make for Cannon Films, she felt *Nuts* might be the ideal vehicle to finally bring them together on-screen. The two stars were seen huddling in conversation in a small New York restaurant in mid-May, and soon word leaked out that Hoffman was indeed interested in playing Levinsky. His financial demands—and perhaps his realization that Levinsky was a provocative but essentially supporting role—led him, after two months of meetings, to turn the part down. "Hoffman's interest in *Nuts* was strong," said columnist Marilyn Beck, "but not strong enough for him to compromise on his financial demands. The deal being negotiated called for him and

Claudia confronts the high-priced lawyer her family has hired to plead her case.

In one of several face-offs, Levinsky insists that Claudia behave herself during her sanity hearing. (Photo courtesy of Richard Giammanco)

Streisand to profit equally from the picture, and when push came to shove, Hoffman insisted on so much that Warners decided it would end up with a budget that would be too big a nut to crack." Al Pacino and Marlon Brando were reportedly interested in the role, but on June 16, Dreyfuss decided to sign, though his casting forced the production to be delayed until October.

To complement the *Nuts* leads, a supporting cast of rare distinction was assembled. Oscar winners Maureen Stapleton and Karl Malden would play Claudia's mother and stepfather; James Whitmore was cast as the judge presiding over the hearings; Eli Wallach would play the prison psychiatrist determined to label Claudia insane; and Leslie Nielsen agreed to play a now-rare dramatic role as the client whom Claudia kills in self defense. (While they were filming their scenes together, Barbra asked the snowy-haired Nielsen if he knew how he had come to be cast in the role. "She had been watching the movie *Airplane!* at home," Nielsen later disclosed, "when she saw me on the screen and said, 'That's the man to play the

john at the bar.' It wasn't really because of the comedy I was doing. Barbra was going for the appearance, and that was it. It's one thing to be the . . . bumbling Frank Drebin and another thing to be the beast that has been turned loose in Barbra's apartment. . . .") Such a gifted supporting cast didn't come cheap, and soon the *Nuts* budget had ballooned to close to $30 million.

When Mark Rydell was still with the project, he had planned on using Vilmos Szigmond, the cinematographer Ray Stark had fired from *Funny Lady* after one day of shooting, but Ritt and Barbra agreed on Andrzej Bartkowiak, whose credits included *Terms of Endearment*, *The Verdict*, and *Prizzi's Honor* and who had pleased Streisand with his photography of *Putting It Together: The Making of* The Broadway Album.

Nuts began filming on an unseasonably warm October 1 in lower Manhattan. Among a crowd of onlookers, Barbra emerged from her trailer to shoot one of the only off-studio locations at the U.S. Custom House, doubling for the courthouse from which Claudia emerges triumphantly at the

179

film's conclusion. Visiting journalist Allison Waldman described the final take of the day capturing Claudia's merging into the throng of pedestrians choking the rush-hour sidewalks. "As the camera crew prepared to shoot the scene, Marty Ritt, Barbra, and Andrzej Bartkowiak conferred . . . [and] it seemed that . . . Barbra . . . didn't like the camera setup. She animatedly discussed the placement of the camera . . . checking it out by looking through the lens, having to stand on tiptoes to reach the eyepiece, and explaining with her hands how she thought the shot should be filmed." Waldman noted that Ritt and Bartkowiak were neither surprised nor annoyed by Barbra's suggestions.

Following the New York location, the company returned to the Warner Burbank lot to shoot the remainder of the film. On-set observers would later claim that star and director seldom clashed, but as filming progressed, Barbra and Marty Ritt began having their differences. Nearing seventy and in poor health, Ritt let Barbra know in no uncertain terms that he would not tolerate the late-night telephone calls her colleagues had come to expect. The director also became peeved when he felt Barbra's other endeavors distracted her from the work at hand. He had expressed frustration that she was preparing the *One Voice* concert—and the subsequent TV airing and album—while *Nuts* was in intense preproduction, and he resented any attention that she gave to outside interests. Once Ritt yelled, "Action," however, Barbra's costars testified that she was as focused as ever. To aid her concentration, Barbra demanded that a strict "closed set" policy be implemented on Stage 15. One of the few who *was* granted access to the soundstages (and with whom Streisand and Dreyfuss posed for publicity photos) was Madonna, on the lot to film the ill-fated *Who's That Girl.*

Whatever professional rifts might have occurred between Ritt and Streisand, Barbra's costars never mentioned them when queried about the production. "Forgetting myself," Karl Malden told *USA Today*, "there has never been a better group of character actors put together to appear in one film than in this one. Every performance, and I mean every performance, could well be called brilliant. And Marty Ritt is just a perfect director." Asked about Barbra, Malden added, "She's a fascinating, energetic woman, aside from

one of the best singers we've got in the country. She's got an awful lot of vitality." Admitting that he had heard the tales about her temperament, he said, "I've heard those stories, too, but I haven't seen any of it. She is not difficult to work with; if anything, you might call her a perfectionist."

Maureen Stapleton also sang Barbra's praises to columnist Shirley Eder. "I met her in New York a few times years ago. I was never an intimate of hers. But from the day I walked on the set, I found her so easy, so open. Everything is up-front with Streisand. There's no subterfuge. She was a joy to work with. You can say anything to her. One day towards the end of the movie, I made a suggestion to Barbra, saying, 'I have a great idea for a cut. We stop right here, see.' I pointed to a page in the script. She looked at me and said, 'You mean we cut that *whole* scene between us? You just want to get home,' she said, laughing. 'That's true,' I agreed, 'but we really don't need that page.' She didn't cut the scene . . . but she was wide open to hear what I had to say. Everybody got along in the company. At least I never saw any dissension on the set."

"Barbra is a case," Richard Dreyfuss told Gene Shalit. "She's very specific. . . . People might argue with facets of Barbra's personality or the personality that she gives off, but what Barbra is, is definite. And because she's a woman, we take issue with that to a greater degree than if she were a man. If she were a producer, star, director of the male gender, we would accept all of her eccentricities in a much more forgiving, normal, unquestioning way. The fact that she is a woman brings all of those things out in very sharp relief, and that's why we're here in a sense discussing Barbra's personality. We wouldn't be discussing Marty Ritt's personality or mine or yours. That doesn't mean that I forgive her eccentricities, by the way; it just means that's the phenomena we're discussing, okay?"

Nuts wound up production on February 3, 1987, giving Ritt, editor Sidney Levin, and Barbra several months to get the film ready to preview in the early fall. Calling on her composing talents, Streisand decided to write a musical theme for a scene in which Levinsky thoughtfully goes through Claudia's apartment and for the picture's finale. "As a courtroom drama, *Nuts* required very little music," she said. "So I decided to give it a shot. The end title music was written to convey a sense of freedom and personal triumph. Later, Alan and

Claudia Draper discovers she must wage a one-woman assault on the bureaucracy of the New York legal system.

In lower Manhattan, director Martin Ritt and Barbra discuss the film's sun-drenched finale.

Marilyn Bergman added lyrics to it, and the song became 'Two People,' [which I] recorded for the *Til I Loved You* album." For the sequence in which Claudia first meets the man she ends up killing, Barbra utilized the melodic line she had composed for the song "Here We Are at Last," one of the few highlights of the *Emotion* album. "If I feel like writing music for a film, I will," Barbra added. "I love art direction and costumes and all that stuff, so why not? It's interesting. As a woman, you are considered an ego problem for some reason. If a man does it, he's just multifaceted. That is sad; I think we have a long way to go."

"No, I don't know what Barbra is doing to the picture," Marty Ritt told Marilyn Beck in June. "I did my cut; we previewed it, and now she's doing whatever it is she's doing. . . . There's always a question of taste involved, and as the producer, she has the right to come and do some editing."

In an interview with British writer Douglas Thompson, Barbra said that some of her editing decisions might go against expectations. "Some of the arguments Marty and I had—even over the final cut—were where I would say: 'Take out that close-up of me.' But then he would say, 'That's a good close-up of you.' Nobody would know [about] those arguments. They would think an actress wants close-ups of herself. And it's ridiculous. I have a lot of rage about things that are misinterpreted."

When the final edit of *Nuts* began previewing in October, the studio was delighted. "*Nuts* had some of the best responses in returned cards from sneak previews of any recent Warner Bros. picture," reported Frank Swertlow for *L.A. Life.* "That was confirmed by the appropriate cheers during an industry screening of the flick. . . ." Advance word on the film indicated not only a hit but an effort that was destined to receive multiple Oscar nominations. *Nuts* opened on November 20 at 542 theaters and added 550 more screens for Christmas week. During its first ten days of release the picture grossed over $11 million, and an opening-day exit poll, conducted by Cinema-Score, indicated that audiences were rating the film as "an A with a 96% chance of being liked." The film drew a mixed reception from critics, though the good reviews raved about the performances of the entire cast.

By the third week of release, a baffled Warner Bros. realized that *Nuts* would not be performing as they had hoped. The film wasn't drawing as expected, some theorized, because audiences were in no mood for heavy drama in the wake of the recent, severe stock-market crash on October 19. The relative failure of other brilliantly acted dramas released at the same time, such as *Ironweed* and *Barfly*, gave this theory some heft. America was instead paying to see such hit comedies as *Three Men and a Baby* and *Planes, Trains & Automobiles*. Other pundits felt that, considering the cast and the title, the public expected *Nuts* to be a comedy, while still others asserted that potential ticket buyers were repelled by the film's poster art, which featured a haggard, grim-faced Barbra overshadowing a bespectacled Richard Dreyfuss. And in spite of good word of mouth about the performances, *Nuts* didn't prove nearly as provocative as its creators might have hoped. "Its trenchant themes have lost a bit of punch in the seven years since Topor's play first shook up theatergoers on both coasts," noted Carol Cling in her *Las Vegas Review Journal* critique. "And its psychological revelations, which once seemed shocking, now appear merely perfunctory. (Which may tell us more about society at large than about *Nuts* itself.)"

To make matters worse, Barbra wasn't available to publicize the film as much as the studio had wanted. Perhaps she felt she had overdone it with *Yentl* or naively thought the film would speak for itself, but for whatever reason, she did almost no print interviews in support of *Nuts*. Her only television exposure was with critic Gene Shalit on *The Today Show*, which ran in three daily excerpts, with Dreyfuss joining her on the final installment. She was more generous when publicizing the picture for its European openings, but by then it was too late.

Even positive comments from Tom Topor failed to generate better ticket sales. "I think *Nuts* is a good movie, a very good movie. It's not the movie I would have made. It's Barbra Streisand and Marty Ritt's movie. When you consider how much they eliminated, it's not bad at all. Except for one sentimental scene when Dreyfuss visits her in the prison hospital, it's an enormously brave picture for [Barbra]." Topor also made it clear that without Streisand's participation, his play might never have been filmed at all: "I mean, her commitment to this project has been unwavering for six years."

Some controversy arose when Warners sponsored ads in the Hollywood trade papers that touted Barbra for a Best Actress Academy Award nomination but listed Richard Dreyfuss in the supporting category. Naturally, gossips assumed that Streisand was behind the disparity, but it was soon disclosed that Dreyfuss himself had asked that he be submitted in the lesser category, for he was hopeful of a Best Actor nod for his work in *Tin Men*. Shortly thereafter, *Nuts* received Golden Globe nominations for Best Film (drama), Best Actress, and Best Supporting Actor for Dreyfuss. It lost all three and a month later failed to garner a single Oscar nomination.

Despite its failure to break box-office records and its poor showing during awards season, *Nuts* stands as a finely crafted—if imperfect—film that delivers a tangy feast of meaty performances, not the least of which is offered by its leading lady. It might not, however, have proved as cathartic for Streisand as she intended. Four years after the release of *Nuts*, while Barbra was being interviewed by Mike Wallace on *60 Minutes*, she broke down in tears and asked that the camera be turned off in response to Wallace's probing questions about her relationship with Louis Kind.

REVIEWS

"*. . . the movie's slow, methodical pacing and almost static visual style—which alternates stately tracking shots, tight close-ups of talking heads and jarring flashbacks—gives* Nuts *a talky, relentlessly stagy feel that further undercuts the movie's potential power. . . . Dreyfuss . . . delivers a canny, understated performance as the put-upon Levinsky—who may be too good a person to be a good lawyer. His portrayal meshes perfectly with*

The distinguished cast of Nuts. *Back row: Karl Malden, James Whitmore, Eli Wallach, Robert Webber. Front row: Maureen Stapleton, Barbra Streisand, Richard Dreyfuss. There were four Acting Oscars and ten nominations among them.*

Streisand's impassioned, all-stops-out bravura. But [she] stops short of the kind of 'Look Ma, I'm acting' grandstanding that all too often marks such roles, capturing Claudia's proud and defiant, yet vulnerable edge."

LAS VEGAS REVIEW JOURNAL

"Nuts *is clearly Streisand's response to the response to Yentl. In the [Motion Picture] Academy's most beloved terms—tastefully photographed adult melodrama—she presents her position: 'You all think I'm mad, but I'm actually not. My power comes from my lucidity, my ability to understand what you can't because you're too mired in sexist ignorance and self-interest. All you perceive are the externals: a woman who makes her own decisions. On the inside, I'm really nice, smart, savvy, funny—a threat only to your image of me as a power-hungry nonconformist. . . . I'm simply misunderstood.' Streisand should defend* herself, because the world doesn't like powerful women. On the other hand, there's a distinct flavor of self-pity to the whole proceeding."

L.A. WEEKLY

"Nuts *is not a musical, but Streisand belts out the role as if it were one of her showstoppers—say, 'Don't Rain on My Parade.' She's always been able to give even trite love-and-pain lyrics a live-wire urgency. She does the same here in a whopping star performance, funny and ferocious, that cuts through most of the movie's moldy courtroom melodramatics. . . . Streisand, in her off hours, also managed to find time to compose the* Nuts *soundtrack. Sure, she is given to grandstanding, but her wicked zest keeps you riveted. Whether she's punching out the family lawyer or shocking the court with her [explicit] sex-for-sale rates, Streisand shows a robust comic toughness."*

PEOPLE

The Prince of Tides

(1991)

A Columbia Pictures Release of a Barwood/Longfellow Production

CAST

Barbra Streisand (*Dr. Susan Lowenstein*); Nick Nolte (*Tom Wingo*); Blythe Danner (*Sallie Wingo*); Kate Nelligan (*Lila Wingo Newbury*); Jeroen Krabbe (*Herbert Woodruff*); Melinda Dillon (*Savannah Wingo*); George Carlin (*Eddie Detreville*); Jason Gould (*Bernard Woodruff*); Brad Sullivan (*Henry Wingo*); Maggie Collier (*Lucy Wingo*); Lindsay Wray (*Jennifer Wingo*); Brandlyn Whitaker (*Chandler Wingo*); Justen Woods, Bobby Fain, Trey Yearwood (*Tom Wingo as a child*); Tiffany Jean Davis, Nancy Atchinson, Kiki Runyan (*Savannah Wingo as a child*); Grayson Fricke, Ryan Newman, Chris Stacy (*Luke Wingo as a child*).

CREDITS

Producer: Barbra Streisand, Andrew Karsch; coproducer: Sheldon Schrager; executive producers: Cis Corman, James Roe; director: Barbra Streisand; assistant director: Thomas A. Reilly; screenplay: Pat Conroy, Becky Johnston (based on Conroy's novel); music: James Newton Howard; production designer: Paul Sylbert; costume design: Ruth Morley; director of photography: Stephen Goldblatt; set decoration: Caryl Heller, Arthur Howe Jr., Leslie Ann Pope; set design: Chris Shriver; art direction: W. Steven Graham; editor: Don Zimmerman; sound: Dennis Maitland, Michael J, Kohut, Carlos de Larios, Shawn Murphy; casting: Bonnie Finnegan. Running time: 132 minutes.

W hile *Nuts* was still in the planning stages, rumors circulated about what Streisand's next film project might be. Finding a worthy vehicle with which to follow such uniquely stellar showcases as *Nuts* and *Yentl* could prove daunting. Barbra reportedly expressed interest in playing the embittered wife of *War of the Roses* and the lovelorn waitress in *Frankie and Johnny*, but those roles went to Kathleen Turner and Michelle Pfeiffer, respectively. Barwood was also developing a script about Margaret Bourke-White, the pioneering photographer who supplied *Life* magazine with its first cover photo in 1936 and who indulged in a turbulent affair with writer Erskine Caldwell. Two other possibilities—both reconfigurations of European hits—were mentioned in *Daily Variety* within three days of one another in July 1986. Producer Faye Schwab announced that she would be remaking *And Now My Love,* the Claude Lelouch romance that had starred Marthe Keller, for Warner Bros. with Barbra in the lead, and David Wolper said he would star her in a retelling of Lina Wertmuller's *Swept Away.* It's not known if Streisand was in any way interested in either remake, but by the end of the year she had acquired movie rights to activist-playwright Larry Kramer's *The Normal Heart,* an off-Broadway play in which she was willing to play a supporting role if she could get the controversial film financed.

As soon as she had *Nuts* prepared for release, Barbra was ready to begin immediate preproduction on Kramer's outspoken indictment of the New York medical establishment as it fumbled through the first outbreak of AIDS within Manhattan's gay community. She spoke with Dustin Hoffman about costarring, but when he proved unavailable, she once again turned to Richard Dreyfuss, who had starred in the highly acclaimed Los Angeles company of *The Normal Heart* prior to his film comeback. Barbra planned on joining Dreyfuss in the secondary, though instrumental, role of a wheel-chair-bound doctor. The proposed film came to a halt, however, when Streisand and Kramer differed on salient points, and the project languished for some time before the author reacquired the

rights in the hope of getting his play filmed elsewhere. (He later told the national gay magazine the *Advocate* that he thought *Nuts* was "a really rotten movie.")

In the meantime, Barbra became aware of *The Prince of Tides,* Pat Conroy's bestselling new novel that was touching readers with its lyrical imagery and healing message. The book was first recommended to her by the sound editor on *Nuts* and later by her then lover, Don Johnson. "He would read me passages . . ." Barbra said in a British television interview, "because it related to his life. And his mother and his childhood. And I was just so intrigued by that, the nature of it and the poetry of it. The beauty of the writing. So I got the novel and read it and thought, I have to make this movie." But while Streisand was falling in love with *The Prince of Tides,* her old costar had beat her to the punch.

Robert Redford was planning to star in the film for M-G-M/UA and produce in association with Andrew Karsch, a business colleague of Pat Conroy's. Redford thought the property might serve as an exciting vehicle in which to reunite with Barbra. Certainly he liked the idea better than joining her in a sequel to *The Way We Were,* which he has stated flatly he will never do in spite of his desire to work with Streisand again. Redford felt *The Prince of Tides* offered him and Barbra a rare opportunity, but it was soon apparent to him that Streisand was more compelled to bring the story to the screen than he was, and since he was having trouble getting a workable script forged from the sprawling novel, he turned the property over to her.

"When I read the book, I saw the movie," she told *Drama-Logue.* "I felt the movie. I felt what would be the important themes: how everyone's relationship has changed through compassion and through love." The announcement that Barbra would direct and star in the film was made on April 9, 1989. As usual, and despite perceptions to the contrary, the project wasn't handed to her without reservations. "I couldn't have gotten it made if I wasn't in it," she said. "I certainly wouldn't have gotten to direct."

A dense novel of almost six hundred pages that spans several decades and generations, *The Prince of Tides* could have easily inspired a six-part television miniseries. But, as winnowed down for its cinematic incarnation, it tells the emotionally charged story of Tom Wingo, a high school English teacher and football coach based on the southern Carolina coast, who learns that his twin sister, Savannah, has once again attempted suicide in Manhattan. Although his marriage is close to crumbling, he agrees to journey to New York in an effort to help Savannah's therapist, Dr. Susan Lowenstein, better understand his sister's troubled state of mind. By finally revealing long-hidden Wingo family secrets, Tom is able to help Savannah (and himself) come to grips with their tortured past. In the process, Tom and Susan—who is trapped in a loveless, demeaning marriage—fall in love and conduct a healing affair, but eventually part so that Tom may return to his marriage, for which he feels new commitment.

"I know therapy has been very helpful to me in my life," Barbra told *Empire* magazine, "so when I read this story about love having the ability to transform in this setting of therapy, I felt passionate about it. The themes that the film deals with are very important to me. Forgiveness, that's a big one. To come to terms with your past, to accept what was and be able to change by acknowledging the problem, not living in denial. . . .

"The first draft of the screenplay only took three weeks," Barbra recalled of working with screenwriter Becky Johnston, "but then there was six months of discussing things with therapists and doctors and another two and a half months of discussing another version of the script. Then the roof fell in. The studio [ran] out of money." M-G-M/UA, in the midst of tenuous financial restructuring, dropped the project, and Barbra was forced to hunt for another home for her new baby, just as she had to do with *Yentl.* Smarting from the disappointment of *Nuts,* Warner Bros. was also not interested. But by January 1990, Columbia Pictures, then under the cochairmanship of Jon Peters, welcomed the project. "Ex-boyfriends come in handy," Barbra quipped in response to the studio's interest.

However, even with Peters supportively in her corner at the studio for which Barbra had made many of her most successful films, she was forced to take half a million dollars less than her asked-for fee of $7 million to produce, direct, and star in *The Prince of Tides*—a bargain in inflation-crazed Hollywood—but Columbia had originally hoped to get her for even less. "They wanted me to [accept] almost a million dollars [less]," she recalled. "I thought that was too much."

"I didn't know [Redford] had given [the rights] to Barbra. So when I started receiving messages to call Barbra Streisand, I thought it was a joke," recalled Pat Conroy to *US*. The author had written a *Tides* screenplay in 1986 but had since distanced himself from the film adaptation. "Finally, I was at a hotel in Los Angeles," Conroy adds, "and Barbra said, 'Why won't you return my phone calls?' It was horrible. I felt like the rudest person in the world. We worked together on the script for two weeks. And she *worked* me. . . . She would give me homework—five or six scenes to look at, at night. . . . Here is what surprised me most about Barbra: The first day I was with her, she asked me question after question about the book. . . ." Including a query about the Carolina shag, a dance Conroy had written about. "So she asked me to teach it to her . . . and it was fun. You see, what I did not know about her was that she has an incredible sense of fun. Like everyone else, I had read stuff about her. I thought, Holy God, I am going to be working with the Bride of Frankenstein. I thought she would yell at me, hurt my feelings, slap me around. I was completely stunned to find out that she was a delight. But all the people who work with Barbra closely have been with her for thirty years. That should have told me something."

Although she would be criticized for it, Barbra felt that the film would be most effective if the romance between Tom and Susan became the screenplay's emotional centerpiece—a decision shared by Redford, who had planned the same approach. Above and beyond how it could pull all the elements of the story into sharp focus, the love affair was deemed crucial by some observers to the potential success of the film. Barbra's most popular movies had pivoted on strong romantic relationships. In fact, there were those who believed that *Nuts* had suffered because—as damaging as it would have been to the integrity of the piece—audiences were disappointed when a love story failed to develop between Claudia and Levinsky. Many of Streisand and Conroy's marathon script sessions concentrated on how best to highlight the Wingo-Lowenstein romance without allowing it to shift attention away from the other aspects of the story. "Streisand's smart as hell to take this novel and break it down into a movie,"

Conroy told Liz Smith. "She's not afraid of anything. Her sheer will is the reason this movie is getting made."

"When I first read the book," Barbra said, "I thought, Jesus, I'm perfect for this part. I identify with this woman completely, even to the line in the book that says she is in the middle of aging extraordinarily well. . . . Except for the hair color, this is me. This could be me!" Casting an actor as suitable to his role as Barbra felt to hers would be nothing less than essential to the success of *The Prince of Tides*. It was, after all, *Tom's* story. Finding someone—who also happened to be a star name—capable of projecting Wingo's physicality, his intellect, a wounded quality he must keep in check for most of the film, plus a sex appeal that would mesh with Streisand's would be a tall order. Column items listed Kevin Costner, Tom Berenger, Warren Beatty, and Dennis Quaid among the possibilities, and it also became known that Barbra offered the role of Tom and his hard-nosed father, Henry, to Jeff and Lloyd Bridges. The elder Bridges felt his son erred foolishly when he turned Streisand down.

"I was surprised when they told me Nolte had been cast," Pat Conroy recalled. "I had just seen him the night before in *Q&A*, where he reached his hand down and grabbed a transvestite's genitalia. I thought, Holy God, he is going to play Tom? I just had no idea he had this range."

It wasn't the Nick Nolte of *Q&A* or *48 Hours* or *North Dallas Forty* that Barbra Streisand envisioned in *The Prince of Tides*. Rather it was the alluring rebel Nolte had played in the landmark 1975 miniseries *Rich Man, Poor Man*. The handsome blond actor had risen to sudden stardom in the highly rated show, and as Hollywood's newest heartthrob in the Redford mold, Nolte exploited his good looks and macho demeanor in hits such as *The Deep*. But in more recent years he had obscured his sex appeal in a number of well-received character roles, including the homeless guru who plunges into the swimming pool (and empty lives) of Richard Dreyfuss and Bette Midler in *Down and Out in Beverly Hills*.

While Nolte had been filming *Q&A* (for which he had gained forty pounds, grown a walrus mustache, and darkened his hair for his role as a foul-mouthed, middle-aged cop with a taste for bigotry and violence), the film's producer, Burt Harris, gave him a copy of *The Prince of Tides*. "I

New York psychiatrist Susan Lowenstein finds she is as in need of emotional — and sexual — healing as many of her patients.

asked him what the deal was . . . because I liked the novel a lot. He said Barbra Streisand is going to direct it." Nolte then managed to read a copy of the script and asked his producer if he would let Barbra know that he wanted to talk with her. "I think there's some Machiavellian material here," Nolte said, laughing. "Barbra probably had been in communication with Burt to find out if I would be interested. So that's how it evolved." In another fortuitous coincidence, Nolte had been hoping for the opportunity to work under the guidance of a female director for several years. "It seems to me," Nolte said, "that a male actor and a male direc-tor—when they approach a scene—get to a certain emotional part and there's an agreement [to move on], that it's completed. With a female director you do the same thing, reach that emotional peak, but then there's the discussion. What are the feelings? So you get into the exploration of feelings."

In Nolte, Barbra found the exact qualities she was looking for. "I saw a lot of pain in his work, in his eyes. And then, in talking to him, he was at a vulnerable place, ready to explore feel-ings; romantic feelings, sexual feelings, and deep, secretive feelings." To secure the role, Nolte gladly shed his excess weight and returned his hair to its buttery hue. By the time filming began, he had recaptured much of the pronounced masculine appeal that had characterized his earliest days of stardom.

With her leading man signed (for $4 million) by February 1990, Barbra began casting the sup-porting roles, and as with *Yentl* and *Nuts,* her choices proved impeccable. To portray Tom's mother, Lila, who ages from a determined young woman to a domineering matriarch, Streisand had originally planned to hire two actresses. But when she met with forty-year-old Kate Nelligan, who had moved her to tears onstage in the 1988 off-Broadway drama *Spoils of War*, she realized she was an actress for all ages. "She's the only one who could pull it off, really," Barbra enthused. To play Tom's wife, Sallie, Barbra called on an actress well versed in Pat Conroy's particular brand of southern prose. Blythe Danner had played a version of Conroy's mother in *The Great Santini*, and she was a family friend. "I know Pat put in a good word [with Barbra] for me," she admitted. "He has a bit of a soft spot for me because I knew his mother." Danner had hoped to be cast as Savannah, but Barbra felt her "warm and homey" qualities were perfect for Sallie. The casting was a lucky break for Danner, as it turned out to be a much bigger part, although Savannah is more prominent in the novel. The choice of moodily handsome Jeroen Krabbe to play Susan's arrogant, unfaithful violinist-husband, Herbert Woodruff, was an easy one for Barbra, but casting a young actor to play their seventeen-year-old son proved more complicated.

Bernard is in conflict with his successful, accomplished, emotionally estranged parents. He is perfectly willing to accept the largesse of their opulent lifestyle, but he is resentful of their expectations; his father wants him to perfect the violin rather than take up football, which Bernard is eager to play in the hope of landing on the varsity team when he goes off to college in the near future. He is willing to take football pointers from Tom Wingo in Central Park until he senses the attraction between Tom and Susan. He responds to their growing attachment with typical adolescent sarcasm.

To play Bernard, Streisand had signed Chris O'Donnell, the fresh-faced juvenile about to burst into stardom opposite Al Pacino in *Scent of a Woman*. During one of her afternoon meetings with Pat Conroy, Barbra showed the writer photographs of actors she was casting in the film. When O'Donnell's eight by ten turned up, Conroy objected. "He was a really good-looking kid. I said, 'Barbra, that ain't the guy.' She told me she had already hired him. I said, 'You can do whatever you want. I'm just telling you, that doesn't remind me of the kid. This kid is supposed to be having trouble. He's kind of snotty.'" Barbra defended her choice: "Look, [O'Donnell's] a good athlete," she said. "This kid [Bernard] is *not* a good athlete; that's the point," Conroy countered. "So she sort of flipped through other kids she'd auditioned. She

Lila Wingo and her children present a tableau of picturesque serenity that contrasts profoundly with the realities of their dysfunctional family life.

finally came to this one kid. I didn't know it was her son. But he showed a snarling, wonderful teenage quality. I said, 'That's the kid right there.'"

Jason had wanted the role from the beginning. For several years, he had seemed more intrigued with directing, editing, and composing than appearing in front of the camera; he had, in fact, been given the responsibility of editing *Yentl* for its commercial television debut. But in 1989 he acted in small roles in the youth-oriented films *The Big Picture, Say Anything,* and *Listen to Me*. As soon as he learned that his mother would be making *The Prince of Tides,* he asked to play Bernard and was turned down. "I resisted hiring him," Barbra recalled, "even though he read the [part] at a reading we had the first time we finished the script and he was absolutely brilliant. But I thought [at twenty-four] he was too old for the part. And I was concerned about the complexities of mother-son direction and so forth." But Pat Conroy's enthusiastic reaction to Jason's photograph sent Barbra back to the novel. "He's described in the book just as Jason looks," she marveled, "dark curly hair, dark eyes, long legs, prominent nose, and full lips, like his mother." After paying O'Donnell a termination fee and being assured by Jason that he could survive the possible cries of favoritism if she could, Barbra signed him in May to play Bernard Woodruff. "I had to be prepared for the criticism . . . of potential nepotism or whatever people want to believe," Jason said. "A lot of other directors have worked with their children and gotten a lot of flack recently."

By June, Barbra had assembled her production personnel, which included cinematographer Stephen Goldblatt, whose photography of *The Cotton Club* had been much admired, and an art department under the guidance of production designer Paul Sylbert. On June 18, filming on *The Prince of Tides* began on location in Beaufort, South Carolina, at makeshift studios set up at the local technical college and the National Guard armory. For two months in suffocating heat and humidity, Streisand and company toiled to capture scenes involving Tom's childhood as the son of a

shrimper, his current family life, his sessions in Lowenstein's office, and Susan's unhappy home life in her Manhattan apartment. Through the magic of moviemaking, nearly all of the film's interiors, including those set in New York, were shot in Beaufort.

The controversy, from which few Streisand projects are completely free, followed Barbra to South Carolina, where she was judged aloof and unreceptive by the Beaufort press. After working fourteen-hour days, she seldom ventured from the antebellum mansion she had rented for the duration of the shoot, disappointing locals, who expected her presence in town to take the form of a glamorous personal appearance. There was an atmosphere of distrust swirling around Barbra as well. Many Carolinians, who had no idea of her fanatical commitment to research and detail, wondered how a Brooklyn-born Jewish superstar could possibly understand, absorb, and portray the peculiar attitudes and rhythms of the South. Beaufort did, however, appreciate the financial windfall the filming brought to the area and the opportunity for some of the citizens to appear in roles of various sizes in the picture.

The actors—and costars—under Barbra's direction appreciated her legendary refusal to settle if she felt scenes could be mined for more emotional truth. "[Her] being an actress is a tremendous help because she knows the dilemma an actor goes through," recalled Blythe Danner. "I had a hard scene on the telephone. . . . It was a very sensitive shot." The actress was eager to get the scene over with as quickly as possible, but her director wouldn't rush. "I lost count of the takes. But she was right. I thought we had it, but it wasn't until one of the last takes. Usually I feel better in the first take or two. But she was absolutely right. She has a great eye."

Kate Nelligan agreed that Barbra "doesn't settle for anything, ever. So you can be confident that the best work is going to end up in the film because she's going to stay there until it happens." For the film's first love scene between Tom and Susan—after weeks of frustration and a dramatic confrontation with Susan's husband—Barbra *wasn't* willing to stay until it happened. As the scene escalated, Streisand sensed that Nolte would have been perfectly willing for the moment to go farther than the script demanded. "When we were doing the love scenes at first, they would just get hot," Nolte says. "Just start to really work and she'd cut! The actress would order the director to cut. And I would say, 'Barbra, why are you cutting it? It's just getting good.' And she'd say, 'Well . . . ,' and get flustered. Then she saw the dailies, and she said, 'If I cut the camera anytime when it's really going good, don't let me do that.' "

Though Barbra felt she needed to draw the line for the sexy scenes, she was apparently not above calling on her feminine appeal when it came to interacting with the predominantly male crew. "I think she flirts with the men," said Paul Sylbert.

"One of her weapons as a woman [director] is that she can deal with the men as a woman. She can be charming and a little intimate sometimes in a kidding kind of way. Suddenly, she'll be flat-out honest with you and say how frightened, how nervous, she is. And of course, what are you going to do? You're going to help her out, protect her." Later, Sylbert and Barbra would clash over the set he had designed for the elegant apartment Susan Lowenstein shares with her husband and son. Sylbert felt its decor should reflect Woodruff's cold, dominating personality, while Streisand wanted it changed to have a warmer, more conventional look. Sylbert came close to walking off the film, and finally Barbra backed down and later agreed that his choices had been right.

As she often does in the wake of such squabbles, Barbra—rightly or wrongly—laid the blame on old-fashioned sexism. "The craft takes so much out of you that it's very important for the soul, the spirit, and the body to be surrounded by a loving support system. I didn't have that on *Prince of Tides*. The grips, the prop people, the gaffers, were wonderfully supportive. But there were a handful of 'boys' clubbers' who were not, and it made my job extra difficult. I want to work with people who say, 'Yes, it can be done.' And I won't be afraid to fire people who constantly say, 'It can't.' " To writer Tom Shales she added, "You know, [for *Yentl*] I had a wonderful crew there in London. No chauvinism. I experienced no chauvinism at all making that movie, and that's probably because they have a queen and they had a woman prime minister. It wasn't such a big deal. This so-called powerful woman didn't scare them."

Location shooting was halted briefly when Barbra had to return to Hollywood suddenly to be with her eighty-two-year-old mother, who was undergoing heart-bypass surgery. The experience forced Barbra to place the demands of filming in perspective. "When I was faced with the potential loss of my mother," she admitted, "the movie became much easier. It lost its importance. It took the proper place—it's much more secondary to life. That's what *The Prince of Tides* is about in a way—learning to appreciate your mother." After a relatively brief location shoot in Manhattan—covering street scenes and those involving Central Park, among other locales—*The Prince of Tides* wrapped production in September. Columbia had scheduled the film for a fall 1991 release; Barbra had more than a year to get the picture ready for public viewing.

To compose the film's score, Barbra had chosen veteran John Barry, who found Streisand even more of a challenge than Sylbert had. "Everyone told me I must be crazy working with her. But I thought it would probably work out. But she had to be involved with everything that I and everyone else on the film was doing. She would never leave you alone. She was a complete control freak, very bossy. . . ." Rather quickly Barry was replaced by James Newton Howard, who had played keyboard on Barbra's *Songbird* and *Emotion* albums and had gone on to compose the score of *Pretty Woman*. "Barbra is a sweetheart," he offered, "but she can be quite blunt. If you're not thick-skinned, then she's not easy to take. I happen to think she's a genius. The process of working with her is a difficult one because her perfectionism is unequaled. She's incredibly demanding, but I can truthfully say that working with her has elevated my own work." During the postproduction period on *Prince of Tides*, Howard and Streisand were rumored to be more than just professional collaborators.

Reliable Marilyn and Alan Bergman added lyrics to one of Howard's main themes from the score to create "Places That Belong to You," which Barbra recorded for the soundtrack. Although the studio hoped she would place the song behind the closing credits, after much deliberation she chose not to. She feared that if her vocal boomed out of theater speakers at the film's conclusion, it might distract from the mood of Nick Nolte's final moments. She also felt that her direction of the picture might not be taken as seriously if her identity as a pop-music icon was reinforced just as her directing credit appeared on the screen. Even after 90 percent of audiences who saw screenings of the film with the song included felt it enhanced the picture, Barbra was adamant that it be excluded.

Previews of *The Prince of Tides* in June indicated that the film had tremendous box-office potential. Columbia was so pleased, it pushed the release date forward in order to present the picture as the studio's prime holiday attraction. Barbra was, of course, thrilled that Columbia placed such faith in her effort, but waiting the extra months for its release made her nervous. "Believe me," she said, "I wanted it out, because I finished it. I think they were more pleasantly surprised than they thought they would be, so they wanted to hold it for their Christmas picture. In my opinion, I would rather it had been released earlier. The angst is awful, you know? It's like, get this out already!"

Although a bitchy item in the *New York Times* by Caryn James tried to imply that advance word on the picture indicated a "vanity production" akin to the costly Bruce Willis flop *Hudson Hawk*, Columbia chairman Frank Yablans came to Barbra's defense. "We were particularly incensed to see this film labeled a vanity production. It is not unusual for talented people—among them Woody Allen, Kevin Costner, and Warren Beatty—to direct and star in pictures. Why is Barbra Streisand, when she chooses to do the same, singled out for such criticism?"

Perhaps having learned from the mistake of underpromoting *Nuts*, Barbra launched a full publicity attack to call attention to her latest film. Aside from tremendous print and electronic-media exposure, she also agreed to appear under Mike Wallace's hot lights on *60 Minutes*, and though the experience proved hurtful when Wallace challenged the discomfort she still obviously carried from her relationship with Louis Kind, it also sent the message that *The Prince of Tides* would be an important film from an obsessively gifted filmmaker. Following its New York premiere on December 9, 1991, and the L.A. opening two days later (with Barbra accompanied by Jon Peters, Jason, Roslyn Kind, and a fully recovered Diana) as well as its general release on Christmas Day, the movie enjoyed a predominance of fine reviews and earned close to $32 million during its first twelve days of release.

Within a few days the film had garnered Golden Globe nominations for Best Drama, Best Actor, and Best Director. Though Nolte proved the only victor for his touching performance, industry insiders predicted that Barbra would be a cinch to become the first American woman to receive an Academy Award nomination for Best Director. Streisand took a step closer to this coveted goal when she became only the third woman in history to be nominated for a Directors Guild Award, alongside Jonathan Demme (*Silence of the Lambs*), Barry Levinson (*Bugsy*), Ridley Scott (*Thelma and Louise*), and Oliver Stone (*JFK*).

By the time the Academy Award nominations

The mutually nurturing love affair between Tom Wingo and Susan became the focus of much controversy in the psychiatric community when the film was released.

were announced on February 19, Barbra was in London launching *The Prince of Tides* amid a blitz of publicity that included a lavish premiere at which Streisand was presented to Princess Diana. When the film received seven Oscar nominations, including one for Best Picture, but Barbra was passed over in the directing category, cries of injustice were issued in *Newsweek* and by the National Organization for Women. Though delighted with her film's nominations—which included recognition for Nolte, Kate Nelligan, Pat Conroy, Becky Johnston, James Newton Howard, Stephen Goldblatt, and Paul Sylbert—Barbra echoed the sentiments of many when she said, "I don't know how they get to the best pictures without nominating the directors." When asked if sexism played a role in this most current Academy snub, she added, "We're still fighting it. It's as if a man were allowed to have passion and commitment to his work but a woman is allowed that feel-

Jason Gould escorts his mother — and costar — to the 1992 Academy Awards ceremonies. Praised by critics, Jason's performance in The Prince of Tides *did not provoke the cries of nepotism he and Barbra feared. (Photo by Bob Scott)*

ing for a man but not her work." In March, while accepting his Directors Guild Award, Jonathan Demme said he wished to remind the assembled filmmakers that he was "the forty-fourth white male to receive this award, which I have confused feelings about."

Attending the Academy Award ceremonies with Jason on March 30, Barbra was touched when Billy Crystal, Liza Minnelli, Shirley MacLaine, and Jessica Tandy made references onstage to the Academy's indefensible snub of her directorial talents. But she was disappointed when *The Prince of Tides* failed to pick up a single Oscar.

The Prince of Tides proved to be Barbra's most successful picture since *A Star Is Born* in spite of criticism that ranged from thought provoking to trivial. Psychiatric watchdog organizations decried Lowenstein's affair with a surrogate patient and the length of her fingernails. Elder rocker Carl Perkins received publicity when he objected to his song "Honey Don't" being used as background to a brutal assault by escaped convicts on the Wingo family during Tom's childhood. In a full-page editorial in *Newsweek*, Barbra pondered why a stylish New York therapist who charges $150 an hour wouldn't indulge in a manicure, and she reminded the public that affairs between doctors and patients— while clearly unethical—happen quite often. Some of the issues the film was criticized for were, of course, delineated in the novel; Streisand may have elaborated on the Wingo-Lowenstein romance, but she didn't create it out of whole cloth.

With *The Prince of Tides*, Barbra fashioned a film that seems destined, like fine wine, to improve with age. It offered wonderful performances (including her own—one of the most self-effacing of her career), pleased many important critics, and touched an emotional chord with audiences. Moreover, as the icing on the proverbial cake, it was a big hit. But perhaps the approbation she most treasures came from the story's author. After seeing the completed film, Pat Conroy sent her a copy of the novel with an inscription that says in part, "You've made me a better writer, you rescued my sweet book, and you've honored me by taking it with such seriousness and love. Great love and great thanks and I'll never forget that you gave *The Prince of Tides* back to me as a gift."

The director takes a rare break during filming. "I've never seen anyone go through a total immersion in a project like she does,"
Pat Conroy said of Barbra. "It completely obsesses her and takes over her life."

REVIEWS

"Far and away the best movie of the year. An emotional masterpiece . . . a totally involving journey of self-discovery . . . exquisitely crafted, with the artistry of the heart and the sensitivity of the soul. Nick Nolte is pure acting power as the man in crisis. Barbra Streisand's direction is as passionate and poignant as her performance."

KNBC-TV

". . . the love affair . . . is played out in romantic postures borrowed from The Way We Were *and* Ralph Lauren *ads for country chic. In these gauzy, soft-focused scenes and elsewhere, Streisand's presence on screen is problematic: her self-consciousness makes it hard to accept Lowenstein as Lowenstein; she's always Streisand. It's easy to pick on the producer/director/star, yet her film about forgiveness ultimately earns ours: Streisand's empathy for the characters is big-hearted and contagious.* Prince of Tides *may be a guilty pleasure, but it's a pleasure nonetheless."*

NEWSWEEK

"Making an uncharacteristically delayed entrance after a 12-minute introductory section about the Wingo family, Streisand puts herself as director, star and character at the service of Nolte, gradually drawing out his family secrets and long-suppressed anger and pain. . . . It's a rare film that can make a male-female relationship so gripping on a non-sexual level, and that's one of the special pleasures of The Prince of Tides—*a film that, unlike* The Way We Were *but like Streisand's previous directorial effort,* Yentl, *finds her a lover who's her intellectual equal. That's one of the advantages of having a woman director."*

DAILY VARIETY

The Mirror Has Two Faces

(1996)

A Sony Pictures Entertainment Release of a TriStar Presentation in Association With Phoenix Pictures of an Arnon Milchan/Barwood Films Production

CAST

Barbra Streisand (*Rose Morgan*); Jeff Bridges (*Gregory Larkin*); Pierce Brosnan (*Alex*); George Segal (*Henry Fine*); Mimi Rogers (*Claire*); Brenda Vaccaro (*Doris*); Lauren Bacall (*Hannah Morgan*); Austin Pendleton (*Barry*); Elle Macpherson (*Candy*).

CREDITS

Producers: Barbra Streisand, Arnon Milchan; director: Barbra Streisand; assistant director: Amy Sayres; story and screenplay: Richard LaGravanese (based on the film *Le Miroir a Deux Faces*); music: Marvin Hamlisch; ("Love Theme" composed by Barbra Streisand; "I Finally Found Someone" by Barbra Streisand, Bryan Adams, Marvin Hamlisch, Robert "Mutt" Lang); production designer: Tom John; costumes: Theoni V. Aldredge; cinematography: Dante Spinotti, Andrzej Bartkowiak; second-unit camera: Richard Quinlan; set decoration: John Alan Hicks; art direction: Teresa Carriker-Thayer; sound: Thomas Nelson; editor: Jeff Werner; casting: Bonnie Finnegan, Todd Thaler. Running time: 126 minutes.

For her second, and last, film of the 1990s (apart from a fleeting appearance in the 1990 documentary *Listen Up: The Lives of Quincy Jones*), Barbra chose to remake a French melodrama that, in its updated version as a romantic comedy, offered her a chance to revisit themes that are dear to her heart: the mystery of appearances, the often precarious relationship shared by mothers and daughters, and the complex dynamics that color affairs between the sexes in the wake of the women's movement and the sexual revolution. The picture also harkened back to the ugly-duckling-to-swan themes of some of her earlier films.

The Mirror Has Two Faces was being suggested as a possible Streisand vehicle as early as 1991, but it was also a property for which Demi Moore was mentioned. And at one point, Rosie O'Donnell was reportedly being pitched the project, with a hoped-for casting of Elizabeth Taylor as her mother. However, by April 1992, Barbra and screenwriter Richard LaGravanese (*The Fisher King* and, later, *The Bridges of Madison County*) were seriously engaged in refining the screenplay. Three years later, the title was firmly on the Barwood preproduction schedule, though it remained in a constant state of rewriting—some done by Carrie Fisher. While *Mirror* was being fine-tuned, Barwood was also attempting to get *The Normal Heart* off the ground. When neither project could be brought close to the filming stage, Barbra took advantage of the delay to embark on her 1994 concert tour.

On April 18, 1993, Streisand had delivered an eloquent, moving introduction to a stage reading of *The Normal Heart* at the Roundabout Theater in Manhattan for the benefit of Broadway Cares/Equity Fights AIDS. Photos of a misty-eyed Barbra hugging Larry Kramer at the evening's conclusion left little doubt that filming a version of the play was once again a Streisand priority. Failing to place the project with another producer after his original falling-out with Barbra, Kramer had returned the property to her in the early nineties, and she once again voiced enthusiasm about it, though with the AIDS epidemic now almost fifteen years old, Kramer's angry message had been robbed of much of its timeliness and controversy. Moreover, even with Streisand's name attached, the project proved troublesome to launch. "[It's] not a movie the studios are clamoring to do,"

Barbra said, "but I'm plowing ahead. I'll probably direct it."

Citing the unavailability of certain actors (Kenneth Branagh, Ralph Fiennes) she hoped to cast and noting that it was difficult raising production money for *The Normal Heart,* Streisand decided in the spring of 1995 to instead proceed with *The Mirror Has Two Faces,* much to the delighted relief of many of her colleagues, who had urged her to return to romantic comedy. Barwood announced an October starting date, with all filming to be done in Manhattan, and in a burst of optimism, Barbra indicated she would start *The Normal Heart,* with Branagh starring, immediately following postproduction on *Mirror.* Ominously, however, *Variety* reported that "[Streisand's] option on the play expires at the end of the year [1995] and to renew she would have to buy the rights in a complicated formula that also involves Kramer's *The Destiny of Me* and the services of the [playwright] as a screenwriter. Sources said the deal could be worth more than seven figures to Kramer and is likely to test TriStar's and [Streisand's] commitment to the project." Indeed, by the following April, Barbra had relinquished rights to *The Normal Heart,* prompting a media tirade from an embittered Larry Kramer.

The Mirror Has Two Faces concerns two Columbia University professors, Rose Morgan and Gregory Larkin, who decide to marry for companionship rather than love. He feels that sexual attraction sabotages relationships; she's eager to escape the clutches of her self-absorbed mother. The requisite complications ensue when Rose undergoes a glamorous makeover after Gregory has spurned her sexual advances. (The theme of a passionless coupling that eventually leads to full-fledged romance has been the basis of several Hollywood films, the most notable of which is perhaps *Without Love,* the 1945 Spencer Tracy and Katharine Hepburn vehicle.)

In the original French screenplay for *Le Miroir a Deux Faces,* the female protagonist undergoes cosmetic surgery as part of her transformation. During preproduction, rumors circulated that Barbra might submit to a face-lift for the film, while another report claimed that she was in talks with technicians at George Lucas's Industrial Light and Magic special-effects studio to see if her on-screen image could be altered in a believable manner that would simulate the results of Rose's surgery. The rumors seemed so ridiculous that (through Army Archerd's column in *Variety*) Barbra let it be known that her movie "is not about a woman who changes herself through plastic surgery. There will be no digital alteration of the famous Streisand profile." Later, she added, "I was more interested in exploring self-esteem from within, not from without. And so I asked LaGravanese to change that. Many, many things about it changed." LaGravanese said, "I wanted it to be about a woman who finds inner beauty and transforms herself out of love of this man." Barbra revealed that Rose would "go to a fat farm, lose weight, wear makeup."

By August 1995, Streisand had firmed up her cast and production crew. Although Harrison Ford had been publicized as a possible costar, Jeff Bridges was signed to play Gregory. "He's a wonderful actor," Barbra said, "and I think he's very sexy. You can just feel his love for women. He has a great mom—a strong, opinionated, funny mom. And so I knew that he would be easy to direct. You know, whether you're going to go out with somebody on a date or you're going to direct him, the first question is, 'What was your relationship with your mother?' That will tell you a lot about his behavior towards women." By joining the *Mirror* cast, Bridges became the latest in a fraternity of boyishly handsome, outdoorsy Streisand leading men (Ryan O'Neal, Robert Redford, Kris Kristofferson, and Nick Nolte) whose qualities inevitably complement Barbra's ethnic, urban appeal.

"[She's] a totally natural choice," Barbra said of her decision to place magnetic screen veteran Lauren Bacall in the mix as Rose's mother, Hannah, while Mimi Rogers, tackling a rare comedy role, was signed to play Rose's beautiful, sexually profligate sister, Claire. Dudley Moore took the part of Gregory's friend Henry Fine; Austin Pendleton, an alumnus from *What's Up, Doc?,* was cast as Rose's long-suffering ex-boyfriend, Barry; and Elle Macpherson took the role of a stunning, superficial bedmate of Gregory's.

In a role Barbra's designer-pal Donna Karan hoped to be considered for, Brenda Vaccaro (an offscreen friend of Streisand's since 1968) would play Rose's best buddy and fellow junk-food aficionado, Doris. "This will be [a] fortunate [way] for me to tell her how much I love her—on film,"

Hannah Morgan helps her daughter Rose prepare for an important first date with Gregory Larkin.

Vaccaro remarked. Months before shooting began, Barbra asked Brenda to put on weight for the role—for a touching scene late in the story in which a still-plump Doris feels uncomfortable in the presence of her friend's sleek new appearance.

To play Alex, Claire's new husband (for whom Rose secretly yearns), Streisand called on Pierce Brosnan. As a condition of his signing for the picture, Barbra agreed to film around Brosnan when he was needed to promote his new film *GoldenEye,* his highly touted debut as James Bond. Dante Spinotti would be photographing the film, while Marvin Hamlisch, fresh from his duties as the musical supervisor of Streisand's concert tour, would compose the film's score. Well-known designer and costumer Theoni V. Aldredge agreed to create the wardrobe. TriStar would release the picture under the Sony umbrella.

The Mirror Has Two Faces began production on October 16, 1995, with a plan to shoot the picture entirely in Manhattan, including interiors built on sets constructed at the armory in Harlem at

Fifth Avenue and West 145th Street. For her first days of filming, Barbra returned to the familiar setting of Central Park, where she had shot scenes for five previous pictures. Forced to do numerous retakes on a scene in which Rose and Gregory are enjoying a picnic, a tense Barbra was hounded by a swarm of persistent paparazzi from newspapers and tabloid television shows. (One shutterbug, shooting from a tree limb, lost his balance and crashed near Barbra's feet.) After attempting to dodge the onslaught and concentrate on the logistics of the shoot for the better part of the day, an exasperated Streisand finally turned toward the photographers abruptly, flung out her arms in frustration, and barked, "Take my fucking picture!" As the group snapped away, she added, "Okay, now you have enough. Okay?" before storming off.

Though production progressed smoothly enough for the next few weeks, the film—and, by extension, Barbra—suffered a one-two punch of unwelcome publicity when Dudley Moore and the film's cinematographer were fired during the hol-

Columbia professor Rose Morgan has all the answers about literary love in her classroom, but she hasn't a clue when it comes to her own romantic needs.

"Artistic differences" were blamed for Dante Spinotti's departure. Barbra allegedly felt he took much too long to light the sets and that his style clashed with the atmosphere she wanted for the film. "[She] had been complaining about the camera work almost from the beginning of the production," reported Bernard Weintraub in the *New York Times.* "There were too many gauzes around the lens. Her eyes, one of her best features, got very soft." Other sources claimed that Spinotti had been dismissed because he failed to properly flatter the fifty-three-year-old Streisand visage. For whatever reason, *Nuts* photographer Andrzej Bartkowiak stepped in. Ken Sunshine, the production's publicist, said, "There's no doubt when Barbra gets involved in a project it takes on a life of its own in terms of publicity. But it's hardly the first time there have been changes during the making of a film. [Spinotti's departure] was a major change, but it was on very good terms. There would be a very different spin on all this if the people at TriStar, looking at the dailies, didn't feel so good about what they're seeing."

Although exterior shooting on *Mirror* fell behind schedule because of inclement wintry weather, interiors set in Bloomingdale's, Tavern on the Green, the Monkey Bar, and other locations were completed without incident. Bloomingdale's was only available for filming after closing, and for an intricate, extended scene in which Rose first interacts with her best friend, then her sister, and finally her sister's husband amid a mob of shoppers and diners, the *Mirror* troupe toiled well into the middle of the night. Her costars were amazed at Streisand's seemingly inexhaustible energy. "She's a really strong girl," Bridges said. "She is

iday season. While on location at the Columbia University campus, Moore found it impossible to remember his lines for a brief encounter with Jeff Bridges. Even after Streisand ordered Moore's dialogue written on oversized cue cards, the actor was incapable of completing the scene. Moore claimed that he was distracted by events in his private life. It was also rumored that Moore's emotional problems were so severe that he was close to uninsurable. Streisand and TriStar had no choice but to replace him, and fortunately, George Segal was able to take over the role with no fuss. The press noted the irony in the situation, as it had been Moore's replacement of Segal in Blake Edwards's 1979 hit comedy *10* that established Moore's Hollywood stardom.

definitely in charge. Yet she has a sense of play about her, and one of the reasons I wanted to do this movie was to work with her because she's a perfectionist and a phenomenal artist. If a man acted the same way that she is, people would just say it's part of his creative process."

The picture fell further behind schedule as certain moments naturally required more time to capture on film than originally anticipated. "The gut-wrenching scenes . . . are going to take longer," said TriStar executive Chris Lee. "It's real tears . . . it's tough to do." One such scene was Rose's bungled seduction of Gregory several months into their marriage. When he rejects her because he fears sex will complicate and ruin their relationship, she assumes it's because he doesn't find her attractive. Deeply hurt, she locks herself in their bathroom, where she breaks down in great heaving sobs. After Gregory has fallen asleep, Rose sneaks out of their apartment to return to her mother. The arc of the scene, going as it does from sexy interplay to slapstick farce to heart-wrenching reality, required courageous authenticity from both actors, but particularly from Streisand, who was, of course, also serving as director. The time she took to get every nuance of the scene right paid off handsomely, for it emerged as the film's emotional climax.

"Rose is attracted to Greg," Barbra explained, "but he didn't think he was attracted to her. He actually feels attracted to her but cannot deal with the prospect of that kind of passion and intimacy and the fear of that ruining his life again. Because when he becomes passionate, he loses his mind, he loses control, he can't function as a professional. He hasn't learned to integrate the two aspects of his personality."

Rose's relationship with Hannah intentionally reflected Streisand's experiences with her own mother, especially in a revealing exchange during which Hannah finds it almost impossible to tell Rose she was pretty as a little girl. "I think she put her own mother in there," Lauren Bacall told *USA Today.* "I'd have to say, 'Barbra, I'm not *your* mother!' But you can't help it. You always inject qualities into characters from what you know." Bacall was careful to play Hannah as insensitive and self-centered but not a monster. "She's full of mixed-up emotions, as I certainly have been in my life. She's not aggressively mean or cruel; she's just so fragile that she's built up a facade of how to

deal with the world. She's interested in her appearance because that's what she's hung on to all her life. If she looks a certain way, it will be okay. She'll make her presence felt and not be passed over."

By the end of March, most of *The Mirror Has Two Faces* had been completed, but because of a seemingly endless winter, the company had to wait until the second week of May to return and capture the film's final romantic scene of Rose and Gregory's springtime reconciliation in front of Hannah's apartment—played against Pavarotti's thrilling vocal of Puccini's "Nessun Dorma"—and their early-morning dance down West End Avenue under the credits. Some local residents were less than tickled by the film crew's four nights of noisy, disruptive shooting, but reports in the tabloid press (which *Newsweek* picked up without verifying) that eggs were hurled at Barbra and company were completely untrue. "They said I was pelted with eggs on the streets of New York," Streisand complained to Oprah Winfrey. "New York is my city. Do you think people are gonna throw eggs at me?"

By the time production wrapped entirely, the film was rumored to be anywhere from $7 to $11 million over budget—an unfortunate first for a Streisand-produced picture. Although much of the overage was chalked up to the uncooperative weather, rumored troubles with local film unions, and the unplanned cast and crew changes, some of the blame had to be placed squarely on Barbra's perfectionistic work ethic. "[She] dissects everything too much," claimed one unnamed source. "She'll decide what she wants, think about it overnight, and change her mind the next day." Another observer added, "Streisand loves living in chaos. Everything has to be tortured, [and] she's frustrated about everything. . . . She's tired. . . . I know she's tired." Ironically, she had tackled the project in the first place because she hoped a romantic comedy would prove faster and less stressful to make. "Barbra feels great about this movie," Ken Sunshine said in her defense. "She's killing herself, but she's having a great time."

"I set myself a certain challenge on this movie," Barbra told *Drama-Logue,* "because *Yentl* took five years of my life, *Nuts* took two-and-a-half years, *The Prince of Tides* took about three-and-a-half years. I really wanted to challenge myself to do movies in less time. I figured that a year is

Cable Guy and *Multiplicity* in the last two months, is eagerly anticipating a long gaze into this *Mirror*."

Set to open nationally on November 15, 1996, *The Mirror Has Two Faces* received a $20 million advertising and promotion budget from Sony/TriStar, and Barbra and her costars agreed to dozens of print and television interviews. By the time the picture debuted, Streisand had chatted it up with Gene Shalit, Katie Couric, Joel Siegel, Jane Pauley, and Oprah Winfrey, among many others. "I Finally Found Someone," Barbra's duet with Bryan Adams, which was finally chosen as the song to close the film, was released to radio stations on November 12 and became an immediate hit—eventually rising to *Billboard*'s Top Ten. (A soundtrack album, released simultaneously, featured an additional Streisand vocal, "All of My Life," not heard in the film.)

In the wake of Streisand's being presented with the Filmmaker of the Year Award from the Showeast association of theater distributors and managers, the New York premiere of *Mirror* at the Ziegfeld Theatre on November 10 turned into a media feeding frenzy when a radiantly smiling Barbra arrived on the arm of James Brolin for their first major public appearance. She and the lanky actor had been inseparable since meeting in July. In every interview she granted on *Mirror*'s behalf, Streisand spoke contentedly about her newfound happiness with Brolin, and the romance could not have promoted the mood of the film more ideally if it had been contrived to do so—which, of course, some cynics claimed it was.

Opening on twenty-four hundred screens

enough time to spend on a movie. After all, it's only a movie! Even though it lasts forever, we hope." Keenly aware that *Mirror* had gone considerably over schedule, Barbra worked around the clock with editor Jeff Werner to get a print ready for previews just two months after shutting down production.

Screenings in July indicated a potential hit, though substantial trimming was still required. The film's score hadn't been completed, and a Streisand vocal, "It Doesn't Get Better Than This," utilized for the film's finale, would be replaced. The movie continued to preview in various incarnations over the course of the summer. An August screening in Pasadena led one insider to remark, "An early cut left the studio decision makers in tears. Happy tears, it's said. And Sony, which has suffered the disconnections of both *The*

nationwide, *The Mirror Has Two Faces* drew in over $12 million for its opening weekend—the highest total of any Streisand picture to date and the top moneymaker for any solo female star of 1996. "*Mirror* definitely reflects Barbra's best," enthused Sony distribution head Jeff Blake. "We expect a steady run that should build, based on [the history of] her other pictures. *Prince of Tides*, which had been her best, opened to $10 million . . . and it went on to make $74.8 million. We expect this could do the same, since adult romantic comedies tend to have a strong holding pattern."

The honeymoon for *Mirror* ended abruptly, however, when the reviews started to surface and it became clear that with a few notable exceptions critics were lying in wait for what many characterized as a classic vanity production, designed solely to exhibit the charismatic allure of its star and director. Barbra had, of course, weathered such criticism numerous times in the past, but the tone of these reviews was more personalized and demeaning—especially regarding her age—and they had more impact than they did twenty years earlier. The days of young fans ignoring (or not being aware of) bad reviews and trouping in droves to see *A Star Is Born*—multiple times no less—were over. Barbra's potential audience was now well past thirty, and they took reviews more seriously. Her devout, hard-core admirers had helped produce strong numbers for the opening weekend, but the film needed more general appeal to succeed. Subsequent good word of mouth, even by moviegoers who were initially reluctant to see the picture because of the notices, wasn't enough to push it into the genuine hit category. By the following February it had amassed worldwide grosses of $62 million—certainly no flop, but it still did not make enough to offset the

picture's reputed cost, including advertising, of over $45 million.

Some of the attacks leveled at *Mirror* centered on the script's emphasis on Rose's looks and whether or not she was conventionally attractive—a theme many critics felt had been played out in Barbra's earlier films and one that was lost on a majority of 1996 moviegoers.

Writing about Katharine Hepburn in 1988, Ethan Mordden said, "Today it's common to think of Hepburn as a natural, even as inevitable. But when she was new she was thought strange-looking, affected, and possibly nutty. Hollywood likes outstanding versions of the norm, not outstanding versions of the outstanding. . . ." The same, of course, might be said of Streisand. Today she is accepted in most circles as an elegant, attractive star whose appeal has been trumpeted by a variety of glamorous men on and off the screen; it's easy to forget just how groundbreaking her movie image was at first. Without Barbra's having challenged the accepted standard of beauty at the start of her career, audiences might not have embraced the imperfect looks of Meryl Streep, Liza Minnelli, Cher, Bette Midler, Anjelica Huston, and countless others. While Ray Stark was trying to find a home for *Funny Girl*, one Paramount exec-

Rose tells Gregory she is no longer willing to settle for the platonic conditions of their marriage.

utive agreed to film it, but only if Shirley MacLaine would play Fanny Brice—so afraid was the studio of how moviegoers might be turned off by Streisand's looks, even in a role she had already made famous.

Most audiences might have felt that Rose looked just fine in her natural state, so accustomed are they now to Streisand's unique features, but Barbra, like her on-screen alter ego, is still—after all these years—not so sure. Naturally she utilized

A near-fling with her sister's handsome husband, Alex, helps Rose realize that superficial beauty can often attract superficial men.

her interpretation of Rose to examine anew the wide range of opinions her *own* looks have generated since she was a child. "What I was trying to say," Streisand stressed, "is that beauty is in the heart of the beholder. You might be attracted to someone who is externally beautiful, but if they're not beautiful in spirit, if they don't have character, if they don't have soul, the beauty is going to fade quickly. So there are many aspects of looking at this subject."

The point of Rose's character was not that she was unappealing prior to the transformation but that she *felt* she was and her self-esteem suf-

fered as a result. What also seemed to elude many of the critics was that the makeover didn't really work; Gregory, at first, was put off by it because he preferred the old Rose, for whom he found himself lusting in spite of his determination not to.

The pressure to complete *The Mirror Has Two Faces* on an accelerated schedule surely accounts for several uncharacteristic technical errors found in the first release prints of the film: Microphone boom shadows are visible more than once, and in a scene set in Alex's apartment, a crew member holding a can of soda can be spotted reflected in the glass pane of a French door. For these and more important reasons, *Mirror* suffers in comparison to Streisand's earlier directorial efforts. She elicits exaggerated, hokey reactions from students in Rose's and Gregory's classes, and the stumbling physical distress Gregory exhibits when confronted by his sexual urges is too silly to be very convincing. In fact, the picture's entire premise was criticized as unbelievable. Just as Streisand has been known occasionally to expend tremendous effort to perfect the recording of a song that is unworthy of her talent in the first place, so, too, might *The Mirror Has Two Faces* have been undeserving of her obsessive attention from the start.

The film does, however, in its finest moments—and there are plenty—strike a graceful balance between gentle humor and drama, and for all of its occasional obviousness, it is suffused with the artfully planned, subtle touches in everything from the score to the decor that have come to characterize Barbra's recent films. Also, her carefully shaded performance further proves that she is a highly effective actress under her own guidance. Even her most ardent fans might argue, however, that the time has come for her to place her talents within the hands of another director. With *Yentl*, *The Prince of Tides*, and now *Mirror*, audiences have seen how she chooses to present herself; it's intriguing to contemplate what still untapped qualities another filmmaker might bring out in her screen persona.

It must also be said that for a director of such alleged selfishness, Barbra has managed to extract Academy Award–nominated performances from four actors in the three pictures she has helmed. On January 19, 1997, Lauren Bacall won a Best Supporting Actress Golden Globe from the Hollywood Foreign Press for her striking performance. "I think . . . had it not been for [Streisand] this movie wouldn't have been made," Bacall said in accepting the award. "Had it not been for her I would not have been cast in this part. And had it not been for her, I wouldn't be standing here now, because of the way she directed this movie and my part in particular." Though she subsequently received the Screen Actors Guild Award and an Oscar nomination, Bacall—the odds-on favorite—lost the Academy Award at ceremonies held on March 24. As one of the composers of "I Finally Found Someone," Streisand received nominations for Best Song from both the Hollywood Foreign Press and the Academy but failed to win either.

REVIEWS

"Less a film than a long, two-hour Barbra infomercial, the movie is meant to be a romantic comedy on the theme of appearance vs. character, but it turns quickly into something far more rancid: an exercise in obsessive mirror-gazing and self-mythologizing that comes to feel icky. It has a toxic taint of vanity uncontrolled. It gave me the creeps, not merely because of its director's fascination with herself, but, just as bad, her lack of interest, her lack of charity, her lack of engagement toward her costars. . . . Alas, [the film] comes to feel hypocritical in the extreme. She doesn't want to be just another pretty face, but she does want to be a pretty face. Which is it? The movie, like its star, contradicts itself all over the place."

BALTIMORE SUN

"The Mirror Has Two Faces is a first-class charmer, a passionate and funny love story . . . that will surely wed critical acclaim with box-office success. Certain to engage a major female audience, Sony will also find when it looks into the box-office mirror that this scrumptiously scruffy film will reflect two faces, male as well as female. Even male skeptics who may initially brand it a 'chick flick' will be seduced by its wide-ranging story appeal and intelligent, good-hearted humor. . . . Under Streisand's accomplished direction [the film] glows. It radiates with an array of complementary textures, most prominently Dante Spinotti and Andrzej Bartkowiak's rich and warm-hued cinematography."

HOLLYWOOD REPORTER

"Framed as a knockabout romantic comedy, the movie is so completely an emanation of its coproducer-director-star that, in a way, reviewing it is a bit like reviewing a marathon therapy session. . . . I can't think of another major movie icon—not even Chaplin in Limelight or Bob Fosse in All That Jazz or Woody Allen in anything—who has so extensively laid bare his or her fears and fantasies. The film is a startlingly brave folly, and even after you acknowledge the healthy dollop of narcissism, mixed in with the bravery, it still leaves you swacked, uplifted, bewildered. It's as if Streisand wanted to pull us all inside her head. . . . After Rose has bombed out trying to get Greg in the hay, she undergoes a makeover that turns her into a regal glamorpuss. (The camera announces Rose's new look as if she were the Statue of Liberty.) Rose rejects Greg; she has a chance for a tryst with Alex and rejects him. There's a wish-fulfillment fantasia built into scenes like these—Streisand is letting us know that even though she doesn't need to be glamorous to be beautiful, she can go the glamour-queen route, anyway, and still knock our socks off. Take that, Elle Macpherson!"

NEW TIMES

Epilogue

From the earliest days of her career Barbra Streisand has insisted that her primary show business goal was to become an actress. Even after being crowned the premier female vocalist of her generation—indeed, one of the all-time greats—she still often calls herself "an actress who sings." It is somewhat ironic, therefore, that acting may be the talent for which she is least remembered.

Her singing, directing, composing, and producing abilities have resulted in ground-breaking contributions. And though she has turned in peerless performances in films for which she was perfectly cast, a protective vanity crept in along the way that has kept her from pursuing the kind of challenges that define great acting careers. Though infinitely more versatile than such vintage "personality" stars as Mae West or Marlene Dietrich, Streisand has not lived up to the early predictions, including those made by Irvin Kerschner and Herbert Ross, that "she can do anything." Missing from much of her screen work has been the audacity that propelled almost all of her pre-Hollywood efforts, and that has remained a hallmark of so much of her singing career.

Not that all of her movie choices have been risk free. *Up the Sandbox* was certainly not a safe project to champion, and the decision to take on so much responsibility in the making of *A Star Is Born,* and her dogged determination to turn an obscure short story with an ethnic theme into one of the most graceful musical films ever made, took genuine artistic bravery. But on balance—especially since her filmography is so short—she has too often settled for the predictable in her acting choices. And though she has proven a surprisingly subtle and effective performer under her own guidance, even her staunchest fans can't help but wish that she would place her talents in the hands of other, perhaps more daring, directors.

And now, as she approaches sixty, Barbra's age naturally puts a limit on the parts that will be available to her. *The Mirror Has Two Faces* is most likely the last film in which she can believably portray a character considerably younger than her age. Lately she has indicated in more than one interview that she will retire rather than undergo plastic surgery to attain a more youthful appearance —a ploy many stars utilize in the hope of broadening the range of roles they may be offered. (There are some firmly entrenched traditions of ageism and sexism that even a force like Streisand is powerless to change.)

She has shown little interest, however, in pursuing the age-appropriate character roles that have elongated and added luster to the careers of such erstwhile box-office queens as Katharine Hepburn, Shirley MacLaine, and Sophia Loren. For her admirers, the only benefit to what may be the end of her on-screen career is that it might encourage Barbra Streisand to direct films in which she needn't star. In the future her most important contributions to Hollywood may be made behind the scenes as director, producer, composer. Perhaps by freeing herself from concerns about her appearance, she will once again tap into the audacious spirit that has always characterized her greatest work.